The Revenue
Operations Manual

The Revenue Operations Manual

How to build a high-growth, predictable and scalable business

Sean Lane and Laura Adint

KoganPage

First published in Great Britain and the United States in 2024 by Kogan Page Limited

2nd Floor, 45 Gee Street
London
EC1V 3RS
United Kingdom

8 W 38th Street, Suite 902
New York, NY 10018
USA

www.koganpage.com

Kogan Page books are printed on paper from sustainable forests.

ISBNs

Hardback   978 1 3986 1678 3
Paperback   978 1 3986 1676 9
Ebook   978 1 3986 1677 6

British Library Cataloguing-in-Publication Data

A CIP record for this book is available from the British Library.

Library of Congress Cataloging-in-Publication Data

2024023372.

Typeset by Integra Software Services, Pondicherry
Print production managed by Jellyfish
Printed and bound by CPI Group (UK) Ltd, Croydon CR0 4YY

Sean: To Molly, Emma, Maggie, my parents, and siblings for their
constant inspiration and support
Laura: To my family for encouraging me to "be the buffalo"

CONTENTS

LIST OF FIGURES AND TABLES

TABLES

ABOUT THE AUTHORS

Sean Lane

Sean Lane is a Founding Partner at BeaconGTM, a consulting firm that helps CEOs and revenue leaders improve their go-to-market execution. He has spent more than a decade building Operations and customer-facing teams at fast-growing B2B software companies. Sean spent over five years building the Operations teams at Drift, the creator of Conversational Marketing (acquired by Vista Private Equity at more than $1 billion valuation), and over five years at Upserve, a restaurant technology company (also acquired by Vista Private Equity). He is the host of the *Operations with Sean Lane* podcast, the source of many of the expert conversations featured in this book. When he's not writing, consulting, or podcasting, you can find Sean in Massachusetts, hanging out with his wife, his two amazing daughters, and his dog. To learn more about working with Sean, visit beacongtm.com

Laura Adint

Laura Adint has 25 years of experience with high-tech companies and consulting across multiple functions with a specialty in Operations, leading organizations, and creating alignment across functions to drive impact. She has a passion and proven capability to tackle large and difficult goals. As Vice President of Field Operations at Drift, she led field operations and sales development through the Private Equity group (Vista) acquisition. As the Vice President of Sales and Services Operations at Adaptive Insights, she helped lead through their S-1 filing as well as through the resulting acquisition by

Workday for $1.6 billion, only days prior to their scheduled IPO At Drift, Adaptive Insights and SugarCRM, she managed the operations and support functions for worldwide sales, services, partner, sales development, and customer success. She has experience in Operations, finance, internal audit, finance technology, project management, service delivery, consulting, and software implementations. Laura's motto in life is "better, better, never done." You can find her in the San Francisco Bay area with her husband, two sons, and a fluffy German Shepherd.

FOREWORD

As I sit down to write this foreword in early 2024, businesses around the world continue to navigate some of the toughest and most confounding market conditions of the last century.

In a few short years, we've experienced wild swings in consumer demand. Inflation the likes of which we haven't seen in 50 years. Supply chains stressed, bent, and broken.

And—as some of the world's pre-eminent business publications have accurately reported—markets that are increasingly punishing. Vicious.

It's long been my professional mantra that the single most important question in business is, "Are you going to meet, beat, or miss on revenue?" In 2024, it couldn't be more clear: Business leaders can no longer afford to *not* be able to answer that question.

And the consequences of an earnings miss? They've never been more severe.

Yet, despite this doom-and-gloom backdrop, I've never been more optimistic about the future of business and its most important function: Revenue generation.

Why? Because tough times have accelerated a profoundly positive shift in the way companies think about revenue. Increasingly, CEOs, boards, and others in the C-suite have seen the light: Revenue is not just an outcome. It's a process. The most important process in business.

And a process needs an Operator.

Enter the Head of Revenue Operations (or RevOps, for short), the fastest growing job in the US in 2023, according to LinkedIn.

It's a new era for the age-old function of sales, and the emerging discipline of RevOps is the linchpin to a future of well-oiled revenue machines that consistently deliver efficiency, predictability, and—most importantly—growth.

RevOps leaders and their teams break down the organizational and data silos that plague most companies. They jettison timeworn ways of working and albatross technologies, supplanting them with company-wide collaboration and governance, data-driven strategies, and advanced technologies like AI to empower individuals and teams to achieve more.

In doing so, they deliver ROI back to the company as no other strategic function can.

RevOps empowers sales leadership to spot revenue breakdowns. Companies lose $2 trillion every year to *revenue leak*—revenue earned but never captured due to systemic failures in visibility, process, and execution. And that doesn't include the losses from fumbled sales opportunities and dropped hand-offs. Fueled by AI, RevOps helps revenue teams pinpoint revenue leak at speed and scale, equips managers with next-level data and cutting-edge analytics, and informs top executives to make better strategic decisions, faster.

RevOps delivers forecast accuracy with incredible precision, which means better financial planning and budgeting, smarter staffing and resource allocation, and more strategic decision-making.

RevOps teams crunch the numbers of customer retention, looking at where revenue is falling out, where deals are being lost, and where the leaks should be plugged. They also put in place strategies for retention, including feedback loops, that drive long-term growth.

RevOps teams see the whole board when it comes to growth opportunities, spotting high-potential upsell and cross-sell moments, elevating them to reps in the moments that matter. And they "blueprint" and operationalize the company's "revenue cadence," ensuring revenue teams maximize every critical revenue moment across the entire customer journey, in every week, month, and quarter.

I know of no other strategic function more worthy of C-suite attention and investment than RevOps. And now, thanks to two of the industry's most accomplished Revenue Operators—Sean Lane and Laura Adint—RevOps has its bible.

The Revenue Operations Manual: How to Build a High-Growth, Predictable and Scalable Business is the comprehensive, yet practical and actionable guide that every Revenue Operator needs. In the pages that follow, Lane and Adint educate, inform, and advise on every aspect of the still-emerging discipline of RevOps. It's the definitive go-to manual *for* Revenue Operators, *by* Revenue Operators and is sure to be one of the industry's go-to resources for years to come.

Andy Byrne, Clari CEO

ACKNOWLEDGMENTS

Thank you to the amazing Operators (and friends of Operators) who contributed their wisdom to this book (in order of mention): Pete Kazanjy, Rachel Haley, Allison Metcalfe, Paul Goetz, Craig Wortmann, Kyle Poyar, Jaclyn Balben, Sara McNamara, Tom Wentworth, Scott Brinker, Angus Davis, Maor Ezer, Kyle Bastien, Meghan Gill, Michelle Palleschi, Kevin Knieriem, Kyle Coleman, Chris Lowry, Paul Shea, Heidi Thompson, Karen Borchert, Bridget Zingale, Kyle Morris, Sylvia Kainz, Jake Randall, Tim Parilla, Stephen Hallowell, Todd Abbott, Karen Steele, Dave Gerhardt, Caitlin Quinlan, Arun Venkateswaran, Kyle Thelemann, Jeremey Donovan, Michelle Pietsch, Zubin Teherani, Crissy Vetere-Saunders, Carlos Nouche, Marcela Piñeros, Anu Krishnakumar, Molly Graham, Max Maeder, Noah Marks, Will Collins, Taft Love, Rupert Dallas, Jason Reichl, and Kate Adams.

Thank you to our partners at Kogan Page, especially Donna Goddard-Skinner for taking a chance on us and Jeylan Ramis for her insights and support throughout the process.

Sean: First and foremost, thank you to my co-author Laura for being such an amazing partner on this journey. To Paul Goetz, Will Collins, Angus Davis, (and Laura), thank you for being mentors who challenged me, supported me, and gave me opportunities to learn and grow. To everyone involved in Venture for America, thanks for instilling in me the importance of adaptive excellence. To David Cancel and Elias Torres, thank you for the lessons and leadership principles that served as inspirations for so many parts of this book. To D.C. and Dave Gerhardt, thanks for allowing me and encouraging me to start the podcast, and to Molly Chill, Dan Meyers, and Elizabeth Hilfrank, without whom the show wouldn't have become what it has. To all my world-class Operations teammates through the years, and an endless roster of internal partners who made me better every day, thank you. To my partners at BeaconGTM, Michelle Pietsch and Nish Murthy, thank you for your wholehearted backing of this project. And to my wife, Molly, thank you for your unwavering support in anything I do.

Laura: Thank you to my co-author, Sean, for lighting the fire to get this from a whiteboard outline to a fully executed book—I love that we managed the entire process with an amazing spreadsheet. To Jeff Kelly, Lisa Ryan, Timblin Kelleher, Jen Bialy, and Fred Gewant for being amazing bosses/mentors and taking a chance on me. To my favorite sales leaders, Scott LaFramboise, Carlos Nouche, Amir Assar, Brian Flaherty, Chris Shea, Rob Douglas, Armen Zildjian, and Brian Bell for sharing with me both your art and science of sales. To my COMPASS colleagues, Rita Welshons, James Mitchell, Nick Seewer, Holly Perry, Susan LeGault-Granewich, Shawn Bulen, Flint Tearney, and Ron Cruz, it really *was* all cupcakes and parades looking back on it! To Melissa Amooi for being the best officemate and customer success leader. To Audrey Zhao, Brett Buchanan, David Vital, Kinnari Desai, and Chris Mausler for being fabulous finance partners. Thank you to John Pasvankias, Stephanie Booker, John Swartz, and the late Rebekah Uusitalo for being my dream team. To the amazing Operators and business partners I've been lucky enough to work with over the years. To my dearest husband, Victor, for believing in me always. And to my family and friends for being my foundation of reality and purpose.

LIST OF ABBREVIATIONS

AI = Artificial Intelligence

ARR = Annual Recurring Revenue

BHAG = Big Hairy Audacious Goal

BCR = Base Commission Rate

CCO = Chief Customer Officer

CMO = Chief Marketing Officer

CRM = Customer Relationship Management

CRO = Chief Revenue Officer

CSM = Customer Success Manager

DITL = Day-in-the-Life

DRI = Directly Responsible Individual

IC = Individual Contributor

ICP = Ideal Customer Profile

IPO = Initial Public Offering

KPI = Key Performance Indicator

G&A = General & Administrative

GTM = Go-To-Market

MBOs = Management By Objectives

MEDDIC = Metrics, Economic Buyer, Decision Criteria, Decision Process, Identify Pain, and Champion

MVP = Minimum Viable Product

OKR = Objectives and Key Results

OTE = On Target Earnings

PPR = Productivity Per Rep

QBR = Quarterly Business Review

RevOps = Revenue Operations

ROI = Return on Investment

SaaS = Software as a Service

SDR = Sales Development Representative

SKU = Stock Keeping Units

SLA = Service Level Agreement

SMART = Specific, Measurable, Achievable, Relevant, and Time-Bound

SPIF = Special Performance Incentive Fund

SPIN = Situation, Problem, Implication, Need-payoff

V2MOM = Vision, Value, Methods, Obstacles, and Measures

WIIFM = What's In It For Me

Introduction: The Revenue Operations Mindset

In January 2023, LinkedIn released its list of the 25 fastest-growing job titles in the U.S.[1] The #1 job on that list? Head of Revenue Operations.

If you're reading this book, that's probably exciting news to you. But here's the thing: Roles dubbed as Revenue Operations can be amorphous blobs, with one company's job description different from the next.

If "firefighter" topped that list from LinkedIn, every applicant would show up to their interview expecting to put out some fires. So why can't we have our own clear expectations? And further, if this type of job is becoming so popular, where is the blueprint for building a thriving Revenue Operations function that lives up to those expectations? That's exactly what we're here to clarify and explore together in this book.

Let's start by actually defining Revenue Operations.

The core reason why people can't seem to get on the same page about Revenue Operations is that it is inherently *cross-functional*. As companies grow, silos naturally pop up between functions. Teams make decisions based on what is best for them to solve whatever challenge is directly in front of them.

And that's not always a bad thing. A sales leader *should* focus on what their own team needs to be successful, but that focus, no matter how well-intentioned, doesn't necessarily yield what's best for the company. A decision made in marketing has ripple effects in sales. A change in sales can be felt by your customer success team.

Revenue Operations, though, is meant to break down those silos and create an objective, comprehensive view of the entire customer journey. Instead of having marketing operations, sales operations and customer operations stand alone as individual functions in your company, RevOps brings together those Operations teams from sales, marketing, and customer success, the three legs of the go-to-market stool in Software as a Service (SaaS) organizations. To further the RevOps identity crisis, some companies have taken an additional step to re-brand their RevOps team as a "go-to-market Ops." team. We'll cover more about different Ops. team models later in the book, but there are three primary motivations for this consolidation:

1 **Efficiency:** Silos between teams create inefficiencies. Break them down and the productivity of your organization improves.

2 **Continuity:** Every hand-off in your customer journey is an opportunity for friction and disjointedness. A team that owns the customer journey from end-to-end can design and instrument the processes and technology necessary to ensure a seamless customer journey, for both your customers and your internal colleagues.

3 **Source of truth:** Every one of us has walked into a meeting where marketing had one version of a report and sales had a different one. Instead of spending half of the meeting figuring out whose report is right, RevOps serves as the source of truth for all go-to-market reporting and analytics.

That's where *most* RevOps definitions end. They talk about the cross-functional nature of the team, the organizational benefits of forming a team like this within your company, and send you on your way. But to what end?

Interest in "RevOps" has exploded. But we worry that people are drawn to it because it's a trendy buzzword or someone told them it's a team they're supposed to have at their company.

Just choosing to invest in RevOps is like signing up for a marathon, but never putting on a pair of running shoes.

Choosing to invest in RevOps is not the finish line—it's the beginning. You have to commit to running your business in a specific way. Otherwise, all you've done is commit to a diagram of an org chart.

If the mere existence of the RevOps team is where we as Operators see our teams' value, we're missing the point. Marketers aren't excited that their company has a marketing team. Building a Revenue

FIGURE 0.1 RevOps Google search volume history

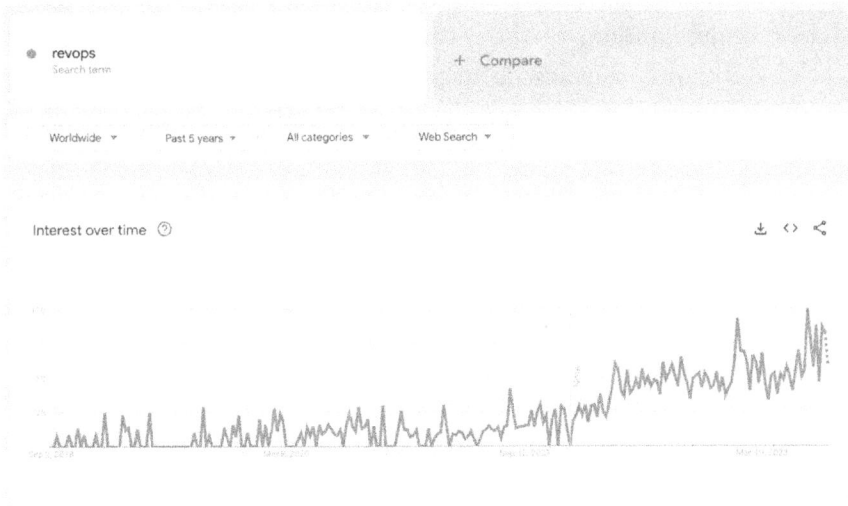

SOURCE Google Trends

Operations function is just an input, not an outcome. Your companies care about—no, they *need*—outcomes.

So what's a better definition? What are the outcomes we should
strive for?

**Revenue Operations transforms siloed, unpredictable businesses
into high-achieving, predictable, and scalable revenue machines.**

Each of the descriptive components of this definition are critical to
your team's (and your company's) success:

- **High-achieving:** This is an easy one, right? We all want to build
  companies that hit their targets. We have a hand to play in that.
  But we also think this component has evolved, especially in shifting
  economic realities. High-achieving doesn't necessarily mean
  high-growth, or growth at all costs. High-achieving should also
  mean financially sound. We as Operators—through our annual
  planning, hiring targets, quotas, comp plans, policies, technology
  costs—play a critical role in making the company financially
  successful.

- **Predictable:** Even if your results are good, that doesn't mean much if you don't understand why. A really strong RevOps team has a clear understanding of the levers available to a business, knows where the inefficiencies lie in the customer journey, and has the ability to push the buttons that will make a difference. That understanding leads to predictability. Operations teams should be able to see into the future. If your results are spiky or you don't have a grasp on how your company's funnels work, you can't possibly predict what's going to happen next.

- **Scalable:** If you build a car that can go 100 m.p.h. on its first drive, but it then sputters and stops the second the terrain changes, why bother building the car in the first place? We as Operators have to look around corners, anticipate where the car will break down, and build accordingly. Sometimes this might mean going a little slower around that corner, and that's ok. You and your company are trying to thrive on a long journey, and Operators are critical to making that happen.

- **Revenue machine:** Operators are the mechanics that know every minute detail of the machine they are building, and they are tasked with simultaneously maintaining and improving that machine.

We'll spend more time in the coming chapters outlining the exact strategies and playbooks to realize this ambitious vision. The mindset shift to outcomes is a critical one for Operators of any kind. Don't invest in RevOps just because you want to solve your internal reporting woes (though this is a lovely side effect). Invest because you are committed to building a high-achieving, predictable, and scalable revenue machine.

You'll be floored by the results when one of these teams is built well. Operational command of the business will increase, more people in your organizations will be comfortable leveraging data to make hard decisions, and when done correctly, the high achievement against your business targets will follow.

And you, the people building these machines, will become among the most valuable employees in an organization. Through the work we do, Operators come to know our business better than anyone else in the company.

The Revenue Operations Mindset

To make these outcomes a reality, it requires a mindset shift for you as an individual as well. If you were to go to the go-to-market leaders in your company today and ask them, "What does RevOps do?", how would they respond? Our guess is that most Chief Revenue Officers (CROs), Chief Marketing Officers (CMOs), and Chief Customer Officers (CCOs) would cobble together some list of responsibilities that includes:

"They handle our tools."
"Oh, they're the Salesforce admins."
"They build our reports."
"They're good with the data."
"They help with forecasting."

Changing the perception and the charter of Revenue Operations starts with challenging these narrow, incomplete definitions. Operators are enablers by nature, so we tend to take on the role of the "fixers," shouldering enormous burdens to make our companies work. Also, our go-to-market colleagues tend to have laughably low expectations about the business acumen we have to offer and the impact we can drive.

Those days are over.

In 2018, before starting the *Operations* podcast, Sean went to a RevOps conference. He was eager to network, to learn, and honestly, he had never seen a conference that was explicitly about RevOps before.

And a funny thing happened: He was disappointed.

While it was great to see Operators stand up and talk about their accomplishments, he found the content boring and mundane. Leaving that conference, he thought there had to be a better way. There had to be a better way to tell Operators' stories, to showcase the work we do in a compelling and interesting way, and to elevate the status of Operations within an organization.

Shortly after that conference, the *Operations* podcast was born, and it has become *the* destination for Operators to talk openly and earnestly about the work they do to drive growth at their companies (you'll hear from many of them in the coming chapters).

This book unapologetically champions the Operator. Operators are at the center of what makes companies run. It's time we embrace that truth, and take our rightful place not in the background, but at center stage. Only after you commit to improving yourself and your team can you play a meaningful role in improving your company.

A *Harvard Business Review* article titled "The People Who Make Organizations Go—or Stop" studied the informal networks at more than 50 large organizations. The researchers found that, "Increasingly, it's through these informal networks—not just through traditional organizational hierarchies—that information is found and work gets done."[2] The article goes on to examine common role-players they found in those networks, focusing primarily on what they came to call "central connectors."

According to the article, central connectors "link most people in an informal network with one another. They aren't usually the formal leaders within a unit or department, but they know who can provide critical information or expertise that the entire network draws on to get work done."

Sound familiar? Revenue Operators are the "central connectors" of your companies. They're the glue. And it's time we adopt and celebrate what we call "The Revenue Operations Mindset."

Like any set of principles, no single tenet of the Revenue Operations Mindset should be blindly adopted in a vacuum. Revenue Operations is a nuanced role; no single statement above will be the silver bullet solution to all your problems. But, when taken together, we believe this approach will change your professional prospects for the better.

The Revenue Operations Mindset means:

- Operators are **strategic** partners, not a support function.

- Operators focus on **outcomes**, not inputs.

- Operators are the perfect blend of **strategic** and **tactical**.

- Operators are **lifelong learners** and not afraid to be proven wrong.

- Operators champion their work and are proud of the **impact** they create.

- Operators believe in constant, incremental **improvements** and a "better, better, never done" approach.

When we look back at how businesses have evolved, there are functions that are foundational to how companies run today that would not have been so widely accepted just 10 or 20 years ago. Customer success teams, for example, rode a wave of category creation thanks in large part to the evangelism of companies like Gainsight. No one would start a company today without a plan for customer success.

Revenue Operations should, and will, be the same.

How to Read This Book

In the coming chapters, we'll give you the blueprint to not only make an investment in yourself and your Revenue Operations team, but to ensure an outsized yield from your investment (for you, your team, and your company).

The book is broken into four sections, the necessary building blocks for a world-class Revenue Operations function:

1 Build Your Knowledge
You're not going to know everything coming into a business. And you can't just replicate what you did at your last company and expect successful results. In this section, we'll offer ways to ask questions, learn the ins and outs of a company, understand your numbers, shadow customer-facing team members, and get out from behind your spreadsheets to take control of your business.

2 Build Your Business

This is where you get to apply what you've learned to start to build out the routines, cadences, and operating rhythms of your business. In this section, we'll explore how to design and instrument your customer journey, learn how processes and tools can support a seamless customer experience (not the other way around), and we'll offer a blueprint for goal setting, ruthless prioritization, and planning so you're only working on needle-moving projects that drive real business results.

3 Build Your Partnerships

The quality of your cross-functional relationships will make or break an Ops. team. This section will offer strategies and tactics to build and maintain those relationships, how you can provide value to your internal customers, and how to earn your seat at the table as a strategic partner to go-to-market leaders, and not just a support function.

4 Build Your Team

Last, but definitely not least, we'll focus on the Operators themselves. In this section, we offer advice on how to design your organizational structure, the traits of the people you want on your team, the importance of seeking out role models, and how to get incrementally better as an individual and as a team every day.

You'll also come across two recurring features in the book, brief interruptions where we'll stop to share relevant stories and lessons:

· **Real World Role Models**

As you'll see in the coming pages, we're strong believers in getting outside of the four walls of your company and seeking out role models you can learn from. Also, we're mindful that no Operators (or authors) have all the answers. To help, we've brought the role models to you, and in the pages to come, you'll hear from nearly 50 world-class Operators across a wide range of roles and companies, so you can learn from their experiences for yourself.

- **Confession Corner**
  Operators are usually pretty buttoned up, but we all have had moments where things didn't go quite according to plan. We've captured such moments throughout the book. Too often we only spotlight when things go right, and we felt it was just as important to share the moments we might not be as proud of. We've kept these stories anonymous to encourage the most vulnerable and real sharing from our contributors.

We don't pretend that this book will have every answer to every problem that someone who works in Revenue Operations might come across. As we've already established, the charter of Revenue Operations is broad, and only widening. So, if your role is specifically focused on sales operations or marketing operations or customer operations, not every single concept in this book will be perfectly applicable to everything in your day-to-day job.

However, we do believe that there is more in common than there is different across any Revenue Operations role. This book is about those commonalities and, in the pages to come, we'll offer proven strategies, practical guides, and hard-earned lessons you can apply to your role right away.

Running your business using the methods outlined in this book will be the difference between a siloed, unpredictable business and a well-oiled revenue machine.

If that sounds exciting to you, then let's get started.

Endnotes

1 LinkedIn News. LinkedIn Jobs on the Rise 2023: 25 U.S. roles that are growing in demand [LinkedIn] 18 January 2023, https://www.linkedin.com/pulse/linkedin-jobs-rise-2023-25-us-roles-growing-demand-linkedin-news/ (archived at https://perma.cc/ZNF5-KXNB)

2 R. Cross and L. Prusak (2002) The People Who Make Organizations Go—or Stop, *Harvard Business Review*, June, https://hbr.org/2002/06/the-people-who-make-organizations-go-or-stop (archived at https://perma.cc/6P9E-GVJU)

PART ONE

Build Your Knowledge

1

When is it Time to Invest in RevOps?

One of the most common questions we hear is, "How do I know when it's time for my company to invest in Operations?"

The most likely answer is, "Yesterday."

Most start-up companies put off investing in any sort of operational function because they view it as a "nice to have" instead of a "need to have." And who can blame them? Founders are trying to get their companies off the ground, find product—market fit, convince some customers to take a risk on a brand-new product, all while making sure they don't run out of money. There's plenty else to distract their focus.

Let's put ourselves in the shoes of one of those founders for a moment. Typically, at least one person on the founding team at a company is responsible for the product. That person's job resembles that of a Product Manager, shepherding the development of the product along and plotting the future roadmap of what's in store. No founder would go for long without having someone in this product management position.

Now imagine that exact same scenario but consider the company itself as the product. Once again, you need someone in charge of shepherding the development of the company along and plotting the future roadmap of what's in store. That someone is an Operations hire.

If your company is the product, your Operations team is the Product Manager.

So, when is it actually time to put a dedicated Operator in place to shepherd the development of the company? We've found that three things should be true:

1 The company has found basic product/market fit.
2 The founder/CEO is no longer the sole seller.
3 There is a proven, repeatable sales process.

When these three things are true, it's time for a dedicated resource to develop a high-achieving, predictable, and scalable revenue machine. That someone is an Operations hire with what it takes to make a difference.

In Chapter 20, we will walk through different options for the structure of a Revenue Operations organization, but it is common for the first investment in Operations to be focused around the sales organization. Throughout this book, we will keep coming back to the necessity of ensuring your investment in Revenue Operations does not stop with just sales. Without a holistic view of Revenue Operations that includes the full revenue lifecycle, you will end up with internal and external silos, broken hand-offs throughout the customer journey, tech stack debt, and issues with reporting accuracy.

REAL WORLD ROLE MODELS

Pete Kazanjy is the author of the book, *Founding Sales*, and the co-founder of Atrium, makers of sales performance management software. In Episode 27 of the *Operations* podcast, Pete outlined his advice on when to invest in Operations.

You should be investing in operational excellence from day zero, but your question is, *"When is there a human who's responsible for it?"*

I think that one of the big shortfalls is when people say, *"Hey, we just got to sell. We just got to sell"* versus saying, *"Actually, **until we have an Operations person**, this is the responsibility of the founder to think about process and efficiency specifically to set ourselves up for success in the future."*

Then the question becomes, *"At what point does it make sense for us to have an individual human who kind of peels off that responsibility from sales leadership or from the founder?"* When it gets to the point where the opportunities for operational efficiency gain make up for the incremental salary expense there, that's really the time to hire. Rather than hiring an incremental salesperson at that point, hire an Operations person. What they're going to do is make the existing salespeople way more effective and help us set the incremental salespeople up for success.

The next question is, *"When does that happen?"* Usually, you could see it as early as six, eight, ten sales humans who are being orchestrated. You could see it as late as maybe 15. If you get beyond that, it's going to get messy and you're going to start seeing things getting broken.

What's really dangerous there is what ends up happening is you die a death of a thousand cuts rather than it being one big mess up. It's one of those things that can be insidiously invisible and so this is why it's got to be somebody's job. Even if it's not somebody's dedicated responsibility, somebody has got to be responsible for thinking about it.[1]

Internal and External Customers

Throughout this book, we'll write about two different types of customers: Internal and external. As Revenue Operators, we must consider instrumenting and operationalizing the full revenue lifecycle for both audiences. External customers, the purchasers of the product or service that is produced by your company, are your first audience. The Operator's objective is to consider how to orchestrate the internal workings of the company to best support the external customers' needs. Of equal weight and importance is the experience of your internal customers, your colleagues in sales, marketing, customer success, and elsewhere who are doing all of the activities to support your external customers. Operators need to have a customer-first attitude for both.

The Goldilocks Principle

In the "Goldilocks and the Three Bears" fairy tale, there is a search for "just right" in porridge, chairs, and beds. In Operations, we search for the "just right" level of people, policies, and processes to prevent damage to the company while being able to efficiently grow our businesses.

Too many strict policies and processes early in a company's life-cycle will stifle growth and undermine a small company's unique strength to be nimble. Overly onerous processes aren't efficient and perhaps you are so concerned about protecting a company that you don't allow it to grow big enough to have something to protect.

If you find yourself in a situation where things are over-controlled, the best avenue to following the Goldilocks Principle is to simplify your existing policies and processes. Find the biggest areas of friction by interviewing your stakeholders, observing where extra processes don't add to the outcome, and proposing simplifications.

On the other hand, not *enough* policies or processes in a growing, medium-sized company can create confusion for your customers who get different answers from different people; they can cost your company money with too many gives and not enough gets, and sow uncertainty into being able to execute on your promises. Don't mistake chaos for agility; you can have reputational or sometimes monetary damage if you don't execute on your commitments.

The goal of the Goldilocks Principle is to hit that elusive "just right" spot, based on where your company is in its journey. It is also to realize that the company will continue to grow and what is "just right" today won't be right in 18 months (maybe less). Use Pete Kazanjy's rule of thumb where the benefit outweighs the cost; just know that you will need to regularly re-evaluate that trade-off.

The Incremental Investment

Ever been asked what the ratio should be for Operations to sales reps? Years ago, Laura was in an interview for a Revenue Operations leader position when the interviewing CRO asked her that question. Her answer was "it depends," but the interviewer was not satisfied. Why does it always feel like the Operator's answer is "it depends"? Well... because it does!

Your company's needs for Operations will depend on a lot of things: Company lifecycle stage, current operational maturity, sales motion, go-to-market complexity, average deal size, and, perhaps most influentially, your scope of responsibilities. For example, if your Operations team is responsible for enablement, the number of resources you'll need will be very different from an Ops team that isn't (more on that particular dilemma in Chapter 18).

In an episode of the *Operations* podcast, Rachel Haley, the co-founder and CEO of Clarus Designs and the former Senior Director of Sales Operations at Snowflake, outlined how she had approached staffing Operations:

> We looked at benchmarks of other studies that had been done, and we landed on a ratio of one sales ops. employee or individual to every 10 quota carrying A.E.s (Account Executives). These were core A.E.s only, meaning when we had 450, we had around 45 people in sales ops.

> The issue with that is sometimes you can do more with less, and that was what our CRO and I would talk about. Okay, maybe this one to ten ratio does hold. However, if you can hire someone who is maybe a little bit more experienced or more senior and can do 1.5X or even 2X the work of someone who is a little bit more junior, even though from a cost perspective it's a lot less, you should probably hire the more senior person. Do more with less, build in leadership, and a good second line leadership level, so that they can also take on some of that burden of management. Loosely, that is what we aligned on, but it didn't always necessarily fit that way.

> Sometimes we would need more. You still have all of the supporting functions within sales that still require your time, right? You have sales management, you have sales engineering, you have SDRs [sales development representatives], et cetera. And those people still take up Operations bandwidth.

> That's a loose ratio that you can operate within, but sometimes you don't need as much and you can do more with less. And then sometimes in different scenarios, you might need a little bit more given that your core A.E.s are not your entire sales team.[2]

Like we said, it depends. Rachel's 10:1 ratio is among the lowest we've seen; we've run teams that were more in the 20:1 range. So your ratio may look like Rachel's or it may look differently. And advancements in technology like artificial intelligence (AI) will only further challenge our assumptions about staffing and headcount ratios. What is important is landing on an agreed upon set of responsibilities and the required resources to fulfill those responsibilities. Whether you support all customer-facing teams or just a couple, or agree on a 10:1 ratio or 20:1, get unimpeachable clarity on this internal agreement, so that it's not something you need to relitigate over and over as your team grows.

Chapter Takeaways

1 **Invest early in Operations:** Start investing in operational excellence early, treating it as a necessity for sustainable growth from the beginning. Invest in an Operations leader when the company has basic product/market fit, the founder/CEO is not the sole seller, and there is a repeatable sales process.

2 **Operations as a product manager for the company:** The analogy of the company as a product and the Operations team as the product manager highlights the essential role of Operations in shepherding the development of the company and planning its future roadmap.

3 **Holistic view of Revenue Operations:** Understand that the first investment in Operations often focuses on the sales organization, but it's crucial to avoid stopping there. Achieving the benefits of Revenue Operations requires the broad perspective of before the sale, during the sale, and after the sale.

4 **Both internal and external customers:** Operators should adopt a customer-first attitude, considering both external customers (purchasers of the product) and internal customers (those involved in supporting activities).

5 **Implement the Goldilocks Principle:** Apply the Goldilocks Principle to strike the right balance in people, policies, and processes. Avoid too many strict policies/processes early in the company's lifecycle that stifle growth, as well as too few that may lead to chaos. Regularly re-evaluate to ensure alignment with the company's current needs.

Endnotes

1 *Operations* with Sean Lane (2020) When to Invest in Sales Operations (Plus the Right Way to Measure Performance) with Atrium Founder Pete Kazanjy, Episode 27 [podcast]
2 *Operations* with Sean Lane (2020) The Art & Science of Snowflake's Sales Capacity Planning, with Rachel Haley, Episode 39 [podcast]

2

Know Your Numbers

Here's a myth we would like to bust:

Every business is different, so I can't possibly understand a new business quickly.

Laura worked in the semiconductor business for 11 years. She worked in an outsourced services delivery business, consulting, and automotive. She worked in software. What do any of these businesses have in common with each other? It is very easy to think the answer is nothing.

But the truth is there are core building blocks that you can use as a foundation for analyzing any business, and then fill in the nuances as you learn more.

An Operator's ability to offer insight transcends the company you are in. To understand the numbers of your particular business, you must start with the business drivers and how they work together.

CONFESSION CORNER

I was really new to a software company and it was the first time that I was asked to sit in the executive staff meeting. It was intense: The CEO was going through the income statement line by line (from memory!) on the whiteboard, drilling into every weakness. Everyone in the room was jumping to answer the rapid-fire questions.

I wasn't familiar with the numbers yet. I wasn't even familiar with the software industry yet. I definitely had imposter syndrome. I was hoping to add value, but at a minimum, I figured I could at least learn.

I had to draw upon my prior experiences to contribute. In the meeting, we were circling around why the gross margins were lower than usual this quarter. In my prior companies, I would have broken it down into product lines, but that wouldn't work here with software.

Finally, someone mentioned the recently increased headcount in the services team and that unlocked something for me that could help explain the numbers. Software margins are much higher than services margins. Utilization of resources is what drives services margins, and new resources are usually not at peak utilization immediately. My experience outside of software, where I closely monitored margin numbers, helped me to isolate a relevant data point, but I wasn't confident enough yet to directly speak up to offer my perspective.

As Operators, we need to "know our numbers." The organization counts on us as a source of truth for those numbers. More than just knowing critical metrics like revenue, retention rate, opportunity conversion, discounting, and services resource utilization, Revenue Operators need to have a deeply rooted understanding of which numbers are important for a particular business to be high-achieving and predictable.

Our goals in this chapter are two-fold. The first is to help the newly hired Operator ramp up quickly in a new business. The second is to expand the perspective of a veteran Operator in their existing business.

Where to Start

When you are new to an organization, where should you look as an Operator to get a handle on the numbers of your new company? That will depend on the current stage of your company.

If your company is public, start with its annual report and, in particular, the "Management Discussion and Analysis" section. Any level of Operator should have already read this before they interviewed at a company, but now is the time to read it in detail along with any supplemental information you learned from the interview process. If external analysts write about your company, review what they are analyzing and what questions they ask during earnings reports. Earnings releases are excellent sources of information of the top-level concerns and success barometers for your company. Each type of business will have different strengths they highlight, which will give you ideas on what should be tracked.

There is also likely a quarterly internal reporting package that is produced and a company meeting presentation that will provide excellent insights into what the key metrics are for the business and what the goals are for the company. Your objective in reviewing this information is to understand which go-to-market areas are being monitored and how actual results compare to the goals set. You can start to form theories on where the areas of concern are and which metrics might offer opportunities for improvement.

If you don't have a lot of experience with financial statements, ask someone in Finance to walk you through the financials of your new company. In Chapter 15, we'll discuss the importance of RevOps' relationship with the finance department. You can begin to develop that relationship from the start by understanding what finance believes the most important company metrics are. You can also learn a lot by asking which additional go-to-market metrics they don't currently have visibility into but would like to better understand.

If the company is not yet public, there will be a wide variety of what might or might not be available. Your job is to consume as much as you can get your hands on. Board meetings, internal reporting packages, dashboards that are used by executives, company meeting slides, annual kickoffs, and quarterly business review (QBR) presentations are all excellent sources of understanding what is tracked, what is communicated, and how the company is currently performing against its goals. In some companies, there will be hundreds of metrics monitored closely; in others, there may be tracking but no goals, and in some, the absence of metrics might be why you were hired in the first place.

You'll notice we didn't initially advise you to ask what your Operations team currently produces. Yes, of course you will also want to ask about that. But we believe it is important to start **first** at the company level. It is easy to perpetuate the siloed mentality by focusing only on what your team already does. But that would mean that you miss out on the big picture and how all of the company parts (and goals) fit together. If we take the "revenue machine" mentality of Revenue Operations, we need to first understand how the full machine works before we begin.

What to Look For

Once you have compiled all these sources of information, it's time to put the puzzle pieces together. Your objectives should be to articulate what your company's key success drivers are, how you are currently performing against your goals, and how well your organization can articulate why your performance is what it is. Each of these areas will start to form your roadmap of where you can focus your efforts. For example, if the goals aren't clear, that might be the first order of business. Sometimes there are so many metrics, you can't tell which ones are the most important. In other cases, articulating why something isn't working may require investment in an analytics function.

Some questions to consider include:

- What are the key metrics of focus? Revenue? New business vs. expansion? Margin? Costs? Customer satisfaction? Customer retention?
- Is it clear what the goals are for each of these and how the company is performing against those goals?
- What are the sources of revenue?
- Are there obvious leading indicators (meaning they will tell you if there are problems/success headed towards the company)?

- Are there obvious lagging indicators (meaning the problems/success already happened)?

- How important are margins, operational costs, and overall spend to the company's current stage?

- Do you have departmental spending targets and where are they discussed?

- Do you understand what the goals are for each go-to-market function?

- What are the specific goals for sales? Marketing? Customer success? Services?

- What are the current areas of concern? How do those tie into what the go-to-market teams do, impact, and are measured on?

- Is there a current understanding of why the company is above or below its targets?

- How well is performance articulated and *understood* in the information you have gathered?

REAL WORLD ROLE MODELS

On Episode 48 of the *Operations* podcast, Allison Metcalfe, the former CRO of Demandbase, provides an excellent analogy of how to think of and manage through Key Performance Indicators (KPIs):

> If you're going to run a proper field organization, you need to imagine yourself walking into a big world bank where you see all the world clocks up on the wall, although you've got to replace the world clocks with the critical KPIs that measure the effectiveness of your field. Then you need to decide what the times should be, and then you look at those clocks and you figure out which ones are really off time, and you execute programs and initiatives ruthlessly against getting that clock back on time.

> Our macro-categories were: Pipeline health, record activity, sales excellence, growth and efficiency, and customer health.

> Now, what I see a lot of organizations do, if they don't do this right, is they start to invest a lot of their time on hunches, and not on hard data.

I'll give you a great example of that in one of my former companies. Before we got this world clock concept in place, when I poked into what the productivity team was working on and when I really pushed them on what metrics they were hoping to change, it was all about CSM (customer success manager) efficiency. And the reality was when we got the world clocks up and we really narrowed in on customer health, our ARR (annual recurring revenue) per CSM, which is how we defined efficiency at the time, was fine. We were happy with it. It could always be better, but it wasn't the number one problem.

The real problem was actually value-based churn. And so one of the first things I did was redirect their attention. This efficiency program was helpful, but it wasn't the most important thing based on what our clocks were telling us. We needed to figure out how we coach our customer success and sales teams on business outcome value, because that was the biggest problem we were having. So we lifted and shifted resources to put the attention back on what would really drive results for our business.[1]

What are the world clocks of your business? What are those critical KPIs that would actually move the needle of the business? The Operator's objective is to create that world clock wall for the business, ensuring the right clocks are on there and that the attention is on what will drive results.

Benchmarks

When you have a child, there are many, many benchmarks available to assess how your child is progressing. There are age milestones for sitting up, crawling, walking, speaking, smiling, letters, numbers, reading, etc. You can measure growth and weight against averages at every month marker.

If only measuring companies were as easy!

We would never assess a puppy against those baby benchmarks. You have to be in the same species for the benchmarks to be useful. The same is true for companies: Find what your company's species is to figure out your benchmarks.

In a mature industry, you will likely be able to compare yourself to public companies whose financials are publicly available. If you aren't yet public but your competitors are, you at least understand what your older siblings are measuring and achieving.

In a private or emerging company, you may have some guideposts provided by private equity companies, investment bankers, and venture capital firms. An example would be the "Rule of 40" for SaaS companies: You want the sum of your revenue growth and profit margin to exceed 40 percent. You can have negative profit as long as your revenue growth makes up for it (and of course, they also want to know the time to profitability). Asset utilization is often used as a benchmark for manufacturing companies. If your company already has a relationship with a venture capitalist group, they may have a set of benchmarks they have gathered from their portfolio companies. Find your appropriate benchmarks for your company's maturity, size, and industry.

It's Beyond the Arithmetic: It's the WHY

Perhaps you are lucky enough to be able to remember all of the numbers and to recall not only last quarter's revenue, but also the prior four, the targets, and what percentages of attainment you had. Perhaps you can do calculations in your head to say what 104 percent of your goal would be down to the penny. If so, congratulations; you have a gift that will help you in an Operator's world. If you can't, that's okay. That's not what we meant by "Know Your Numbers."

An Operator needs to know:

1 Which numbers are important.

2 What those numbers "should" be.

3 How to calculate them in detail.

4 What can cause those numbers to veer off course.

5 What actual results tell you to do differently.

Many Operators will stop at the first three. World-class Operators push to deeply understand, communicate, and *impact* the last two. Understanding what the drivers are for a business will help you track the right things. Understanding what the indicators are telling you about your business is how to create a high-achieving, predictable, and scalable revenue machine.

Knowing your numbers is actually understanding the why of your numbers. If revenue is flat, do you know why? Was it a particular segment? Was it volume? Was it price? Was it new business or existing business? The answers to these can help guide you on what to evaluate or possibly change.

Indicators

We mentioned lagging and leading indicators in the questions to consider. Lagging indicators are like looking in the rearview mirror on what happened. Revenue growth is generally a lagging indicator. Leading indicators are like looking through the windshield at upcoming road conditions that give you warnings to change course. Lead volume is generally a leading indicator for revenue (and a lagging indicator of marketing campaigns). When you understand the drivers of your business and how to track them, find a balance of both leading and lagging measures.

Understanding the time horizon of your company's sales cycle will give you ideas on how to identify leading indicators. If pipeline is a leading indicator of revenue, how long does it take for that pipeline to turn into dollars? Or let's say you are changing the pricing of your product. In businesses that have short sales cycles, you can see the impact of pricing changes on revenue very quickly; so, your average sales price becomes a helpful lagging indicator of that decision. For longer sales cycles, though, changes in pricing will take longer to show up in revenue, but you can see quoting discount behavior changes as leading indicators of that average sales price.

Customer success is another area where leading indicators are critical so that you aren't simply looking forlornly through the rearview mirror at customer churn. In many businesses, it is too late to do anything when a customer leaves you. Leading indicators for customers may include things like product adoption, usage, satisfaction, and support tickets.

If you have a recurring revenue model, even your lagging indicator of retention rate can hide nuances to understand what happened or is happening in your business. For example, a company had a number of different products and the customer success organization was allowed to swap out one product for another. So when renewal time came, the new product counted as "add-on" but the swapped-out product did not get recorded as a loss because the total value of the customer was the same. The compensation plan paid on total renewed dollars. While CSMs were getting paid for these flat renewals, the hidden truth was that the company's products weren't proving sticky with customers. Sometimes the simple calculations can mask problems and it is the Operator's job to sniff these out.

How Low Can You Go?

Most of us have heard the term "analysis paralysis." How do you know when you have gone deep enough into your numbers to understand what's happening? What's most important is to understand: 1) The directionality of a change, and 2) whether the analysis indicates that further action is necessary.

Sometimes it's all in the details.

The first thing you need to do is make sure you're aligned on the metric you're measuring and *how* it is measured. For example, oftentimes "opportunity win rates" and "opportunity conversion rates" are used interchangeably, but the calculations of these can be different and can give you conflicting messages about what is happening in your business.

Win rates are generally calculated as the total number of wins divided by the sum total number of wins plus losses for a specific period of time. It can be calculated as an opportunity count or dollar amount ratio. However, if you don't have processes where the sales team has clear and consistent criteria on when to open opportunities as well as to regularly monitor and close old opportunities, this ratio could be less useful as an indicator of successfully closing business (e.g., if you have a bunch of stale opportunities that are still open but are never going to be won or closed, the win rate you're looking at will be inflated).

Opportunity conversion rates can be calculated as the wins for a given time period over the total pipeline cohort for that time period. This metric can be broken down into components to give you indicators on whether you have "tumbleweed" pipeline that moves from quarter to quarter and how much in-period business (a.k.a. "Create and Close") you rely upon to hit your numbers. Opportunity conversion rates are best used in longer sales cycles with strong pipeline hygiene practices. In this scenario, it can serve as an excellent leading indicator of whether you have enough pipeline to hit your revenue goals. Or it might demonstrate the strength or weakness of a particular cohort of pipeline that was created from a specific campaign (e.g., you created a bunch of pipeline from that trade show you went to, but none of it ended up closing so maybe you skip that show next year). On the other hand, if the majority of your opportunities open and close within the same period (or you just have lax pipeline hygiene), the beginning of quarter indicators can be misleading.

WIN RATE VS. CONVERSION RATE

Win Rate = Wins / (Wins + Losses)
Conversion Rate = Wins from a Given Pipeline Amount / Total Pipeline
    Amount

As Operators, we need to understand not only how to measure and calculate our companies' metrics, but we also must consider the adjacent factors, scenarios, and drivers that will affect the outcomes and the validity of those metrics.

Chapter Takeaways

1 **Start at the company level:** When entering a new organization, begin by looking at the big picture at the company level. Thoroughly review internal and external reporting available. Understanding the key metrics, goals, and areas of concern at the company level provides a foundation for diving into team-specific details later.

2 **Create a world clock wall:** Visualize and manage KPIs as if they were world clocks on a wall, as explained by Allison Metcalfe. Focus on hard data rather than hunches, and align programs and initiatives ruthlessly with the most critical KPIs for your business.

3 **Go beyond arithmetic; understand the WHY:** Knowing your numbers goes beyond merely memorizing figures. An Operator should understand why certain numbers matter, what they "should" be, how to calculate them, and what can cause deviations. Delve into the drivers of the business, comprehend leading and lagging indicators, and seek to understand the underlying reasons behind the numbers to drive meaningful results.

Endnote

1 *Operations* with Sean Lane (2021) A CRO's World Clocks for Running a Business with Demandbase's Allison Metcalfe, Episode 48 [podcast]

3

Know What Your Company Sells

Are you familiar with the TV show, *Severance*? The fictitious company in the show uses a mindwipe procedure to separate the consciousness of their employees between their lives at work and outside of it. Characters in the show have no awareness of what goes on in their "other" life.

What's more, even at their jobs, the employees are kept in the dark as to what the work they're doing even means. They sit in their cubicles, doing mindless work, oblivious to the impact of what they do every day.

This is the exact opposite of what we believe you need to be an excellent Revenue Operator. Plenty of people put on blinders when they are at work and just focus on their job or the tasks they are asked to complete. To embody the philosophy and realize the benefits of Revenue Operations, we simply can't ignore what the rest of the company does. In fact, the Revenue Operations Mindset requires the exact opposite.

When Laura worked in a semiconductor business, she took an internal class offered on how semiconductors are manufactured to learn all about ingots, wafers, bake-in times, testing machines, packaging, etc. Sounds thrilling, right?

Did she need to do this for her sales operations jobs? Probably not. However, it did give her a better appreciation for what the teams she supported did. It also helped her decipher the wealth of information packed into the stock keeping units (SKUs), which would reap rewards for years.

Those tidbits that you pick up by being intensely curious about everything in your business can make a difference. Laura was able to use that SKU knowledge multiple times to assist with investigations, CRM design, and most importantly, to help the sales teams get paid accurately.

Perhaps SKUs aren't important in your world, but getting sales compensation correct in **any** business is one of Revenue Operations' top priorities. Here's the point: Knowing the details of what your company sells will help you make better decisions.

As an Operator, you need to know what is important in your business and what is important to your customers. That knowledge will help you navigate everything from what goes into the systems you build to solving the sticking points for your customers and internal teams. It can also provide insights into how you should structure your internal teams to best serve your external customers. For example, you might find that with a more technical product and experience, you need specialists on your customer success team or solutions consulting/pre-sales as part of your selling teams.

You will also generate more genuine empathy for your internal customers by walking a mile in their shoes. Even in extremely technical and complex products, ensuring that your Revenue Operations team is well educated on what the business sells and how they sell it will help them to better advocate on behalf of their internal customers.

Empathy can:

- help make process changes more user friendly and customer sensitive
- have an impact on how effectively you communicate changes to the organization
- inspire your Operations team to proactively solve problems that your internal customers didn't even know they could help with.

WHAT SHOULD OPERATORS UNDERSTAND ABOUT WHAT YOUR COMPANY SELLS?

- **Your customers:** Who are they? What are their roles? What are they measured on? What are they looking to solve by buying what your company sells?

- **Your market:** How are you different from your competitors? How do you fit in your market? How price sensitive are your buyers? What are the trends affecting your market?
- **Your product:** What do you sell? How do your buyers buy it? What problems are they solving? What are the switching costs? What else do buyers use it with?
- **Your commercial offering:** What do customers typically start with? How do they upgrade? Buy more? Use more? How do they buy again/renew?

So, how do you reach this level of empathy and understanding? First things first: You have to get out from behind the spreadsheets (and likely outside of your natural comfort zone). Here are a number of different ways we've used to help us and our Revenue Operations teams to learn the business and be able to answer the questions in the box.

Customer-Facing New Hire Training/Sales Bootcamps

Sign up your Operations team for the new hire training for customer-facing teams. We've even had a number of our team members go through sales bootcamp training, including a requirement to stand and deliver a sales pitch deck. Operations folks don't always want to do this and plenty of our team members have asked to opt out, but we believe you should hold your ground and ask them to do the pitches. The nerves they experience in a low-risk environment of bootcamp provide more empathy when they eventually run reports on adherence to the new sales process or design how the CRM stores information that could help improve the sales process.

Sales/Product/Message Certifications

Depending on the complexity of your product, sales cycles, and industry, some certifications might be worthwhile for your Operations team to complete. If your company offers a product certification to customers, then your Operations team should be certified on that product as well.

Investing a few hours in a certification is well worth building real knowledge of what your customers are experiencing. At one of Laura's companies, when a marketing messaging certification was rolled out with a new campaign, she had all of her Operations team members certify on the new messaging early. It not only raised the confidence of her Operations team members, but it also demonstrated leadership to other departments, especially the customer-facing ones, that the new messaging was important for everyone to nail.

When we as Operators participate in the certification processes of our internal customers, we align ourselves as true partners to them. Operations teams aren't always on the front lines of selling (although both of us have been at companies where we were pulled in to speak with Operators at customer accounts), but being educated on what our internal customers are having to do/say/sell provides valuable context to our operational activities.

Operators should also consume marketing training or presentations on the ideal customer profile to understand how to identify potential customers. What better way for your analyst to score the best accounts than having them truly understand what an ideal customer looks like? (Much more on firmographic account scoring and territory planning in Chapter 9.)

Sales Pitches

New hire training doesn't always provide your team with an opportunity to perform or see other sales pitches. If not, pick some sample pitches for your team to watch, or watch them during one of your staff meetings if you have a tool like Gong or Clari (if your company isn't consistently recording sales calls, start now!). If you don't have recordings, get creative on how to ensure your team sees some live sales pitches. Your team knows who the best sellers are from the data. As a team, watch what the superstars do differently from their peers.

It's tempting for observers to criticize, especially if they haven't gone through it themselves. Temper the critiques with analyses of why certain things are done during the pitch.

Product Demos

Product demos are where the theoretical value of a product is tested by the reality of presenting that value to a customer. Whether you're looking at a highly-produced demo designed by marketing or a live call with the sales department, you and your teams should be watching these. How effectively is the team pairing the customers' problems with your product's story? Where do the individuals providing the demo struggle? What do the prospects react strongly to? When are they bored or (worse) apathetic? What questions are asked during the demo? What stands out?

Some products don't lend themselves well to product demos or may be more complex than what your Operations team has the background to understand. In these cases, don't throw up your hands and give up. How can you be creative in understanding how your product is used and how your internal teams demonstrate its benefits to prospects? The best product demos show how your product solves the prospects' problems. Does your Operations team understand the problems being solved? If not, lean on your partners in marketing to coherently articulate what those problems are.

Customer Success Meetings

It is one thing to sell a product once; it's quite another for the promises of that product to be realized (not to mention additional sales milestones like annual renewals, upgrades, or expansions). Regardless of the business model, you need to understand how your customer success and support teams speak with customers to keep them engaged. If these meetings are recorded, watch a recording as a team. If they aren't, ask if you can have your team join a meeting to learn what resonates with customers, what is covered during the meetings, and what tools and resources are used by your CSMs to provide value. Operators should look for insights into what information is helpful for customers to visualize and tangibly access demonstrable value. These insights can drive future reporting, process improvements, system enhancements, and even new product features.

"Ride-Alongs" with Customer-Facing Teammates

At one of Laura's companies, she noticed that her SDR group was having a really hard time meeting certain service level agreements (in an SDR context, SLAs are typically an internal agreement on how fast SDRs follow up on leads). The SDR leaders were working with SDRs who were most out of compliance: The metrics were up front and visible, everyone talked ad nauseam about why it was so important to get to leads fast, but there were still leads that just didn't get responded to within the SLA timeframes. After weeks of head-scratching, Laura decided to go to the office herself to observe what the SDRs were experiencing alongside them. She picked a few that were on the "SLA naughty list," but always hit their numbers, to see what she could learn. Her intention wasn't to "catch" anyone, but rather to walk through how they process the leads and where they look for information.

Through her observations, Laura discovered that some leads were being sent to the SDRs that shouldn't have been and, in the interest of being efficient, the top performers were just moving on and not marking them. She also discovered that some of the leads were missing obvious markers that would have identified them as high value leads: The highly converting indicators were missing from the lead screen and only the low conversion sources were showing. Because the marketing operations team had thoroughly trained her on how to understand the lead signals, she could see the gap in the lead information visible to the SDRs.

She asked the marketing operations team to suppress the false flags and amplify the good signals. The team also educated the SDRs on marking false flags better so that feedback on the lead quality could make it to the marketing team, rather than making it a battle about SLAs.

There is no better substitute than to sit, literally or virtually, with your internal customers to see how they do their job and how you as an Operator can make their lives (and the experience of your external customers) better.

While Operators can't be experts in everything, we believe that deeply understanding what your company sells has to be a priority in fulfilling the mission of Revenue Operations. How can you be the expert mechanic of your company's revenue machine if you don't fundamentally understand the engine?

Chapter Takeaways

1 **Understand your company's offerings:** To excel in Revenue Operations, it is crucial to have a deep understanding of what your company sells and how it sells.

2 **Cultivate empathy for internal customers:** Gaining knowledge about how your company sells can help Operators develop empathy for internal customers. Empathy helps Operators create user-friendly processes, enhance communication, and proactively address issues.

3 **Participate in training and certifications:** Providing training and certifications to your Operations team can enhance their understanding of the product and ideal customer profiles, and how to communicate value to customers.

4 **Watch what your customer-facing teams do:** Regularly observing sales pitches, product demos, and customer success meetings can provide valuable insights into internal and external customer needs.

5 **Seek first-hand experience:** Participating in "ride-alongs" with the teams you support can help Operators identify operational issues and opportunities for improvement, ultimately benefiting internal and external customers.

PART TWO

Build Your Business

4

The Importance of Operating Rhythms: The Routines, Meetings, and Cadences to Help You Hit Your Numbers

As you read this, new technologies, new tools, and new use cases for those technologies and tools are exploding. It's nearly impossible to keep up with every trend or the latest application of the most cutting-edge technology. Even trying to cite an example in this book would likely be woefully outdated by the time you read it.

So, what are Operators supposed to do? Do we stick to proven but potentially stale ways of doing things? Or do we spend all of our time constantly replacing tools, processes, and strategies with the latest shiny toys?

Like most things in Operations, the answer lies somewhere in-between. We believe that Revenue Operations teams can and should push for new, more efficient ways of leveraging the latest technologies, but to do that, you need to have a disciplined foundation upon which to build. We also believe that high-performing go-to-market teams are built on disciplined operating rhythms. Regardless of the latest trend or the hottest new tool, you have to *run your business*.

Disciplined operating rhythms start with "inspecting what you expect." You may have heard leaders preach this mantra in your career, especially during times of explosive growth or change. When your company is undergoing a lot of change, it can be tempting to launch a new product, a new team, or a new process, and then immediately move on to the next thing that requires your attention.

And that thing you just spent a bunch of time, money, and resources building gets neglected.

Fast forward a few months, and everyone is *shocked* that the results everyone expected from the new initiative didn't magically materialize on their own.

You need to "inspect what you expect."

Building and running your business means having "operational command" over that business. Not only do you as an Operator need to know what's going on, what's working, and what's not, so too do all of your internal customers and stakeholders.

One of the fastest ways to instill operational command in a business is through routines. This doesn't mean meetings for the sake of meetings. It's about bringing together the *right* people at the *right* cadence to review key aspects of the business.

And unless you have an incredibly simple business, it's unlikely you can cover the entirety of your Revenue Operations spectrum in a single routine. So that creates a perfect opportunity for us, as Operators, to build consistent operating rhythms in which all of the go-to-market teams can participate.

Plenty of people claim they "hate meetings," or that their company runs just fine without them through asynchronous communication methods like email, Slack, or even short video recordings. If you can pull this off, congratulations. But when companies reach a certain size, that scale creates opportunities for miscommunication and misalignment.

Operating rhythms are the perfect antidote to misalignment. And they are perfect forums in which your various revenue leaders can demonstrate their operational command (or, seize the opportunity to improve it). By checking in on what matters, discussing problem areas, and driving action towards solutions *together*, your company can catch and resolve issues before they have the opportunity to negatively impact business results.

We have learned from experience that there are effective and ineffective ways to run these routines; so, in this chapter, we're going to outline not only the different types of operating rhythms we recommend, but also, and perhaps more importantly, how to run them effectively.

So, what are some of our favorite routines that you can implement in your business?

The Operations <> Internal Customer Alignment Routine

Whether your team is called RevOps, sales ops., or (insert your special flavor) ops., one of the most important things you can do is to stay aligned with your internal customers and stakeholders. There should not be any difference in the project priorities of a sales team vs. a sales ops. team. This routine (likely on a weekly basis) is your time to get—and stay—aligned.

Purpose

Review goals, key projects, and priorities for the Operations team and their internal GTM stakeholders.

Benefits/Expected Outcomes

- Leave no ambiguity about what each team is working on and the priorities of all parties.
- Maintain alignment between Operations and internal go-to-market leaders at all times.

Attendees

You likely don't need every single member of your Ops. team or your internal customer's team. Limiting this to key leaders from each group is a productive way to both protect your team's calendars and encourage full transparency in the meetings. It's also a great opportunity to invite junior team members to present in front of leadership when they have something specific to share. If your Operations team has multiple internal customers (like marketing, sales, and customer success), don't try to serve all audiences in a single routine. Break it up into multiple meetings so that each meeting can focus on a single function. This means more meetings for your Operations team, but a better, more productive experience for your internal customers.

Sample Agenda

- Review progress against key goals and projects.
- Prioritize/re-prioritize upcoming work based on business needs.
- Share work in progress for feedback and validation of direction.
- Discuss key personnel items: Performance management, hiring, ramp, etc.
- Offer business insights based on proactive analysis by Ops. team.

The Pipeline Generation Routine

Notice we didn't call this the pipeline review routine. We'll talk about deal reviews a little later for how you might be able to add value on specific deals that the sales team is working, but there are plenty of other forums where reps and their managers can review open deals (for example, in their 1-on-1s or in team meetings). The pipeline generation routine (likely bi-weekly) is about accountability—specifically two-way accountability between marketing and sales. For marketing, are we generating enough meetings and pipeline for reps to be successful? For sales, are we making the most of those opportunities? A Revenue Operations team is the perfect owner and arbiter of this routine because we can be objective facilitators in a relationship that can be tenuous.

Purpose

Review progress against pipeline creation targets and create mutual accountability between marketing and sales.

Benefits/Expected Outcomes

- Improved visibility and understanding of sales pipeline creation vs. targets.
- Identification and resolution of bottlenecks to accelerate deal progression.
- Effective resource allocation for proven marketing campaigns and optimization of the sales process.
- Increased win rates.

Attendees

These should include key leaders from marketing, sales, and operations. If you have an SDR team, the SDR leader should absolutely be included in this routine as well.

Sample Agenda

- Review meetings and pipeline creation performance vs. targets:
  - Marketing: Provide learnings/insights on recent and upcoming campaigns that will help achieve targets (what's working, what's not).
  - Sales: Provide learning/insights on recent opportunity creation and open pipeline advancement (what's working, what's not).
- Review pipeline coverage for current period vs. targets:
  - Review of open sales pipeline progression and its current status.
  - Review performance by source vs each source's expected contribution.
  - Discussion of strategies to move deals forward: Surface learnings on resources/tactics on specific opportunities that have been working well in advancing/closing pipeline.

CONFESSION CORNER

The pipeline generation routine is by far the routine I've struggled with the most in my career. I think it's because the core purpose of the meeting is accountability. When things are going well and you're hitting your goals, this meeting is easy. When things are hard and you constantly find yourself falling short of the company's targets, that's when the finger pointing begins.

Meticulously crafted agendas can blow up in your face. Insightful revelations from well-executed analysis ignored. Instead of seeking out solutions to problems, this meeting can quickly devolve into unproductive conversations:

"That report is wrong."

"The goals don't make sense."

"I don't agree with our attribution definitions."

"Sales isn't following up with the leads."

"The marketing leads are garbage."

I've tried every version of this meeting possible: Every agenda, every unique combination of attendees, every format/system of record from which to run the meeting. I've had plenty of times where I left this meeting hopelessly frustrated with our lack of progress or questioning why we had the routine at all. What value were we actually getting from it?

What I've come to believe is that above all else, you need well-intentioned, open-minded participants who *want* to solve problems. If you too find yourself struggling with this routine, one experiment to try is shrinking the number of attendees. People are typically less inclined to get to the heart of tough issues in front of a big group, and they also might feel targeted in the face of tough feedback in front of their peers. If the attendees of this routine view themselves as partners who are accountable to one another (including Operations), then the benefits of the meeting are real.

The Forecasting Routine

We're going to explore all things forecasting more deeply in Chapter 8, but it's undeniable that a weekly forecast meeting is one of the most common routines in a revenue organization. This meeting can carry a lot of baggage and even generate some visceral reactions from folks who have been through poorly run versions of this routine. When run well, though, this should be a critical muscle to flex within your organization.

It's almost as important to share what this meeting is *not* as it is to share what it is. The forecasting routine should not be "reading the news"—meaning, if your leaders show up, regurgitate some information from someone else on their team, and then you move on, you've missed the point of coming together. It's also not "story time," where leaders share long-winded explanations of why that one deal slipped or offer excuses for why they missed their forecast yet again. The meeting is an opportunity for each leader to demonstrate the command they have over their business, articulate how their team will contribute to business results, and raise areas where they need help.

Purpose

Review and discuss the forecast vs goals for a particular time period.

Benefits/Expected Outcomes

- Understand how we are pacing to our goals.
- Proactively identify any areas where teams are stuck, mitigate potential risks.
- Forum to ask for and provide additional resources for the team to be successful.
- Improved accuracy and reliability of forecasts.

Attendees

Forecasting is often viewed as a sales routine. In a Revenue Operations context, though, you need to think about forecasting more than just new bookings or revenue. How you forecast renewals, churn, or any other service offerings are all relevant in a routine like this. You need leadership from all revenue functions to make this routine work.

Sample Agenda

- Update team forecast calls for the current period, and the review of the previous period's forecast accuracy.
- Discussion of any significant changes in the sales pipeline.
- Identification of risks, opportunities, and adjustments for the upcoming period.
- Alignment on strategies and actions to meet sales targets.

Note: This is not story time, nor is this time to solve deal-specific issues. Teams can and should ask for help on specific deals, and set up next steps or deal reviews to fulfill those requests outside of the forecast meeting.

The Deal Review Routine

It's important that all of these routines are viewed as "value-adds" by your teammates, and that none of them feel tedious or "Big Brother-ish." This could not be more true of the deal review routine.

A deal review is a forum in which sales can take advantage of all of the resources in the organization to help them close more deals. It should not be an interrogation or an inquisition; it should be a collaborative meeting with the end goal of closing more business.

For this to happen, the sales rep needs to come prepared to answer the most important questions about their deal and where they need help. If your company uses a sales methodology (like Challenger, SPIN, or Command of the Message) or a qualification criteria (like MEDDIC), these methodologies should be embedded in every routine you have, particularly deal reviews. If the company (looking at you, Operators) has documented exactly what happens in a productive deal review and trained the team on how to prepare, then coming without the necessary information to make that routine productive is completely unacceptable.

While you want to make this routine so enticing that reps volunteer to take advantage of it, you may also want to consider standard thresholds where a deal review is required or strongly encouraged. High-value deals, complex deals, deals with custom product requirements, or abnormal discounting requests are all good candidates for a deal review.

Not all deal reviews are the same. Sean's former boss, Paul Goetz, the CRO at Upserve, coached his teams on a few different types to consider:

- **Pursuit (go/no go) deal review:** Determine whether we should pursue a specific deal or not.
- **Solution deal review:** Planning the right solution, value proposition, sales strategy, and tactics to win a deal.
- **Commercial deal review:** Final pricing, negotiation, contract, and risk decisions in the closing stages of a deal.

Purpose

Spend dedicated time strategizing about an individual deal.

Benefits / Expected Outcomes

- Leverage the company's resources (in sales and elsewhere) to increase the likelihood of winning the deal.
- Embed creative problem solving and deal strategies in your organization.
- Increase win rates.

Attendees

The rep who owns the deal, that rep's manager, and any other relevant sales leaders should be in attendance. If there are cross-functional partners or stakeholders (like a CSM, renewals manager, or members of product/engineering, services, or finance teams) who can add value to your deal, they should be there as well. Inviting leaders from non customer-facing teams like product or engineering is a great way for them to hear first-hand the types of challenges your customers are facing and bring that intel back to their respective teams.

Sample Agenda

- Discuss client needs and current pain points that your product is uniquely positioned to solve.
- Discuss and craft the best fit solution for that customer.
- Review the customer's decision-making process and criteria for success.
- Review the buying committee, their roles, and the relationships the company currently has and doesn't have with prospective buyers.
- Review the timeline for a decision and the mutual success plan to advance from the current state of the deal to closing.
- Review any unique legal, security, procurement, or risk factors that will impact the strategy to close the deal.

The Quarterly Business Review Routine

The QBR provides an opportunity for individuals on your team to both reflect on the previous quarter's performance and look ahead to thoughtfully plan for the upcoming quarter. This is a routine that should happen at every level of seniority in your organization, and while it's most common in sales, the QBR can be just as effective in functions like customer success, professional services, and yes, Operations.

This is also probably, all-in, the most time-consuming routine on our list. QBRs take significant investment not only from the presenters (about 20 to 30 minutes of content and discussion per person, not to mention the prep time), but from all of the stakeholders, managers, and executives who attend them. Because of this, it's critical you make QBRs as effective a use of time as possible, and design the agendas accordingly.

When designing the agenda of your various QBRs, it's important to include both individual contributors and managers in the design process. They will have different views on what will be the most useful conversations for them, and again, these routines are about utility.

CONFESSION CORNER

I have a confession: I hate QBRs.

I know as Ops. I'm not supposed to say that, but I do. Or I should say, I hate *some* QBRs. Sometimes, the stars can align and you can get a team that is focused on what needs to be done to succeed. Participants are balanced and fair-minded about what happened and why, everyone who attends leaves with a better understanding of the business, and you even build stronger team rapport and overall company morale. I do love *those* QBRs.

The QBRs that I don't love are the ones where you spend half of each presenter's time trying to figure out why their numbers aren't right. Or ones where it is just a very large (and expensive) audience for a deal review. Or ones where no one keeps time and they run on into the evening or one of the last people only gets five minutes for their presentation. Or ones spent looking at the past results only, reliving the hits and misses of the last quarter with no look forward or discussion on how to hit the numbers for this quarter. Or ones that repeat the exact same requests from the last three quarters that no one bothered to record or act on the last time around.

The good news is with some thoughtful design, preparation, and partnership with the field, Operators have the agency for making QBRs that are worthwhile.

It's quite normal for a lot of the data preparation and logistics of QBRs to fall on Operations. Don't shy away from this responsibility—embrace it. This is a great opportunity for Revenue Operations teams to stay close to the data, their end users, and ensure the accuracy of what's being presented. In fact, when we have prepared for QBRs in the past, our Operations team compiled *all* of the data for every QBR to simplify the data compilation work for the presenters themselves. This isn't to let presenters off the hook when it comes to understanding their data. Instead, it's to ensure they spend their time on reviewing, digesting, and extracting learnings from that data for their presentations (not to mention a great way to build trust and appreciation with your internal customers when they don't find themselves pulling the wrong reports at midnight the night before their presentation).

It's also important that Operations (or Enablement in some cases) has a clear plan for capturing, prioritizing, and reporting back on all of the feedback and requests that come up during QBRs. If teams feel like they ask for the same things quarter after quarter with no transparency or updates on those asks, they will quickly come to resent this critical routine and put less thought into the feedback they give.

Purpose

An opportunity for individuals to reflect on the previous quarter's performance and learnings, and to look ahead to thoughtfully plan for the quarter to come.

Benefits/Expected Outcomes

- Operational command of each person's role in the business (they are the CEO of their role!).
- Reinforce the data points and trends that matter (e.g. rep productivity, forecast accuracy).
- Start a new quarter with a thoughtful plan in place for individuals to achieve that quarter's goals.
- Forum to surface asks and feedback to leadership and the broader organization of what you need to be successful.

Attendees

There are pros and cons to running QBRs in a larger group setting vs. just one individual presenting to their direct manager. We believe that group settings are best because it encourages sharing learnings across team members and creates a more collaborative environment (think about a brand new rep who gets to watch the most successful reps deliver their QBRs). That being said, these can take up a load of time on the calendar. If your company has a large sales kickoff or other routines at the beginning of a new year, for example, that might be a good opportunity to trim down that quarter's business reviews. Another recommendation is to have cross-functional partners attend your team's QBR Marketing, product, engineering, and customer success should all have some type of representation at sales QBRs. And yes, Operations should too! AI can help summarize themes and requests from recordings of QBRs; so, you should leverage the tools available to you, but you should be there to ask the relevant follow-up questions and build critical relationships with the presenters. In the past, we've created coverage schedules to make sure that at least one representative from Operations attends every single QBR.

Sample Agenda

- Reflect on the previous quarter's performance: Quota attainment, funnel metrics, forecast accuracy, and lessons learned.
- Look ahead to the upcoming quarter: Open pipeline, path to quota, current forecast, and most important opportunities/customers.
- Asks for leadership or the organization: Product feedback, systems or tool improvements, training needed, and marketing collateral/support.

A NOTE ABOUT SYSTEMS AND ROUTINES

As you think through the right mix of operating rhythms for your business, it's important to think about the supporting systems or materials you will use to run them. Each routine, especially those that rely heavily on data and reporting, should leverage your company's system of record (most likely your CRM). Instead of putting data points in a Google Doc or manually creating graphs in a slide deck, run your pipeline creation meeting from a dashboard in a CRM like Salesforce or HubSpot, or a business intelligence tool like Looker or Tableau. Instead of running your forecast meeting from a spreadsheet, leverage a pipeline management and forecasting tool like Clari. Creating one source of truth for the company's routines is a critical function of Operations.

The more you optimize your routines to run from your systems, the more prepared everyone can be without significant manual work prior to each routine, and consequently, the more aligned everyone will be on expectations for that routine as well.

Leveling Up Your Routines

The routines and cadences with our internal customers are critical to the partnerships we have with those teams. But it's not just about the agendas and the content of these meetings. What's arguably more important is how Operators present and articulate that content. The words we use, the energy we bring to the conversations, and the consistency with which we approach them—they all matter.

How you start any routine sets the tone for that meeting. If you are going to schedule a meeting and expect people to carve out a portion of their day to attend your routine, you need to make it abundantly clear to them your reasoning for doing so.

Enter the Purpose, Benefit, Check™.

Craig Wortmann, CEO of Sales Engine and the Founder and Academic Director of the Kellogg Sales Institute at the Kellogg School of Management, Northwestern University, offers a simple, effective way to make sure everyone is aligned at the beginning of any meeting.

Wortmann explains that you offer "… your stated purpose for the meeting, what benefit there will be to having this meeting, and a 'check' to make sure that the purpose and benefit are okay."[1]

For example, in a forecasting meeting, you might say, "The purpose of this meeting is to review and discuss our forecast for the upcoming quarter. The benefit will be to understand how we are pacing to our goals and identify any actions we can take to help the team be successful. Everyone on board with that?"

The utility of the Purpose, Benefit, Check™ is not just to gain initial buy-in at the beginning of the meeting; it also gives you permission later to gently bring everyone back to the core purpose and agenda when somebody inevitably starts to sidetrack your discussion.

There are countless books, podcasts, and articles out there about the concept of "managing up." Chances are if you read one of them, it's going to be about the relationship between an individual and their manager (or their manager's manager). But that concept is just as applicable when you're talking about the relationship Operators have with our internal customers and stakeholders.

While most advice on "managing up" is about giving and receiving feedback with your boss, or managing expectations on projects and goals, Operators need to expand the definition of managing up. "Managing up" as a RevOps team is about managing the *perception* that others have of you, the work you do, and the routine you're running. How people perceive you, your team, and the value you add to the organization is all a product of managing up.

Now, don't confuse *perception* with *politics*. This isn't about misrepresenting data or offering rose-colored glasses to make yourself look good. It's about taking advantage of the opportunity that these routines present to you to secure your position as a strategic partner in the business (more on this in Part Three: Build Your Partnerships).

Three Ways to Level Up Your Routines

With that definition of "managing up" in mind, there are three concrete ways you can level up your routines, and therefore, your interactions with revenue leaders.

1 You're the owner of this routine. Act accordingly.
Whether you believe it or not, if you're the one who schedules and organizes the operating rhythms of your team, you own those routines. If other people are going to think that way, you might as well think that way yourself.

Start the meeting with the Purpose, Benefit, Check™. Clearly articulate why people are giving up precious time to be there. And bring passion and excitement to the work you're discussing. Operators often play down what they deliver or even apologize for the routine itself. Don't! Clearly articulate a pain point you found and proudly present the problem you resolved. These are your customers that you're talking to—treat it that way!

2 Be knowledgeable, but concise.
Humans like to show off everything they know. When we're asked questions, we want to convey our expertise and depth of knowledge. This is a trap that Operators fall into in our routines. We're asked, "What's going on with net retention in enterprise?" and we suddenly find ourselves four minutes into an answer about the multi-faceted approach we're taking with our new customer health score that no one understands.

We hate to be the ones to break it to you, but your audience likely doesn't care about that crafty workflow or that new validation rule you built late the night before. They care about *outcomes*.

The key in these routines is to convey the most important information in the most concise way possible. If you have something that takes 60 seconds to say, see if you can find a way to say it in 30. Practice this so that every time you speak, people know to listen. And then, when the inevitable follow-up questions do come, you can demonstrate your depth of knowledge and understanding. Come prepared to speak to anything, but don't feel compelled to speak to everything.

3 Tie the work you're delivering back to business results.
Each of the routines we outlined in this chapter is there to help run the business better than you could without them; therefore, you must take the time to tie everything you're talking about back to business results. If you made a change in the forecast meeting, did

forecast accuracy improve? If you increased the volume of deal reviews you ran last quarter, did win rates improve?

In Chapter 11, we'll explore what it means to effectively set goals in Revenue Operations. Use these routines to articulate not just the deliverables your team is producing, but the impact of those deliverables on the business's goals.

Bonus: Feedback and Recap After Each Routine

None of your routines are going to be perfect. And none of your routines are going to stay the same quarter after quarter. Acknowledge this and build in opportunities for reflection, feedback, and improvement.

After each routine is over, get in the habit of quickly reviewing how the meeting went with your Operations teammates or key stakeholders. Ask each person two questions: 1) What went well? And 2) What can we do better next time?

This might feel awkward or forced the first couple of times, but once you get in the habit of doing it, you'll come to find these moments for feedback as motivating reminders to always seek out opportunities for incremental improvement in the work we do as Operators.

How you run these routines, how you manage up, and how you present and articulate the work you're doing *matters*. Keeping these strategies in mind and always holding a quick recap on how the interactions went will go a long way towards transforming your routines into highly valuable operating rhythms, and cementing your seat at the table as a strategic partner to your internal stakeholders.

Chapter Takeaways

1 **Establish disciplined operating rhythms:** There is a need for consistent operating rhythms in Revenue Operations.

2 **Key operating routines:**

- **Operations <> internal customer alignment routine:** Conduct weekly alignment meetings between Revenue Operations and internal stakeholders to maintain alignment, transparency, and collaboration on shared goals.

- **Pipeline generation routine:** Foster mutual accountability between marketing and sales through this routine; optimize resource allocation, identify and resolve bottlenecks, and ultimately increase win rates.

- **Forecasting routine:** Leverage forecast meetings as opportunities for leaders to demonstrate their command over their business, effectively predict business outcomes, and proactively identify and resolve challenges.

- **Deal review routine:** Create a collaborative forum for sales to leverage organizational resources, increasing the likelihood of closing deals and sharing creative problem-solving strategies.

- **Quarterly business review routine:** Conduct quarterly reflections and forward planning sessions at all levels to reinforce operational command, enabling teams to set thoughtful plans, discuss challenges, and align on goals.

3 **Adapting to challenges in your routines:** Acknowledge and address challenges in routine execution. Emphasize the need for well-intentioned, open-minded participants for successful outcomes.

4 **Purpose, Benefit, Check™ approach:** Implement the Purpose, Benefit, Check™ strategy to kickstart and maintain effective routines. Clearly articulate the purpose and benefits of a meeting, and check for alignment to keep participants focused and engaged.

5 **Leveling up routines:** Encourage routine owners to act with a sense of ownership, communicate knowledge concisely, and consistently tie routine outcomes back to business results. Foster a culture of feedback and reflection after each routine to drive continuous improvement.

Endnote

1 C. Wortmann 3 Tips for More Productive Meetings, Inc., 8 May 2014, https://www.inc.com/craig-wortmann/3-tips-productive-meetings.html (archived at https://perma.cc/SH6G-W6KG)

5

Designing and Instrumenting the Customer Journey

Have you ever heard the parable about the blind men and the elephant? In the story, an elephant is brought to a village with a group of blind men who have never come across an elephant before. Each of the men approaches the elephant and touches a different part of the animal. Predictably, having never encountered an elephant before, each of the blind men has his own distinct interpretation of what an elephant is. One touches the trunk and thinks it's like a snake. Another touches the tusk and compares it to a spear. A third touches the ear and thinks it's like a fan. A fourth feels the leg and thinks it's a tree... you get the idea.

All in all, six blind men come away with their own distinct perspective on what an elephant is. In John Godfrey Saxe's poem version of the parable, he writes, "Each in his own opinion / Exceeding stiff and strong, / Though each was partly in the right / And all were in the wrong!"[1]

If you were to go to different parts of your organization and ask them about the customer journey for your company, do you think you'd end up with answers as disparate as the blind men with the elephant?

Unfortunately for many Operators, the answer is yes.

Designing and instrumenting the customer journey at your company is one of the core responsibilities of a Revenue Operations team. Every interaction, every conversion point, every hand-off, every lifecycle stage must be thoughtfully considered and purposefully crafted.

So, what is the customer journey exactly? The customer journey is the series of needs, interactions, and exchanges your customer experiences on the path from prospect to customer and beyond (notice that the journey doesn't end when they become a customer).

In RevOps, we have—or should have—a unique view of this customer journey. The reason it's unique is that it's comprehensive, while many teams only focus on the specific section for which they are responsible (their part of the elephant). And that focus, that narrowed vision, isn't necessarily a bad thing for those other teams. If anything, you want a front-line sales leader to focus on what's best for their team; you want a front-line customer success leader to care more about their team's customers than anyone else's. But someone (looking at you, RevOps) has to look at the whole elephant.

As Operators designing the customer journey, it's important to remember what we learned in Chapter 1: We have two distinct sets of customers, external and internal. Our external customers are our company's customers, and our internal ones are the internal stakeholders we partner with to run the go-to-market motions of our companies.

For both groups of customers, there is a common enemy that Operators must defeat: Friction. If there's one key lesson that we took away from our time at Drift, it's that the companies that remove friction for their customers are the most successful. Companies like Uber, Airbnb, Netflix, and Shopify are all famous for upending their industries by removing friction from some aspect of their customers' lives that was previously painful. Your customers have high expectations for seamless experiences: Meet them and you'll be successful; fall short and you'll lose the opportunity to win or keep them as a customer.

We'll spend more time in Part Three of the book on internal partnerships and how to learn directly from your end users where this friction exists. In this chapter, we'll focus on:

- Different views of the customer journey.
- How to start designing your own.
- How to instrument your customer journey to be able to learn from it.

Different Views of the Customer Journey

When Operators approach the topic of the customer journey, it's easy to default to the thing we all know and love best: The funnel. You're probably familiar with some version of a sales and marketing funnel similar to the one in Figure 5.1.

Everyone has their own slight variation on this funnel: Different terminology, different milestone definitions, but ultimately, most B2B organizations have some version of this that drives the key assumptions of their customer journey.

If only it were as simple as those five funnel stages, right?

As much as we'd like the buying process to be linear and straightforward, it usually doesn't work quite like that. According to Gartner, Inc., the research and advisory firm, the buying process looks more like what you see in Figure 5.2. Multiple stakeholders get involved, champions and power users change jobs, there are numerous engagements across a plethora of marketing and sales materials, budgets get cut, procurement and legal complicate things—the list of deviations from the perfect path to purchase is endless.

So, what should Operators do? Do we throw up our arms in defeat? Do we try to anticipate and accommodate every possible entry point and interaction in the complicated web of a customer journey?

FIGURE 5.1 Traditional marketing and sales funnel

Prospect

Marketing Qualified Leads

Sales Qualified Leads

Opportunity

Customer

FIGURE 5.2 B2B buying journey

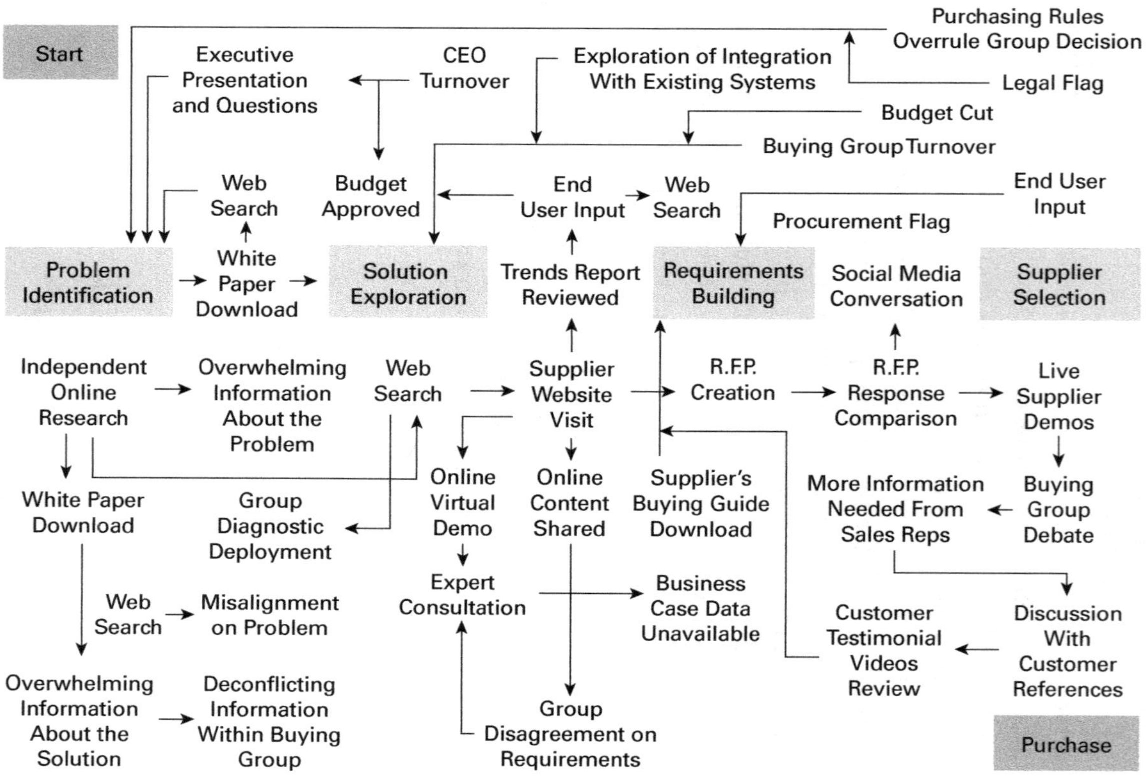

Start

Problem Identification

Executive Presentation and Questions
Web Search
White Paper Download

Independent Online Research
Overwhelming Information About the Problem
Group Diagnostic Deployment
Misalignment on Problem

White Paper Download
Web Search
Overwhelming Information About the Solution
Deconflicting Information Within Buying Group

Solution Exploration

Budget Approved
CEO Turnover
Exploration of Integration With Existing Systems
Buying Group Turnover
Budget Cut
Overrule Group Decision
Purchasing Rules
Legal Flag

End User Input
Web Search
Trends Report Reviewed
Supplier Website Visit
Online Virtual Demo
Web Search

Requirements Building

Procurement Flag
End User Input
Social Media Conversation
R.F.P. Creation
Supplier's Buying Guide Download
Online Content Shared
Business Case Data Unavailable
Expert Consultation
Group Disagreement on Requirements

Supplier Selection

Live Supplier Demos
R.F.P. Response Comparison
Buying Group Debate
More Information Needed From Sales Reps
Discussion With Customer References
Customer Testimonial Videos Review

Purchase

SOURCE Courtesy of Gartner, Inc.[2]

The answer, as it usually is in Operations, lies somewhere in-between. We don't have the option to simply say it's too hard, but we also can't realistically design processes and systems for every possible scenario. Instead, what we can do is focus on key milestones in a process and design a framework within which both our internal and external customers can operate and succeed.

What does that version look like?

First, you have to acknowledge that not all funnels or customer journeys will act the same. You might have different expectations based on where the customers come from, which products they are buying, or which segments of the market you're serving. For example, we have frequently referenced Gartner's double funnel, as shown in Figure 5.3, as a foundational element for designing both the customer journey and the operating plan assumptions around it.

In this model published by Gartner in 2021, the "account based" funnel is driven by your ideal customer profile and reflects the target accounts you have explicitly selected to pursue (you might call this account-based marketing, or ABM., at your company). The "volume" funnel refers to all other leads that enter your company's funnel, but weren't explicitly selected as targets. You can see how having a starting point like the "double funnel" creates opportunities to craft distinct experiences for each entry point to the funnel, to have different assumptions, and perhaps even staff the teams who work with them differently.

FIGURE 5.3 Double funnel

Volume

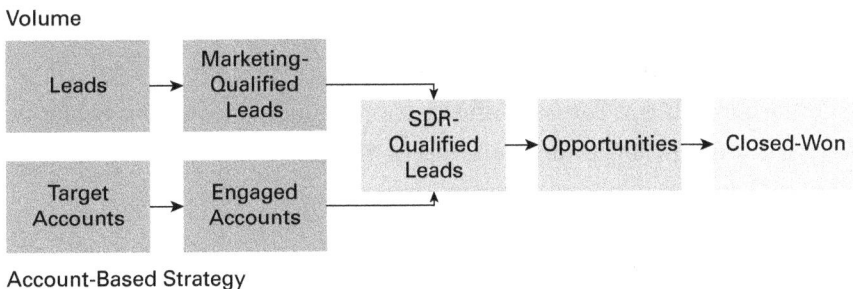

Account-Based Strategy

SOURCE Courtesy of Gartner, Inc.[3]

FIGURE 5.4 Comprehensive customer journey loop

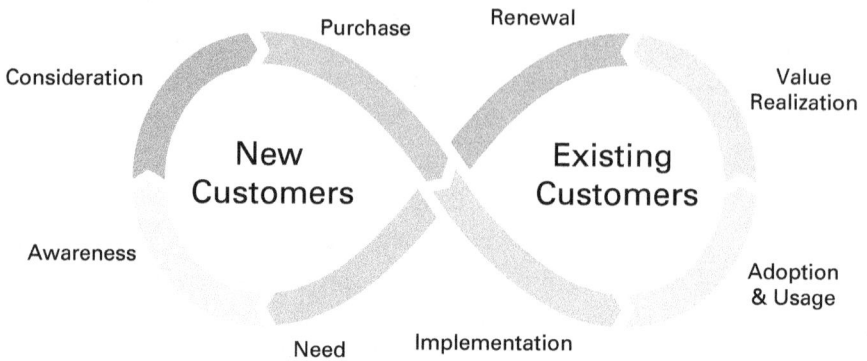

Second, you need to expand the lens of your customer journey to look at more than just acquiring new customers. Too many companies—especially early-stage ones where new business revenue is a key driver of growth—over-emphasize new customer acquisition and don't spend nearly enough time considering how to effectively onboard, retain, and grow their existing customer base. We believe in designing for all of it. Figure 5.4 demonstrates our own approach for how you can bring both the new business and existing customer journeys into a single view.

In this example, you are consistently looking for new needs, opportunities, and ways to provide value to your prospects and to your existing customer base. For example, when it is time to renew one of your customers, if you've done an effective job creating value for that customer throughout the length of the contract, you should be well-positioned to understand any additional needs the customer has and create potential opportunities for cross-sell or upsells.

Whether you opt for our infinity loop visual or not, now that you have a foundational understanding of the customer journey options available to you, it's time to start designing your own.

How to Start Designing Your Own

Plenty of people will tell you they see the value in designing a seamless, cohesive customer journey, but don't actually put in the work to build one. As simple as it sounds, the most important first step is documentation. Grab a piece of paper, a whiteboard, or a flowchart design tool like Lucidchart or Miro, and start at the beginning. Some questions you and your team can ask yourselves:

- Who are our target customers and who are not?
- How do customers find out about us and what are the different entry points to our customer journey?
- What are our different go-to-market motions (e.g. direct vs. channel)?
- How do leads get captured?
- Which leads make it to our sales team and how are they distributed? By region? By product? By grade? What rules govern this process and who manages them?
- What are the key ingredients to an effective evaluation and sale of our product?
- If and when someone decides to buy, what type of implementation is required?
- How do we ensure adoption and successful use of our product?
- What happens when the customer has a problem?
- What opportunities are there for renewal, cross-sell, and expansion after the initial purchase?

This list will get you started with a discrete set of activities and interactions, which means it's then time to assign out the responsibilities of all of these interactions internally. When is an SDR responsible versus when do they pass ownership over to a sales rep? When you have a new customer, does someone from customer success act as the project manager of the implementation or is there a separate onboarding team to handle that? When can you leverage technology versus when does a human need to be involved? Keep in mind the answers to these questions might be different for different products or different go-to-market motions.

If you're looking for places to eliminate friction, any hand-offs in the customer journey between humans or between humans and technology are great places to start. Product-led growth (PLG) has grown more popular as a go-to-market strategy because it often complements or replaces human-assisted interactions with technology-driven ones.

Kyle Poyar, author of the popular newsletter *Growth Unhinged* and Operating Partner at OpenView, shared his perspective on PLG on an episode of the *Operations* podcast:

> The way we think of it [PLG] is that it's an end user-focused growth model that relies on the product itself as a key driver of the acquisition, conversion, and expansion of your customers. I call it more of a dimmer switch rather than an on/off switch. There are ways that any company, even an enterprise-focused company following the traditional SaaS playbook, can start to incorporate elements of PLG to drive a better customer experience, and ultimately more efficient growth too.
>
> One way that folks can think about it is you might want to look for bottlenecks, where there's a bunch of humans in the funnel that might create a lot of friction, slowness, or a bad experience for your customers. Are there ways that you can start putting more of that into automated processes or product experiences, so it's on demand, self-service for your customers? That's a win-win for everyone.[4]

Whether it's through go-to-market strategies like PLG or others, a documented customer journey will allow you to easily identify points of friction. Then it's your job to root them out. As we mentioned, it can be difficult to anticipate and accommodate every slight permutation of the customer journey; so, it's best at this time to pick the major milestones in your customer journey, and align with your team on the definitions of those milestones.

Keep the milestones as limited in number and straightforward in complexity as possible. This can be as simple as the things you know you want to count (like leads, meetings, or customers) or it could be the hand-off points between different teams (like SDR, sales, onboarding, customer success, and support). The most important thing, though, is alignment on the definitions. You must spend time during this customer journey design to align on what everyone means when they use terms like "MQL"; otherwise, this entire exercise is a waste of time.

We as Operators have to help drive and facilitate these alignment conversations, and document the decisions that come out of them so that the same conversations don't have to happen over and over again. Even if the final definition of every milestone isn't exactly the way you envisioned it, you have to disagree and commit to the outcome (and help others to do the same). Jaclyn Balben, COO at Bamboo Health, stressed the importance of this exercise as a prerequisite to the actual work of running the business. She explained:

> The most important piece of it is to ensure that we're aligned so that when we do set goals and we start to report on them, we're not continuously debating the thing that drives success. We've already decided on the metrics of success, and so then we're actually discussing where we stand and how we're progressing against our goals.
>
> What we should be asking is, "Do I have enough pipeline today in order to hit my number tomorrow?" Let's not debate what pipeline means anymore. We should have that landed and now we should be talking about what it is that we can be doing as a team to make sure the answer is, "Yes, we do have enough." Make sure that we are crystal clear on the metrics, how we define them, and then focus on solving problems and generating the pipeline that we need instead of getting caught up in rehashing old conversations.[5]

What constitutes pipeline (or opportunities to sell) is a perfect example of a milestone that is critical to your internal customers. To make this concrete for them, document and share objective criteria for creating pipeline that everyone must follow. It might look something like this:

- **Role/authority:** Director-level or above is aware of or supportive of this evaluation.
- **Pains/needs:** Must have a problem that our product can solve (list out your product's specific use cases or value proposition).
- **Timing:** An active evaluation is in progress or looking to make a decision within X days/months.

Once you have documented your customer journey, defined key milestones, and identified the internal teammates that will service each of those milestones, it's time to move on to instrumenting that customer journey.

How to Instrument Your Customer Journey to Be Able to Learn From It

If a tree falls in a forest and no one is around to hear it, does it make a sound?

If something happens in your customer journey but you don't have a way to measure it, did it really happen? (We promise no more parables or idioms in this chapter.)

RevOps teams are best positioned to take your newly documented journey and start to instrument your internal systems, your product, and your overall data architecture to be able to measure what is happening in your customer journey.

This process is vital, but can also get unwieldy quickly if you're not careful. There is no limit to the number of ways you can slice data or dissect every possible conversion point in your customer journey. And if you don't take control of this instrumentation, your internal customers will ask you for far more "slices" than will actually be helpful to them or the business.

So, here are a few key recommendations to follow and pitfalls to avoid as you instrument your own customer journey.

1. Keep it Simple

Start with the milestones you defined in the previous step with your customer journey design. You have to be able to count the volume of prospects/customers that reach each of these milestones to give you your level 1 metrics. All other metrics will stem from these, and you can't get any more sophisticated until these are in place. Build basic reports in your CRM for each milestone (we used to keep our core reports for each milestone in a folder in Salesforce, creatively named "Reporting Essentials").

If you're working with a sales team, for example, you might have level 1 metric reports for the number of:

- Sales activities
- Meetings booked
- Meetings held
- Qualified opportunities created (# / $)
- Closed won deals (# / $).

2. Think Long-Term

When it comes to instrumenting your customer journey, it's important to match the complexity of your metrics with the current stage of your company while simultaneously laying the long-term foundation for how you capture, store, and report on data. This isn't an easy balance, but it is one that Operators must strike.

For example, if you can't yet count your customers and the revenue associated with them, it's probably not yet time to be talking about EBITDA. Don't stress about crafting the perfect weighted health score before you understand the basic usage metrics for your product.

To effectively think long-term, you want to anticipate what data the company might need later, and design data architecture to support those needs. For example, you may want to invest in a data warehouse tool like Snowflake or Amazon Redshift so that you can store not only the current values of all your key milestone data, but also snapshots of what they were in the past (more on this in Chapter 6).

3. Inspect What You Expect

Don't allow yourself or your team to spend time instrumenting things that no one will ever look at again. Take the time to properly scope what you're building, ask questions about why the data is necessary and what questions you're trying to answer, and then, most importantly, leverage some of the routines from Chapter 4 to regularly check in on what you instrumented.

One prime example of the need for inspection pre-sale is "Speed to Lead." In B2B companies, the speed with which sales and marketing teams follow up with high-intent inbound leads is paramount to increasing the likelihood of conversion. So, it makes sense that a company would want to measure that speed. At prior companies, we set up SLAs between our sales and marketing teams for how fast leads were expected to have a human follow-up (yes, we had automated follow-ups, too!). Instrumenting this well was actually a significant amount of work; so, to ensure everything was working as expected, we had daily stand-ups for a while to review performance. That may seem like overkill, but we needed to: 1) Ensure the way we had instrumented everything was working as expected, and 2) the teams were exhibiting the behaviors we expected. Hope is not a strategy; don't leave these critical inflection points in your customer journey to chance.

As we've stressed, post-sale instrumentation is just as important. Sometimes you might find that the basic milestone metrics are helpful, but aren't providing the insights and guidance you need. At one company, we found that just getting a product implemented and used by a customer wasn't enough. There were key ingredients that, when completed, had a direct impact on the retention of that customer. So we created a metric of our own: The "Onboarding Completion Percentage." It consisted of eight unique ingredients: If you completed at least six of them, the net dollar retention of those customers was over 130 percent, which meant it was wildly important to have an onboarding completion percentage over 75 percent (6/8). We created ways to track each of the eight ingredients, put that information front-and-center, and measured each post-sale team member on this critical metric. Soon, everyone in the company was looking for ways they could increase the onboarding completion percentage and give our customers a higher likelihood of success.

4. The Customer Journey is NOT just quantitative

We'll continue to stress metrics and data throughout Part Two of the book, but it's important as you look at your newly documented customer journey to recognize that there will be needs for qualitative instrumentation as well.

Qualitative instrumentation?

Those hand-offs we mentioned, where friction builds up and balls go to be dropped, are a great opportunity for qualitative data to be passed from one teammate to another.

Here's a common example: During a typical sales process, a customer offers up a load of information about their company, their pain points, why they are considering your solution, and how they plan to potentially use your solution to meet their needs. If that prospect ends up buying your product, they should not have to then repeat all of this same information to whoever gets assigned to work with them post-sale. That's a terrible customer experience.

Revenue Operations must seek out ways to help their teammates capture this information uncovered during the sales process, synthesize it, and ensure it is accurately conveyed to any other colleagues who might be working with this customer. You should have an aspiration internally that a customer never has to repeat themselves. Accomplish that, and you'll set your customer journey apart from the rest.

5. Automate, Automate, Automate

Humans are great, but they aren't the most reliable source for data collection. In fact, they're pretty bad at it. For every metric or milestone you instrument across your customer journey, seek a system-driven, automated way to capture that information before asking a human to do it. Not only will this increase the quality of your data, but your internal customers will thank you for it as well and they can get back to doing their actual job.

Your product is a great place to start when it comes to automating what you want to measure within the customer journey. Specifically, how are your end-users interacting with the product itself? If you have a physical product, this is a little different than a piece of technology, but if your company sells a software product, take the time to instrument your own product in a way that will teach you valuable insights about your customers.

If you're unclear on whether or not technology can help you automate something in place of human data collection, spend time researching the options available to you. How do you find and implement the right technology to help you with this automation and to support the entire customer journey? That's next in Chapter 6.

Chapter Takeaways

1 **Understanding the customer journey:** The customer journey encompasses the series of interactions a customer experiences from prospect to customer and beyond, emphasizing that it doesn't conclude upon purchase.

2 **Importance of comprehensive view:** Revenue Operations should adopt a holistic view of the customer journey, unlike other teams that may have narrower focuses. This broad perspective aids in identifying and removing friction points for both external customers and internal stakeholders.

3 **Designing the journey:** Operators should create a structured framework to understand and cater to the needs of their customers, considering both acquisition and retention. Key steps include defining target customers, identifying entry points, establishing go-to-market strategies, understanding product evaluation and implementation, and ensuring post-purchase success.

4 **Instrumenting the journey:** RevOps teams play a crucial role in instrumenting the customer journey by integrating systems, products, and data architectures to monitor and measure interactions. Recommendations include simplifying metrics, anticipating future data needs, regularly inspecting and validating

the instrumentation, and emphasizing both quantitative and qualitative data collection.

5 **Emphasis on automation:** To enhance efficiency and accuracy, automation is pivotal in capturing data points across the customer journey. By leveraging technology, especially within the product itself, companies can gain deeper insights, reduce manual errors, and optimize the overall customer experience.

Endnotes

1 J. G. Saxe (1873) "The Blind Men and the Elephant," *The Poems of John Godfrey Saxe*

2 Based on Gartner. Improve Digital Engagement to Support B2B Buying Journeys, analyzed by S. C. Ceurvorst, Gartner, 8 January 2024, https://www.gartner.com/en/documents/5083031 (archived at https://perma.cc/UZX8-VDKW) [GARTNER is a trademark of Gartner Inc. and/or its affiliates.]

3 Gartner, Tool: Measure Account-Based and Volume Go-to-Markets With the Double Funnel, Chris Moody, 23 June 2021. This Gartner report is archived and is included for historical context only.

4 *Operations* with Sean Lane (2021) Under the Hood of Product-Led Growth with OpenView's Kyle Poyar, Episode 65 [podcast]

5 *Operations* with Sean Lane (2021) Live from Modern Sales Pros: Why Operations is the Key to Sales and Marketing Alignment, Episode 70 [podcast]

6

The Building Blocks of the Modern Tech Stack

In 2011, there were 150 marketing technology companies. By 2014, the number had grown to just shy of 1,000. As of November 2023, there are over 13,000 martech software tools available in the market.[1] Yes: **13,000**.

No problem for all you Operators out there, right? Just learn how all 13,000 of those work, and of course, how they seamlessly integrate with one another.

The technology landscape is vast, and only exploding more with advances in AI, vertical and niche-specific tools, and a shrinking barrier to entry for creating new tools in the first place. As Revenue Operators, our job is to find the right technologies that best support the customer journey, not to force the customer journey into specific technologies.

Too often people become enamored with a specific tool or capability and don't stop to think through the problem they have and the use cases that need solving. Designing the modern tech stack isn't about achieving a high score in the number of tools you can duct tape together; it's about picking the right ones.

Which Tools Do You Need?

In Chapter 1, Pete Kazanjy taught us the basic rule that the impact of a RevOps hire must exceed the cost of that person. Any technology

FIGURE 6.1 Number of martech software apps since 2011

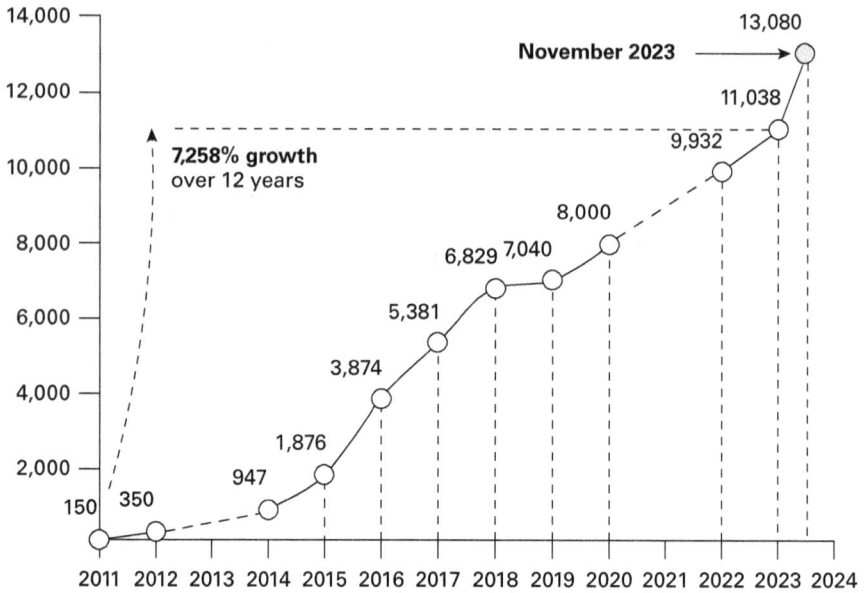

SOURCE Courtesy of chiefmartec and MartechTribe

you invest in has to follow the same rule. When you examine a problem in your customer journey, you need to be able to quantify the cost of either not solving that problem or addressing it manually. For example, if you are manually distributing every single lead that comes into your company, you're not only paying for the salary of the person doing that manual work; you're missing out on the potential yield of higher conversion rates if those leads were distributed and followed up on faster. As long as the cost to build a lead distribution mechanism or purchase a tool that does it for you is less than the alternatives, do it.

So how do you figure out which tools you need and when? To start, take the customer journey infinity loop map that you created in Chapter 5 and identify where in that journey technology could increase efficiency, reduce costs, or increase productivity. Figure 6.2 demonstrates where some of those needs and solutions might be.

Like in building a house, RevOps needs to lay a strong foundation for the company's tech stack. That foundation should include two core components: 1) A customer relationship management (CRM)

FIGURE 6.2 Customer journey with potential technology needs

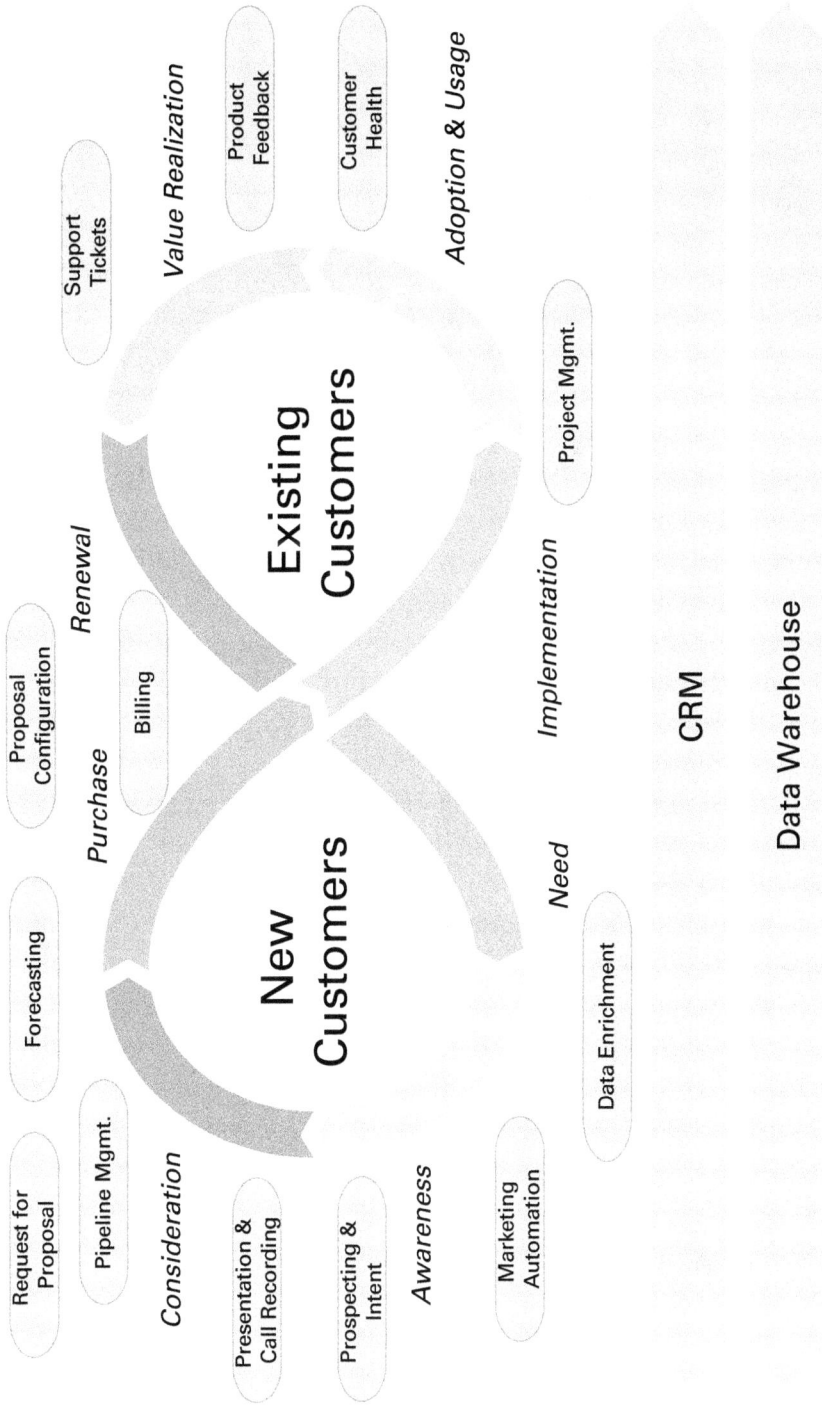

tool, and 2) a data warehouse. Think of your CRM as your window into everything you know about your business right now, and your data warehouse as the subterranean basement where you store everything you've ever known about your business, ever. These are non-negotiable sources of truth for your organization—the sooner you invest in these tools, the sooner you'll engrain a data-driven culture in your company.

When you go through your customer journey, you may end up with a dozen different opportunities where technology might offer some improvement. Next, you need to prioritize the areas that will have the biggest impact on the business and make the most sense for your company's maturity and go-to-market motion. If you're at an early-stage company that is still figuring out how to consistently generate demand for your product, you probably don't need the fancy multi-touch attribution tool; you need a data enrichment provider to help you target the right contacts and accounts to prospect. If your company is drowning in product bugs and support issues, you probably need to invest in a customer service ticketing tool before buying the fancy weighted customer health score offering.

You'll notice that we aren't going to provide you with any specific company recommendations or a list of our favorite tools. That's for you to assess on your own (and also, with the pace of change in technology, plenty of our recommendations would be woefully outdated by the time you're reading this page).

The technology marketplace is also cyclical and is not immune to the economic trends of any marketplace. For example, according to Recorded Future CMO Tom Wentworth, once-popular single "best of breed" solutions are being displaced by all-in-one platforms:

> I would have said until very recently that technology is the best as
> a best-of-breed game. Find the best combination of tools for your

business, stitch them together, orient them around a central thing like your CRM That's how you build a stack. But lately, I've become more convinced than ever that that's actually the wrong approach going forward. We are now seeing a shift to integrated suite platforms. Buying a bunch of point solutions isn't going to get you to the promised land anymore. And I think we're in a new world right now. From here, you're going to want a single vendor to do all of this for you and apply their unique data set to the sets of problems that you have. I can't predict what's going to happen in the go-to-market landscape. You're going to be sitting there with the equivalent of a Model T in an era of Teslas. It's interesting, but it's also frightening how fast stuff is going to evolve.[2]

Regardless of industry, economic conditions, or company stage, what you can do is start your tech evaluations by asking yourself the following questions:

- What is the problem I'm trying to solve?

- Do I already have a tool available to me that might solve this problem?

- What are the outcomes I'm hoping to drive by purchasing this tool?

- How do those outcomes compare to the cost of this tool? What's my expected return on investment (ROI)?

- Which features are must-have and which are nice-to-have?

- What do companies like mine say about their experience with this tool?

- What is this company's track record for product reliability, innovation, and customer satisfaction?

- What is the effort required to implement this tool?

- What is the effort required to maintain this tool?

- Does this tool play nicely with other critical tools in my tech stack?

- How does it fit into the existing day-in-the-life (DITL) of my end users or how does it alter it?

The more times you go through this exercise, the better you'll get at it. You're bound to make mistakes, so seek out those who have confronted similar problems or made similar purchases in the past (more on seeking out role models in Chapter 24). They give out awards for tech stack design! You can Google an entire company's tech stack; so, even if you're brand new at this, the answers to the test are available to you.

Where things start to get more difficult is when you are faced with the challenge of stitching together the internal experience of all of those different tools. Just as RevOps is meant to break down the silos between different teams in your organization, we are also tasked with eliminating (or at least artfully hiding) the gaps between the different tools we use.

REAL WORLD ROLE MODELS

Scott Brinker is the VP Platform Ecosystem at HubSpot and Editor at chiefmartec.com. He also produces an annual Martech report and the well-known MarTech Map graphic. On Episode 120 of the *Operations* podcast, he helped make sense of the ever-expanding landscape of tools available to Operators:

> For a long time, marketers have largely purchased commercial software to do a particular thing and the software works a certain way out of the box. It's kind of take it or leave it. Maybe there's a little bit of margin on the edge to configure or tweak, but it's largely, "I've got this package that does X, and I've got some other package I get that does Y, and this other app that does Z."
>
> But I've thought about it and for any given customer experience that I'm trying to create, maybe I want elements of X, Y, and Z to participate in that. And today, that's usually been hard. But in an ideal world, what people really want to do is they want to lift above the actual software packages. They want to think of this through the lens of, "What is the ideal workflow I want for my digital operations? What's the ideal customer experience that I want to deliver at a particular touch point?" And to then have this freedom to say, "I've got data here, here, and here, and I've got this service here and here. I'm bringing those together and have them work seamlessly in this particular way." And this is what composability is really about.

I can structure a workflow, and if it crosses multiple A.P.I. boundaries, that's fine. If I have a particular use case I want data for, I'm not restricted to just the data of one particular tool or another particular tool. If any of the data got into the cloud data warehouse, I now have the ability to pick and choose a set of data that I can leverage for this specific use case I have in mind. This is really powerful because it starts to get us into a mode where individual businesses and individual Operators can start to use their creativity and their imagination. Instead of being restricted to what any one particular software vendor thinks I should be doing, it's what I want to do, and how I want to differentiate what we do.

The expertise of a lot of Revenue Ops. people is to act as the translation layer between what the organization actually wants to do strategically and tactically, and how to map those goals to the capabilities that the underlying infrastructure and systems offer. The more time, the more freedom, the more underlying power that Ops. people are given to really focus on the use cases, and compose things in a very creative way. Oh man, that's golden.[3]

Integrating the Tools

When designing the integrations and connections between different tools in your tech stack (and therefore different stops in your customer journey), remember that you are also creating interdependencies and potential points of failure between those tools. Take the time when implementing new tools to document as much as possible about what the tool does, how it is meant to function, and why you made the design choices you made. Documentation is the least sexy safeguard you can put in place, but it's the most enduring institutional knowledge available to you (more on what happens when things break in Chapter 13).

Sara McNamara, who has experience leading Marketing Operations at companies like Salesforce, Slack, and Cloudera, explains the potential pitfalls of non-standard integrations. "We spend a lot of time trying to develop custom integrations or finding work-arounds, but when we look at tools, we just need them to work. If it requires some kind of custom build, we can do that, but then it needs to be reliable. When we have to put a bunch of duct tape together, to me, that's a red flag that we either need to look at the process or look at the tool and figure out why it's so fragile. It doesn't make sense to duct tape something together if it's something that's important enough that the company's revenue is going to depend upon it."[4]

Building your tech stack and crafting these connections between tools in your customer journey takes careful consideration and thought. Have you ever made a change in one of your systems or one of your tools only to realize that whatever you just changed broke something else? And then you go to try to fix the thing that you broke and something else breaks? Whether it's because of poor planning or lack of historical documentation and context, Ops. teams can often find themselves in a precarious game of tech stack Jenga, hoping that we can pull out the next block carefully enough so that the whole tower doesn't come tumbling down upon us.

CONFESSION CORNER

When I got a new job as a Director of RevOps, my first project was to implement products and price books—standard functionality for Salesforce, but they weren't using it at the time. I was like, "I got this. Perfect. Done this a hundred times. This is fantastic. Great first project to really get my feet wet here."

I spin up a sandbox. I build my solution and get the thumbs up from all the executives and all the VPs and all the end users. I deployed all my change sets to push my solution to production at 12:01 AM on a Tuesday night, and did more testing like a good Salesforce admin does. I felt great about it, and I could sleep.

I woke up the next morning at 06:00 AM to text messages, voicemails, phone calls, emails, Slack notifications. "What is going on with Salesforce? What is happening?" Because of one small blind spot that I didn't see, because I didn't know how all these systems were interconnected, I wiped out our revenue, which is not a fun thing to happen.

At the time we were roughly an $18 million run rate company. And nobody is happy with you when you take something from $18 million to zero million dollars.

Think about the downstream, almost catastrophic impact that is made by wiping out essentially all opportunities and all the revenue associated to them. Our sales reps couldn't manage their pipeline. Our marketing team couldn't run reports on which opportunities we have in our pipeline, and which ones we should target for different advertising strategies. Our CSMs had no renewals to manage because they all had $0 beside them. Finance couldn't bill anybody. The impact of all that is catastrophic to your entire go-to-market and just overall company.

Customer-Centric Design

Just like with everything else in this book, we have to design the tech stack with our internal and external customers in mind. Technology is the highest leverage tool in your toolkit to best serve both audiences. And if the aim of using technology is to create that leverage, AI might offer Operators the most outsized opportunity that we've ever had to accomplish that in ways previously not possible. Manually sifting through S-1 filings, accounts with outdated news alerts, flawed lead models, or even just analysis that was reserved for the most technical colleagues all will become problems of the past.

But being able to effectively design and use any tool requires that you fully understand your customers' needs and pain points.

For example, one of our favorite recommendations is to design a "day-in-the-life" (DITL) dashboard for every role you support. A DITL dashboard is a series of actionable reports and views purposefully designed to mimic the priorities and responsibilities associated with a particular role. When someone sits down at their desk each day, the DITL dashboard should act as their home base.

When training customer-facing team members, we would encourage them that this dashboard should be open on their screen at all times. An SDR's dashboard might focus on the highest intent leads that require action, sales activity inputs, and meeting and pipeline outputs. A CSM's dashboard might focus on high-risk customers, upcoming renewal events, or open support tickets they need to be aware of. The key is to not just expose them to things that have already taken place. Showcasing results is valuable, but a DITL dashboard should aim to facilitate the next best action by any team member in any role.

What goes potentially unnoticed and certainly unappreciated about designing an internal customer experience like a DITL dashboard is all of the upstream decisions you must make to bring that "home base" to life. Before these technology-driven workflows see the light of data, Operators must make data quality decisions, integration choices, and have the foundational business context we learned in Part One to make them useful at all. The closer you get to your internal customers' needs, the more you'll learn about the seemingly small, but persistently painful moments of pause in their days. These moments of pause are ripe for an Operator's creativity.

We encountered one of these painful moments of pause in the hand-off between SDRs and the A.E.s they book meetings for. Every organization wants to measure and understand the quality of the meetings their sales team is holding, regardless of whether an SDR scheduled the meeting or not. But the question of quality is intensified when the ascribed value and compensation of an SDR team depends on whether those meetings were any good or not.

Every place we've ever worked has had issues capturing the data that answers this meeting quality question. The process for designating that the meeting took place and was qualified might be cumbersome, or sometimes sales reps forget to verify how the meeting went, and go on with their busy day. Then, to make matters worse, the SDR will chase down the A.E. for answers that creates tension for both parties—one waiting to get paid for booking the meeting, the other worried about closing business from the meeting... to also get paid. The typical solution is to chase and chase these answers, wasting even more time and energy.

Nothing about this process was easy, intuitive, or reduced friction. It only created friction. So, we asked ourselves, is there a better way to reach the sales executives where they already are and answer this important question about meeting quality? For us, Slack was where our sales executives were. It was how we communicated at the company and was deeply embedded in the culture. So, could we bring together this rep-friendly medium with the needs of the business, and ensure proper data capture in the CRM?

To solve this challenge, our Operations team used an integration platform called Tray.io to create a bot that would send a Slack message after a meeting was held to ask the sales rep the outcome of the meeting and whether an opportunity should be created. If yes, the rep could then click a couple of buttons and create an opportunity in the CRM without ever having to leave Slack. We continued to make the experience better and better over time: More options after the meeting, real-time guidance on opportunity creation criteria that should be met, and even a feedback loop back to the SDR (whether things went well or not). We calculated that we saved reps 2 minutes and 22 seconds per meeting based on this workflow, which may not seem like much for a single meeting, but add that up across an entire sales organization, and we gave the team months back in time, which they could spend better serving our customers. The ROI of these efforts was clear and measurable. We met our users where they were and fast-tracked the path to booking higher quality meetings based on the data and feedback loop available to us. Chalk it up as a win for the tech stack.

Of course, the closer you get to your end users and the more efficiencies you create in their DITL, the more those end users will demand. People were floored and wildly excited about the Slackbot solution for about two weeks before it became the norm. You should expect your internal customers to start to approach you with other technology suggestions. Maybe there's a tool they loved at their previous company, maybe they got a cold email and they're passing it along to the RevOps team in charge of tech stack decisions, or maybe a prospect of theirs is looking for the dreaded quid-pro-quo and wants you to give their solution a shot.

Our job as Operators is to objectively (and perhaps ruthlessly) assess all of the questions and factors we've outlined in this chapter. You're going to have to say no a lot. As Sara McNamara puts it:

> It's a masterclass in not only emotional management, but also the bedside manner of how to educate people and help them understand why things are a certain way or why we should approach things a certain way. The best Operators are like doctors. You don't want a doctor that runs into the room frantically and says, "*Oh, you want*

this medication? Let me just throw it at you." There are questions to be asked about a project or a need before giving a solution. We ask questions to gain a better understanding of what really is the problem so that we can create the best long-term solution. The real solution that they're looking for is almost never what they're trying to initially prescribe. There's something behind the curtain that they're not aware of that is the real source of the problem.[4]

While designing and implementing your company's tech stack is a critical part of your role as a Revenue Operator, you can't allow it to consume you. That's not what your company hired you to do. If you spend a majority of your time performing tech stack maintenance and putting out integration fires, you're never going to fulfill the aspirations of the Revenue Operations Mindset.

Sean once had a CRO who told him, "No one wins an award for going out of business with the best systems." Embrace technology and all of its potential, but remember, technology is there to serve the customer journey, not the other way around.

Chapter Takeaways

1 **Explosive growth in technologies:** There is continued exponential growth in technology solutions. This growth poses a challenge to navigate and integrate a vast array of tools in the tech stack, but also significant opportunities for Operators through breakthroughs in technologies like AI.

2 **Strategic tech selection:** Focus on selecting the right technologies that align with the customer journey and deliver tangible value. Rather than being enamored with specific tools, the emphasis is on understanding and solving problems in the customer journey, ensuring that technology investments provide a positive impact exceeding their cost.

3 **Foundational components:** Building a strong foundation for the tech stack is crucial, involving non-negotiable elements like a

CRM tool and a data warehouse. These components serve as sources of truth, fostering a data-driven culture in the organization.

4 **Integration challenges:** Evaluate tools based on specific business needs. There are challenges in stitching together different tools and the importance of careful documentation to prevent potential points of failure.

5 **Customer-centric design:** The tech stack design should consider both internal and external customers. Create a DITL dashboard for each role, aiming to provide actionable insights aligned with individual responsibilities. It's important to understand end-users' needs and creatively leverage technology to enhance their experience.

Endnotes

1 S. Brinker and F. Riemersma. (2023) Martech for 2024, https://martechmap. typeform.com/martechfor2024 (archived at https://perma.cc/ADP5-JHP3)

2 *Operations* with Sean Lane (2023) How AI is Driving the Shift from Best of Breed to All-in-One Solutions, with Recorded Future CMO Tom Wentworth, Episode 107 [podcast]

3 *Operations* with Sean Lane (2023) Why "Composability" is the Key to Designing the Modern Tech Stack, with HubSpot's Scott Brinker, Episode 120 [podcast]

4 *Operations* with Sean Lane (2019) Emotional Management vs. Tech Stack Management, with Cloudera's Sara McNamara, Episode 21 [podcast]

7

How to Make Internal Changes that Actually Stick

"How much would you pay to wake up tomorrow and know how to speak Japanese?"

Maor Ezer, CMO at WalkMe, posed this question to Sean on the *Operations* podcast.[1]

It's a fascinating question. Not "How much would you pay for the privilege to learn Japanese?", but instead, "How much would you pay to just wake up and know Japanese?" WalkMe is a digital adoption platform; so, Maor thinks about how people learn new things every single day.

And according to Maor, "It's not about learning, it's about knowing." When we get into our car, he explains, we don't use a GPS because we want to learn the best way to get somewhere. We use it because we just want it to tell us how to get there.

Your internal customers at your company are no different. According to Maor, salespeople now have an average of 13 different applications they need to use to go from prospecting to closing a deal: 13!

It's easy when you're building a company to encounter a problem and immediately jump to trying to solve that problem through technology. And with advancements in AI, the temptation to just "know" the answer (and paths to get there) are only growing.

Researching, evaluating, and purchasing software effectively on behalf of your business could be an entire book on its own, so let's instead explore what triggers you to look for software in the first place and how to make the most of it when you do buy something.

Sometimes the idea to add software into a process is correct, and you had the best of intentions when you purchased that new shiny tool. But as Maor explains about these tools, "They might have been great, I understand why each one was implemented to optimize the process. But let's be honest, a salesperson wants to get on the phone, close the deal and, when the deal is done, they want their commission and paycheck. They don't want to do your 13 software applications. And that's where you start thinking about challenging the ways of technology consumption and implementation."

So if even the first step of adding software can be a dangerous one, what's the right balance? How do we balance wanting to "just know Japanese" with developing the key skills and disciplined processes you might pick up through the process of learning Japanese?

While the goal of most software is to make humans more efficient, let's be honest: Sometimes the decision to buy software is driven by pure laziness. So, before you decide that your problem is painful enough that technology is a potential solution, force yourself (or the person asking you to explore the tool) to try the manual version first. This exercise will either validate that the problem is truly painful, or it will reveal that the problem is superficial and doesn't merit being a priority for you to solve.

In Episode 27 of the *Operations* podcast, Atrium co-founder Pete Kazanjy taught Sean that the goal of any sales organization should be that reps are "engaging in the highest quantity of highest quality" activities.[2] Our job as Operators is to eliminate the low-quality activities.

The same is true for our own work within Ops. In a growing Operations team, much of your work will start out manually in spreadsheets or well-intentioned flow charts. Territory planning, forecasting, and workflow automation all start this way—and ultimately can be made more efficient through technology, both for ourselves and our internal customers.

The 747 Problem

So, let's say you have properly validated your pain point, researched and evaluated competing solutions, and ultimately purchased a tool to make your company better. Now what?

When you buy a new tool, your organization is not only placing a considerable investment in purchasing the tool itself, but also investing in the Operators like us to implement and run these tools. And yet so many tools go unadopted or underutilized by the companies that buy them. It's a pretty wasteful, ineffective, and somewhat ironic way to spend money on software that is supposed to have the opposite effect on your organization.

Angus Davis, Sean's CEO at Upserve, called this "the 747 problem." You end up with all of these fancy tools sitting on the runway that only a very small group of people know how to fly. (By the way, this is just as true for new processes as it is for new tools.)

So, how do we, as Operators, avoid the 747 problem?

Kyle Bastien, the former VP of Sales Readiness at Drift, explained on the *Operations* podcast, "Behavior change is hard... You think about what you need to do to land an organization-wide behavior change across a hundred sales reps and sales managers. We need to teach them how to do it. We need to make sure they actually do it. We need to make sure that it works."[3]

Operators often mistakenly reach for a technical solution in circumstances like this. But the answer to the 747 problem has almost nothing to do with how technical you are or how creatively you can bring disparate pieces of technology together. Those are helpful skills, but you could know the tool inside and out and still end up with no utility from it.

Instead, the solution lies in how well you understand the motivations of your end users whose experience you're trying to improve, and your approach to changing that experience.

A Blueprint for Change

There are four key steps you can use as a blueprint to launching a new tool or process that people will actually use.

Step 1: Focus on the "why" and keep reiterating it over and over again.

With any new tool that you're launching, it's important to spend time figuring out and refining what's in it for the users, who you're hoping will ultimately adopt and see value in it. For each role that you're expecting to adopt this tool, how will they use it? How will it fit into their workflows? Why will it make their lives better?

Just like any sales or marketing message, the more you can refine and clarify this "why," the better. Then, once you have it, work this messaging and list of benefits into every meeting, every presentation, and every conversation you have about the tool and its launch. If you're not sick of hearing yourself list off the benefits of this tool, you're not reiterating the "why" enough.

Put yourself in your internal customer's shoes and ask, "What's in it for me?"

A great example of this came when Laura and Sean implemented a forecasting tool called Clari. Forecasting, which we'll explore more deeply in the next chapter, can carry a pretty negative connotation with a sales rep. A tool specifically for forecasting? Forget it.

But when we presented the "why" for purchasing and implementing Clari, it had very little to do with "calling your number." Instead, we focused on why pipeline management and forecasting were critical muscles to build in an organization, and what specifically this tool did to make things easier for reps. We presented them with challenges they had told us themselves about their day-to-day work, and then we framed aspects of this new purchase as solutions to those problems. It looked like Figures 7.1 and 7.2.

Our "why" had nothing to do with specific features or functionality of the tool. It had everything to do with the expected outcomes for our audience when they used it.

Step 2: Make sure you have buy-in from leadership.

An Australian study by Majharul Talukder looked at the factors affecting the adoption of technological innovation by individual employees, and found that "perceived usefulness and managerial support are the two dominant variables in explaining adoption."[4]

FIGURE 7.1 Our challenges today

- Opportunity management is too complicated—it takes too much time.
- Expectations and terminology are different from manager to manager.
- Spend too much time on system updates and not enough time on valuable conversations (deal reviews, 1:1s, etc.).
- Forecast accuracy is poor.

FIGURE 7.2 Expected outcomes

- Simplify reps' lives and save time.
- Align definitions and forecast expectations across the entire business.
- Enable better conversations between reps and managers (deal reviews, 1:1s, etc.).
- Improve forecast accuracy.

Let's stick with the scenario that you're rolling out a new tool to your sales team. The most important people in the organization to convince that this tool is valuable are your sales leaders.

In a perfect world, your CRO or most senior sales leader is an internal executive sponsor for the implementation who can lend their voice to articulating the "why" behind the purchase in the first place. But even without that highest ranking advocate, the broader sales leadership group is where you can really set yourself up for success. Not only is this the audience that allows you to reach your intended audience of end users, but this is also the group with whom you can start to test your messaging of the benefits of the tool, and build a ground-swell of support for your launch. Leaders can make or break your roll-out. If they aren't bought in, or their team can sense that they don't agree with the "why" behind your tool, you might as well put that 747 out on the tarmac now to collect dust.

Leaders are the ones you want to defend and advocate for your tool when you're not there to do it yourself. Spend time with your leaders, taking them through the justification of the business case, validate your approach, and outline for them the exact project plan and timeline for the launch. Also, don't forget that post-launch, you'll need them to be your best evangelists for reinforcement, adherence, and more reinforcement.

One specific way that we achieved this with sales leaders was that we made the use cases real for them as well. In a group setting, we presented real-life sales opportunities to the sales leadership group and challenged them to collectively forecast a deal. Together, we all debated and explored the nuances of sales stages, forecast categories, qualification criteria, and workback plans, ultimately landing at a collective understanding of how to properly manage and forecast our pipeline. This exercise accomplished two things: 1) It confirmed the existing challenges around forecasting, and 2) aligned our highest-leverage audience on a common language for how we talked about our deals.

Step 3: Create a pilot group.

Once you get your leaders on board, the next group to identify and bring together around your new tool is a pilot group of users. These will be the most important internal customers and users you have.

First, be thoughtful as you pick your pilot users. It's important to get a variety of perspectives in your group—you don't just want the people who are always your early adopters. You want a range of participants from different teams, different tenure lengths at the company, and yes, even those folks that always find something wrong, no matter what.

Then, it's time to ask your pilot group to start using the tool and giving you feedback. Take their feedback and implement it as much as possible. Not only is their feedback going to be super valuable and insightful for your launch, you're also building champions of the product for after the launch.

As Kyle Bastien explains, "When it comes to enablement or broad process change, anytime you want a sales rep or team to do anything differently, they will say, 'How do I know this is going to work? How do I know that this is better than what I'm doing today?' Because you're implying that the way they're doing it could be improved."[3]

Kyle's suggested reply to this line of question is simple: "This is what we changed. This is what we learned during the experiment. And these are the results that we're getting that tell us that this is better than what we're doing today. And don't take it from me. These are the folks that were trying it, let's see what they think."

When their peers are skeptical, the pilot group of users should be the ones advocating for a new change's value on your behalf. Any end user is far more likely to trust the word of one of their peers than they are someone else. Figure out who in your pilot group can be your champions to others in the company and set them loose!

Step 3.5: Train your Operations Team.

Okay, we're cheating a bit with a bonus step here, but we don't want to make any assumptions. You have to ensure you are training a few pilots within your RevOps group to fly your new 747. Depending on the size of your team, think about who will own, administer, and update your new tool without creating single points of failure. At a minimum, inform your full Operations team on the new tool and train a few key users. This offers a great opportunity to test out your training material on a friendly audience, and your RevOps team-mates can point out any blind spots you missed up until this point.

Step 4: Pick KPIs to measure the success of your launch,
and measure them!

This last step is an easy one to skip even if you've done a great job on Steps 1, 2, and 3. But it's so important. Because you've already done such a great job of defining the "why" behind your launch, picking out the KPIs to measure should be easy. All of those benefits and value-adds you clearly articulated for your users—that's exactly what you should be measuring.

You've spent all of this time, money, and effort to buy and implement this tool. It would be such a waste of your own work not to clearly identify how you'll measure success.

When you pick out your metrics, make sure they are outcomes that leadership and your users care about, and then clearly articulate when you're going to come back and measure them. Is it one month after launch? Six months? It's easy in Operations to quickly move on from one project to the next thing on the "to-do" list, but having the discipline to revisit your original hypothesis and expected impact is critical. Spending the time defining these metrics will make it easier for you to declare victory or make the necessary adjustments after your initial launch.

If we revisit the Clari example, we pitched the sales team on some concrete expected outcomes, as listed in Figure 7.2. So, how do we make these outcomes measurable? As you'll learn about in Chapter 11, Operators need to be able to translate fluffy value propositions into measurable outcomes. Table 7.1 shows how you might do that.

Only after you've meticulously followed these four steps is your tool ready for general release. No one wants to have those 747s sitting on the runway with no one to fly them. Follow this blueprint, and it will save you the pain and headaches of any failed takeoffs.

TABLE 7.1 Translating potential value into measurable outcomes

Fluffy Value Proposition	Measurable Outcome
Simplify reps' lives and save time	Use improved Clari interface to reduce opportunity management admin time by X%
Align definitions and forecast expectations across the entire business	Document and train sales org on forecast category definitions and sales stage exit criteria by June 30
Enable better conversations between reps and managers (deal reviews, 1:1s, etc.)	Survey reps on 1:1 efficacy on a scale of 1 to 5; improve average rating from X to Y in first three months post-launch
Improve forecast accuracy	Improve forecast accuracy from X% to Y% in Q3

Chapter Takeaways

1 **Change management is hard, and technology is only part of the solution:** Operators often first reach for a technical solution when faced with inefficiencies, but adoption of a new tool or process has little to do with how technically gifted you are and everything to do with your approach to gaining that adoption.

2 **Understand the "why" of tool adoption:** Prioritize understanding the benefits and integration of a new tool before its implementation, emphasizing its value to end users and how it improves their workflows.

3 **Secure leadership buy-in:** Gain endorsement from organizational leaders, especially in the context of sales tool adoption, ensuring their understanding of the tool's benefits and support for its successful integration within the company.

4 **Create a pilot group and obtain user feedback:** Select a diverse pilot group to trial the tool and provide feedback, fostering a group of internal champions who can advocate for the tool's value and address skepticism among their peers.

5 **Measure and monitor key performance indicators (KPIs):** Define and measure KPIs aligned with the expected benefits of the tool to assess its effectiveness, allowing for adjustments and improvements to maximize the tool's impact on the organization.

Endnotes

1 *Operations* with Sean Lane (2022) The True ROI of Digital Adoption with WalkMe's Maor Ezer, Episode 88 [podcast]

2 *Operations* with Sean Lane (2020) When to Invest in Sales Operations (Plus the Right Way to Measure Performance) with Atrium Founder Pete Kazanjy, Episode 27 [podcast]

3 *Operations* with Sean Lane (2022) The Genesis of Drift's Sales Lab with Kyle Bastien, Episode 85 [podcast]

4 M. Talukder (2012) Factors affecting the adoption of technological innovation by individual employees: An Australian study, *Procedia – Social and Behavioral Sciences*, 40, 52–57

8

The Art and Science of Forecasting

Michelle Palleschi was the Director of Worldwide Sales Finance at Apple. As part of her role, she was responsible for helping to forecast the sales of the newest iPhone set to hit the market. She and her team had to make forecasting decisions three years prior to the phone's actual launch date. And it wasn't just how many to make—the forecasts needed to precisely anticipate the volume, geographic distribution, and even the color of the future demand. Michelle explained:

Imagine anywhere you can buy an iPhone. Someone is literally planning how much inventory and supply that exact store gets. You don't want too much supply sitting in one place and not enough in another. And that might just be in San Francisco, right? How much is China getting? How much is Norway getting, and how much is going to every single location there? How much is going to sell in the first weeks of launch, and how much do we need post-launch? Just like anything, you have to be watching the data and the trends to ensure that you are making the most relevant decisions today. For instance, when iPhone launched its rose gold phone, predicting how much demand would be in China and allocating supply based on geographic tastes and demand was a huge debate. Rose gold flew off the shelves in China, and that was one of the biggest decisions that was made there, but deciding how much needed to go, what would be the mix between silver, black, white, rose gold, those become new decisions and can be big mistakes. You could miss a color allocation pretty big and not have enough of the right phone, and not be able to sell through it.[1]

Forecasting the exact volume of the demand for iPhones is a science supported by an army of smart people with billions of dollars at stake. That may not be the case for you and your company (yet!), but that doesn't diminish the importance of confidently forecasting the outcomes in your business.

Why Forecasting Matters

For some people, they hear the word "forecasting" and their eyes immediately glaze over. They view it as a necessary (or perhaps unnecessary) evil that doesn't bring any value to their own day-to-day responsibilities; it's simply a required exercise to appease management. That couldn't be further from the truth.

Kevin Knieriem, President of Strategic GTM at Clari, has one of the best explanations for why forecasting matters. He writes:

> Sales forecasting is one of the most important business processes to running the business. It determines how the company invests and grows and can have a massive impact on company valuation... The sales forecasting process is so much more than just calling a number. It represents the entire operating rhythm of the whole company. When the team is hitting their number quarter after quarter, the company can invest and grow with confidence. That means more marketing campaigns, increased headcount, and new technology to not only sustain, but also boost that growth trajectory... Done right, sales teams perform at their best, and everyone wins. Done wrong, there's finger-pointing and distrust, and everyone loses. Sales is a team sport, and a great forecasting process can vault team performance to new heights.[2]

Forecasting represents the entire operating rhythm of the whole company

We view forecasting as a critical muscle that you have to build in your organization. Practice that muscle and it will only get stronger with repetition and time; leave it unattended and the muscle will atrophy. We also recognize that forecasting in many businesses is not purely scientific. There is a balance of art and science. The art comes from your knowledge of specific deals, your industry, your customers, your product, and the business context you've developed over time. The science is backed by actual historical results, conversion rates, and data-backed outcomes. Both are required to produce an accurate forecast and, once again, Revenue Operations is uniquely positioned to be experts in both.

As Kevin has explained, forecasting cannot be an exercise exclusively designed for sales. As companies grow and mature, they realize that just forecasting bookings or revenue leaves them blind to other critical business metrics like pipeline or retention. To fulfill the promises of a Revenue Operations function, you need to design and implement forecasting motions that benefit the entire business.

The Foundations of Forecasting

Before you can even think about calling a number, you need to lay the foundations for effective pipeline management and forecasting within your go-to-market teams. In Chapter 5, we outlined the importance of clearly defining the different milestones in your customer journey. For example, we recommended having objective criteria for creating opportunities (or pipeline) in your new business sales motion. It might look something like this:

- **Role/authority:** Director-level or above is aware of or supportive of this evaluation.

- **Pains/needs:** Must have a problem that our product can solve (list out your product's specific use cases or value proposition).

- **Timing:** An active evaluation is in progress or looking to make a decision within X days/months.

You can't possibly forecast the outcomes of your opportunities if everyone has a different definition of what an opportunity is. Once you have this baseline foundation in place, start to define the different stages of what happens in the rest of the customer's buying process. Some people have very strong feelings about the names of these stages, or whether they should be explicitly tied to the buyer's process or the seller's process, but the most important thing is to arrive at a common language that everyone in the company uses. If a sales rep and their manager are talking about a deal, they should be able to quickly root themselves in what's happening in the sales process based on their shared understanding of that language.

As you design your sales process, map out what happens at each stage. Work with your teams to think about what needs to be true in order to advance from one stage to the next, and document the exit criteria for each stage. Table 8.1 shows an example of what those stages might look like.

TABLE 8.1 Sales stages example

Deal Stage	Exit Criteria
Discovery	• Problem and need are understood • Buying committee has been scoped
Solution scoping	• Product demo has taken place • Fully scoped use case and confirmed technical needs • Confirmed budget and buying timeline • "Why change? Why now? Why us?" is understood and documented
Solution validation	• Achieved technical win and fully validated use case with all relevant stakeholders • We are confirmed vendor of choice for decision maker • There is a documented mutual action plan (timeline, legal, procurement, security, etc.)
Negotiation	• Legal, security, and procurement are all fully signed off • Proposal has been sent for signature
Out for signature	• Signature completed!
Closed won	• Fully executed agreement!
Closed lost	• No meeting in the last 30 days and nothing scheduled for the next 30 days • There is no longer a problem/pain that we can solve • The opportunity has gone stale and there is no clear timeline for making a decision • Prospect has communicated a different vendor of choice

Look, we're Operators, so we appreciate a good table with explicit, bulleted definitions more than most, but we also recognize that customer-facing interactions don't follow a straight line. Decision makers change roles, procurement introduces unexpected requirements; buying committees balloon and delay your agreed upon timelines. This is where the concept of forecast categories enters the conversation. If your deal stages are there to guide you through the process of selling, forecast categories are your confidence intervals for how likely that deal is going to happen. Table 8.2 offers an example of what those forecast categories might look like.

This is where the "art" in forecasting can shine through. While many forecasting tools make it easy for you to associate specific sales stages with corresponding forecast categories, we believe this misses the point of why you need both concepts in the first place. If being in the "Negotiation" stage automatically means that deal is in "Commit," why bother having forecast categories at all? The forecast category

TABLE 8.2 Forecast category example

Forecast Category	Definition
Pipeline	• < 30% likelihood to close during currently forecasted close date period
	• Criteria to move to Best Case are not yet met
Best case	• > 60% likelihood to close by the currently forecasted close date
	• We are confirmed as preferred vendor by a champion, and we have path to economic buyer
	• Timelines for legal, security, and procurement are not fully confirmed
	• Business case and success metrics are in place, but not fully confirmed
Commit	• *This is you committing this deal and its revenue to the business!*
	• > 90% likelihood to close by the currently forecasted close date
	• We are the confirmed vendor of choice by economic buyer
	• Legal, security, and procurement processes and timelines have all been agreed upon
	• Success metrics and timeline of implementation are all fully confirmed

TABLE 8.3 Sample do's and don'ts of forecast categories for sales reps

DO	DON'T
• Use the definitions as guidelines for your forecast; discuss the definitions often with your manager	• Overthink them—the definitions are meant to be guidelines; you know your deal better than anyone else
• Reverify or update forecast category following each customer call	• Be afraid to advance deals
• Align with opportunity team: Lean on your manager, and other teammates involved in the opportunity for help in gauging where the deal is at	• Forecast in a vacuum—your teammates are there to help you

offers opportunity owners a place to include their unique perspective and expertise into what's happening in the deal, and all of the nuances that come with selling. This also means that every single deal won't fit perfectly into the bulleted forecast category definitions in Table 8.2. In fact, we recommend teams use these as guidelines, not gospel. Again, it comes back to leveraging the agreed-upon common language.

Educate your sales teams on what the common language is for both your sales stages and your forecast categories (see Table 8.3). Consistently using and maintaining accurate forecast categories can be a hard adoption curve, but de-mystifying the definitions and removing the stigma around why they're helpful are great starting points in getting higher quality inputs for your forecast.

So what do all of these inputs add up to? At a certain point, you have to actually make your forecast call. In a common sales scenario, this means "calling your number," or predicting the revenue you're likely to close. This is also an area where you need to be incredibly prescriptive with your guidance and your expectations. For example, many sales organizations ask for a "commit" number (what you're committing to the business will happen) and a "best case" number (what might happen if some things go your way).

Every organization has its own unique quirks and factors to consider, but we find it's simplest to start by just calling a single number. Why overcomplicate things or open yourself up to odd behavioral incentives to low-ball a "commit" number? The business is asking for accuracy, and so, think of your job as getting "closest to the pin." A helpful formula for this might be:

Forecast = Closed Deals + Committed Deals + Highest Confidence Best Case Deals

"Best case" deals aren't just there to offer upside to your forecast; they should also serve as potential backfills if (and when) things go sideways with a committed deal. The best reps and sales leaders anticipate that things won't go perfectly according to plan and prepare appropriately.

Humans, of course, will be imperfect at all of this. As AI-powered tools continue to advance, we will be able to lean on the insights from call summaries, email exchanges, and overall prospect sentiment to further inform our forecasting. We'll be able to train models on our own unique sales processes, buying intent signals, and examples of successful and unsuccessful outcomes.

Regardless of how the inputs of your forecast are derived, one final consideration in the foundations of forecasting is the operating rhythms you build into your forecast. In Chapter 4, we offered a sample agenda for a weekly forecast call. Think of that routine as Forecasting 101—the very first and most basic exercise on the path to strong forecasting muscles.

In addition to that call, expand your thinking and consider a more comprehensive approach to the cadences with which you forecast your business.

REAL WORLD ROLE MODELS

Kyle Coleman, CMO at Copy.ai and former CMO at Clari, has spent a lot of time asking companies about their forecasting rhythms and has come to believe that the most sophisticated organizations approached every single week with intention. He explained his findings on Episode 87 of the *Operations* podcast:

> A lot of companies, unfortunately, think of forecasting as this basic process where you're just rolling up a spreadsheet, and that is not what forecasting is.

Of course that's a component of it. You're rolling up a call. You want to understand what individuals and teams are calling, and your leaders are responsible for triangulating. The reason this is the way that people think about forecasting is because 10 years ago, 20 years ago, it was the only way to do it. It was all gut. It was salespeople just calling a number, putting it in a spreadsheet, and crossing your fingers and hoping for the best.

The fact of the matter is we have way more data now. And so, forecasting is not just that bottom-up roll-up. It is also a very analytical exercise. It's looking at your conversion rate trends. It's looking at the current health of your pipeline. How old are the deals in the pipeline? What risk exists? Where are there risk and momentum indicators across those deals? It's looking at buyer engagement, looking at relationship maps, and seeing if they are responding to our emails. Are there files out that are waiting to be signed? What is the exact state of this business?

This approach allows everybody, from individual reps to frontline managers to VPs to our CRO, to have a lot more confidence that they're triangulating a number appropriately, and not just [carrying out] "finger-in-the-air" guesswork. That's what forecasting is. It's an analytical exercise, it's art, and it's science. It requires a really firm understanding of where you've been, but also where you are in order to predict where you're going.

What we found is that the most sophisticated companies put together what they refer to as a 13-week cadence for running revenue. What happens in week one? What happens in week two? All the way through week 13 of the quarter, they had different processes that were cadenced across that weekly calendar.

QBRs are in week two; so, in week one, it's all about deal inspection and clean up, so that when we enter QBRs, it's not an interrogation exercise. It's a strategic exercise to say, "We've already vetted the real from the not-so-real deals, and now we need to focus on those real deals and have a strategic conversation with all of the folks we have in the room about how we're actually going to turn this into revenue."

And then they go into this cadence where week three is the in-quarter forecast, and then week four is your out-quarter forecast. So they start looking out one quarter in the first month of the current quarter, and then have a rotating cadence every other week between the current and upcoming quarter.

Along the way, there are a bunch of other things. They look at slipped deals, and they start to understand why deals are slipping. Then as you get closer to the end of the month, week 4, week 8, week 13, they have what they call 'sequence of events' calls. The sequence of events is what has to happen, by what date, with what stakeholders, to actually get this deal done.

Every week of a 13-week quarter has revenue-critical moments that they are focusing on and optimizing along the way. It creates a flywheel where the more you focus on all these sub-processes across the greater revenue process, the better you become, the more data you collect, and the more you can optimize.[3]

EXAMPLE OF A 13-WEEK REVENUE CADENCE

Week 1:   Deal inspection and clean up

Week 2:   QBRs and slipped deal analysis

Week 3:   Current quarter forecast

Week 4:   Next quarter forecast; sequence of events call for end of month push

Week 5:   Current quarter forecast

Week 6:   Next quarter forecast

Week 7:   Current quarter forecast

Week 8:   Next quarter forecast; sequence of events call for end of month push

Week 9:   Current quarter forecast

Week 10: Current and next quarter forecast

Week 11: Current and next quarter forecast

Week 12: Current and next quarter forecast

Week 13: Current and next quarter forecast; sequence of events call for end of quarter push

---

Data-Driven Forecasting

Once you have designed and implemented the foundational components and cadences of your forecasting motions, it's time to make something of all the data that you're collecting. There's no faster way to encourage dirty data inputs than to never do anything with the data you're collecting. Accurate forecasting can be a massive accelerant on your journey to building a high-achieving, predictable, and scalable revenue machine.

So where do you begin? We learned in Chapter 2 how to get a handle on the critical data points in your business. The same lessons apply to utilizing data in your forecast, and we, as Operators, aren't simply facilitators in the forecasting process—we have to participate in it.

At Drift, our Operations team built and iterated upon an internal forecasting model that regularly predicted outcomes within five percent accuracy. The two primary architects of that model were Paul Shea (who built and designed the core components of the model) and Chris Lowry (who later advanced and added more sophistication and reliability to the model). In a conversation on the *Operations* podcast, both Paul and Chris broke down the evolution of the model, its successes, its pitfalls, and how we triangulated our Ops. call with the rest of the business. The key steps to building our model were:

1. Clean Data Before All Else

All of the foundational elements we outlined in this chapter must be in place in order to build a working forecast model. As someone new to the business, Paul had to spend time with the right people to make sure this was the case:

> I really tried to spend as much time with the different sales leaders, with the sales reps to understand how they viewed the business, and then a lot of time with the data. Getting into Salesforce, seeing how opportunities were progressing, seeing how the stages were set up. And really getting into the weeds of the data and to get a well-rounded perspective on the business before jumping in.[4]

The other foundational data design choice we made was setting up our data warehouse and taking a daily snapshot of our Salesforce instance so that all historical CRM data would be available to us there. This way, we could look back at any single moment in the company's history and instantly know the status of all pipeline on that particular day.

2. Leverage Historical Conversion Rates

With clean historical data at our disposal, the next thing we did was build two different models based on our historical conversion rates: One that was stage-driven and another based on forecast categories. This way, on the first day of a quarter, we could ask, what is the expected conversion rate of the pipeline in the "Solution Validation" stage or the "Best Case" forecast category? These conversion rates dynamically changed throughout the quarter because what was true on Day 1 of a quarter was very different from Day 70 of a quarter. Typically, the further along you are in a given forecasting period, the higher confidence levels you have in your forecasted opportunities.

Initially, we also broke our model into three different types of deals that we wanted to forecast: 1) Create and close (new business deals created and closed in the same period of time), 2) Carry-over (new business deals we started the period with that were created in the previous period), and 3) Upgrade/expansion (opportunities with existing customers). Each of these sub-models would evolve over time (new products, new market segments, longer time horizons), but even in the earliest days of a growing business, the conversion rates and expected behavior of these three groups were different enough to merit their own unique lenses.

3. Share Early and Often

Like everything else in this book, we have to, as Operators, share what we're building with our internal stakeholders, especially when our view of the business might be different from theirs. You may have multiple forecasts in your business at any given time. For us, we always had three: 1) Our Operations model call, 2) The sales leadership call, and 3) Our forecasting tool's AI-driven call.

Our role as Operations was to then triangulate the official company forecast based on those three inputs and facilitate the conversations around those calls. Both Paul and Chris were incredibly skilled at having meaningful, productive conversations with individual sales leaders about their forecasts. Chris explained:

> Our forecast model was the source of truth for our Operations call so I would walk managers through the specific inputs that were getting us to that number. We would look at each individual rep rolling up to that manager, their starting pipeline in previous quarters, their historical conversion rates, and be able to show bookings we can expect from their starting pipeline. Eventually, managers can see how to get to the number, they better understand the actual performance of the reps they are managing, and it really builds that trustworthy relationship. They really value the input that we have when it comes to our forecasting.[4]

When sales leadership's call is higher than the Ops. call, we as Operators can offer a reality check based on historical performance; at the same time, sales can provide deal-specific outliers or details that can't possibly be solved through any model. It's a system of checks and balances, which continues to strengthen the company's forecasting muscle.

4. Adapt with the Business

Just because you have a few successful months or quarters in terms of your forecast accuracy doesn't mean the job is done. Business conditions will change. How can you adjust your forecasting assumptions if your company is moving up-market and selling to more Enterprise-style customers? What needs to shift if you launch a new, untested product or expand into a new geographic region? Or, hypothetically, a pandemic upends every assumption you had about your conversion rates?

For our model, Chris expanded its capabilities both technically and functionally. He was never satisfied with the current state. He explains:

> I think one thing that I started to realize throughout the quarters was that there was a give and take of different options. Do you want more

data? Do you want higher quality data? Do you want to look at the last four quarters and maybe a little less data, but more accurate conversion rates? Or do you want to use the last two to three years' worth of data? Each piece was something I wanted to optimize as we grew.[4]

For Chris and the team, they added more confidence in forecasting multiple quarters into the future, added complexity to the way they looked at renewals, upgrade, and expansion opportunities, and used inputs like rep headcount to more accurately anticipate pipeline creation outputs.

Your business will likely have its own unique needs, so it's important to seek out role model companies with similar forecasting needs to your own (more on role models in Chapter 24).

REAL WORLD ROLE MODELS

Not all go-to-market motions are created equal. Meghan Gill is the SVP Sales Operations and Sales Development at MongoDB, a company that underwent a shift from a typical SaaS bookings business to a consumption-based model. In Episode 66 of the *Operations* podcast, Meghan explained how she and her team tackled the challenges of forecasting a usage-driven business:

In the bookings model, it's very binary. Did we get the deal? Did we not get the deal?

Instead, for us, it's usually a question of, "Will that customer expand and bring on new applications that will significantly increase their consumption?" If anything, I actually think the run rate customers are a little bit easier to predict, and over the broad portfolio, it tends to be a little bit more predictable than the booking side of the house.

It's a slightly different way of forecasting because you have to think about multiple different variables. A lot of the sales leaders tell me that end-of-quarter is not quite as exciting as it was in previous iterations of MongoDB or in other companies because by the end of the quarter, a lot of the elastic run rate deals, which are often the big deals, have already been accounted for. The counter to that, though, is that if you're looking at your annual number, then you have to be more strategic. At the beginning of the year, how many new logos am I going to get onboard that will ramp up consumption over the course of the year? It's definitely a completely different mindset.[5]

It's Not All About Sales

As we've stressed throughout the book, we can't just fixate on sales. Far too often, growing companies focus entirely on new business acquisition, and wake up years later only to realize they have a meticulously-crafted, comprehensive New Business funnel, but don't have any idea how to retain and grow their existing customer base (theoretically easier and cheaper to do!).

For forecasting purposes, spend the time to design how your company will track, manage, and execute the existing customer lifecycle, particularly when it comes to renewal events. We've interviewed countless customer operations professionals, and you'd be shocked how many of them have zero customer retention forecasting infrastructure in place at all.

There are some key questions you should be able to answer when examining the retention of your existing customer base:

- How many customers (and how many dollars) are up for renewal in a given period of time?
- Which of the opportunities you're forecasting are tied to a renewal event vs. not?
- What percentage of your upgrade/expansion dollars come at the point of renewal vs. in-term?

By starting with the questions you know you're going to have to answer, you can make all of your instrumentation and CRM architecture designs from there. To get started, there are a few critical data points you'll need to instrument for the renewal process and ultimately your churn/retention forecast:

- Total renewable value: The customer value up for renewal on this opportunity.
- Total change in account value: The net change in this customer's total spend with your company.
- Total new contract value: The value of the new agreement at the point of renewal (this will be helpful when calculating your net renewal and net retention rates).

• Total gross renewed value: Total value renewed up to the total renewable value (this will be helpful when calculating your gross renewal and gross retention rates).

Just because you're building something for your post-sale stakeholders doesn't mean you shouldn't beg, borrow, and steal from all of the lessons you've learned in building your sales forecast. If anything, building renewal or retention forecasts should be accelerated by your existing routines and infrastructure for sales. Build in dedicated time to draft specific goals for your post-sale forecasting work to make sure it doesn't get drowned out by other priorities.

Forecasting is a long-term investment. It's an art and a science. It's a muscle that requires thoughtful and repetitive exercise, and can be a springboard towards your high-achieving, predictable, and scalable revenue machine.

Chapter Takeaways

1 **Forecasting's business impact:** Forecasting can have a transformative impact on a company's investments, growth trajectory, and overall valuation. Forecasting isn't just about predicting numbers, it influences the entire operating rhythm of the business.

2 **Balancing art and science:** Forecasting is a delicate balance between art and science. Successful forecasting requires a combination of industry knowledge, customer insights, and business context (art), along with reliance on historical results, conversion rates, and data-backed outcomes (science).

3 **Foundations of forecasting:** Before calling numbers, you must have well-defined customer journey milestones and sales stages. A shared language among team members is crucial for effective communication. The introduction of forecast categories provides confidence intervals, reflecting the likelihood of deal closures and allowing room for subjective insights.

4 **Data-driven forecasting:** Leverage clean data in forecasting. Historical conversion rates, early sharing of insights with stakeholders, and continuous adaptation to business changes are key.

5 **Non-sales forecasting:** Extend forecasting efforts beyond sales. Design and implement strategies for tracking, managing, and executing the existing customer lifecycle, particularly in terms of renewal events. Building infrastructure for retention forecasting is a key element for overall business success.

Endnotes

1 *Operations* with Sean Lane (2019) Apple Product Launches and 10,000 Handwritten Notes, with Michelle Palleschi (COO of Sendoso), Episode 6 [podcast]

2 K. Knieriem. The Importance of Sales Forecasting and How It Impacts a Company [blog] Clari, 27 August 2019, https://www.clari.com/blog/the-importance-of-sales-forecasting (archived at https://perma.cc/XK4T-6A64)

3 *Operations* with Sean Lane (2022) How Hypergrowth Companies "Run Revenue" with Clari's Kyle Coleman, Episode 87 [podcast]

4 *Operations* with Sean Lane (2022) How to Forecast within 5%, with Paul Shea and Chris Lowry, Episode 125 [podcast]

5 *Operations* with Sean Lane (2021) Building MongoDB's Complex Go-to-Market Motion, with Meghan Gill, Episode 66 [podcast]

9

Annual Planning and the Art of the "Fiscal Year Flip"

When Sean was just getting started in his Operations career, he was doing what every Operator does best: He was worrying about something. That "something" was the upcoming year's operating plan and corresponding compensation plan. He had questions he couldn't answer, dependencies that were unresolved, and the unavoidable reality that January 1 was going to come after December 31.

But when he presented this imminent reality and concern to his boss, he heard something unsettling. "Don't worry about it. Most companies I've been at are lucky to get their comp plans out by the end of the first quarter."

Whether it was inexperience, naivete, or just plain ignorance, Sean couldn't believe this was the "normal" experience on a sales team at a fast-growing company. And, more directly, he couldn't accept that this would be the "normal" experience where he worked.

Fast-forward a few years, Sean was the VP Field Operations at Drift. Instead of rolling out new territories and new comp plans in the third month of the new year, his Operations team put the finishing touches on this critical work on the third day.

A new year at a company brings with it uncertainty, questions, and doubt. Sales reps wonder if the new company strategy will succeed or fail, if the new products being launched will resonate with customers or fall on deaf ears, if their territory will be rich or barren, and most importantly, whether they will make money or not.

Delays in answering those questions only breed more uncertainty, and no matter how unfair the expectation, everyone expects all of the underlying systems and processes to "just work." Not delivering as an Operations team at this critical moment is simply unacceptable.

So, lean into it. The title of this chapter is not just fun alliteration. The "Fiscal Year Flip" (Figure 9.1) is a brand we developed, embraced, and embedded into the go-to-market teams we led. Throughout this chapter, whenever you see us reference the Fiscal Year Flip, know that it is not just the turning of the calendar from one day to another. It's an approach, it's an opportunity, it's a celebration. This chapter will teach you how to treat it as such.

What Makes for a Good Fiscal Year Flip?

The ideal outcome is there is a switch that you flip when you get to the first day of the new fiscal year and magically everything works—your reports, your new compensation plan, systems, new policies for discounting, new territories, new quotas, forecasting goals, lead routing, and any number of other fun things that you and the management team decided to change for the new year. If just reading this sentence gave you anxiety, you are a true Operator. In this chapter, we guide you on how to execute an efficient, comprehensive, and effective planning process. Performing a graceful Fiscal Year Flip is similar to the high-flying acrobatics of gymnastics; it requires planning, practice, and a lot of work before you get to the podium.

An organization can waste weeks or months of a new fiscal year buried in the unknowns. If your sales team doesn't know how they will be compensated, if your customer success team doesn't know which accounts are theirs, if your managers don't know what they have authority to approve, if your leads don't route to the right person, if your reports can't tell you how you are doing against your new goals, how on earth can your organization execute well?

The rollout of the Fiscal Year Flip is the outcome of an annual planning process that starts about halfway through the previous year. A well-executed flip is proactive, includes a cascaded communication

FIGURE 9.1 Fiscal Year Flip LinkedIn post

Sean Lane · You
Operations Leader | Founding Partner at BeaconGTM
1w · 🌐

Happy Fiscal Year Flip to those who celebrate! May your data be clean, your territories be plentiful, and your comp plans be rich.

While the big year-end push for our friends in Sales ended yesterday, the Super Bowl for Ops starts today. Good luck to all the Ops teams doing the hard work under the hood today.

How quickly can you make the transition from Planning to Execution, and kick the new year off with results? That's the measure of success today.

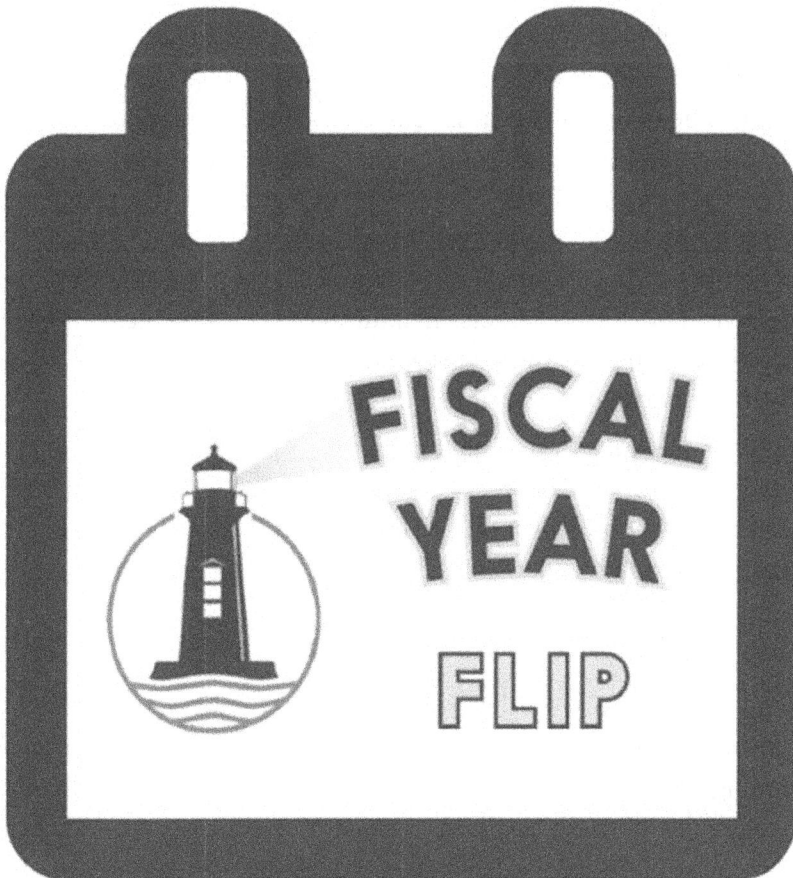

schedule, and provides a smooth entry and operational readiness for your new year. Begin your annual planning process with this desired end in mind, and you're off to a good start.

Our best Fiscal Year Flips have happened with the following ingredients:

1 **Clear end goal**: Create a Fiscal Year Flip execution script that identifies who, what, where, when, and how. Staff your Fiscal Year Flip such that each step of the execution script is assigned, measured, and you can monitor during launch.

2 **Project management**: Assign a project manager to own the project plan. Identify your dependencies and "long poles" of the plan: What are the key activities that take the longest and have the most dependencies? Have an initial draft of your project plan by the start of the second half of the year.

3 **Comprehensive approach**: Document strategic shifts and big bets for the company in the coming year. Coordinate with the financial operating plan. Include your systems work and dependencies. Identify any policy changes by the third quarter. Design org structure and roles to support the new plan. Align on quota capacity and hiring targets. Include territory management plans, books of business for customer success, and compensation/incentive planning.

4 **Communication strategies**: Gather feedback from last year on what worked and what didn't. Hold regular cross-functional reviews with your stakeholders. Include a communication schedule. Align all departments on key due dates.

Project Planning

We know it may sound crazy to start your planning process at the beginning of Q3, but it just takes that much time for most organizations to make all of the decisions needed to execute on week one of a new fiscal year. It can be hard to evaluate the success of your bets from last year with just six months of data, but last year's planning should have established key milestones of success for your bets. If it didn't, it's never too late to start.

Start your project planning by identifying your project manager. Later, in Chapter 19, we will talk about staffing your Operations team with the right mix of skill sets, but find the project manager on your team who loves to run a process and tie up loose ends. They must be able to shepherd cats throughout the planning process and into your fiscal year launch, all while still running the business and executing on the current year's plan. Have them draft an outline of the plan by the end of your first half; this plan will serve as one of your most important resources and best communication tools throughout the process.

We have included a template for a Fiscal Year Flip project plan in Figure 9.2 that you can customize to match your business. The planning for your company may need some additional components that we don't list here, but why start from scratch when you don't need to!

FIGURE 9.2 Project plan template

Functional Area	#	Deliverables
Prep	1	Exploratory interviews: Managers, directors, VPs
	2	Socialize summary of informational interviews with senior staff
	3	Scope firmographic score regression work
	4	Current territories analysis
	5	Prep quota file copy
	6	Communicate Account Assignment blackout period
Rules of Engagement Updates	1	Finalize updated segments
	2	Finalize new role definitions
	3	Update rules of engagement for new roles
	4	Determine data source for Primary/Primary Sub Industry
	5	Update employee count enrichment policy
	6	Update territory naming conventions
	7	Finalize compensation guiding principles
	8	Launch territory carving dimensions section

	9	Rules of Engagement Leadership Review
	10	Rules of Engagement Leadership Sign Off
	11	Updated Rules of Engagement Training
Data Enrichment	1	Enrich employee count, audit, overwrite field, calculation
	2	Stamp Prior Fiscal Year Fields and update formula in Sandbox
	3	Update role titles in Quota File, CRM, and forecast tool
	4	Audit hierarchies
	5	Firmographic scoring audit
Sales	1	Kickoff meeting with Sales Management
	2	Formalize headcount/capacity plan
	3	Finalize team structure
	4	Finalize headcount for specialized roles
	5	Align on territory design for all roles
	6	Align on compensation for all roles
	7	Finalize quotas
	8	Finalize regions
	9	Share holdover sheets with reps
	10	Finalize v1 territory proposal
	11	Block for territory reviews, office hours, feedback
	12	Territory sign off
	13	Territory Sandbox Upload
	14	Send comp letters + upload into forecast system
	15	Conduct training preview with sales management
Customer Success	1	Flip over Individual Contributor Pacing Doc (follows Quarterly process)
	2	Flip over Capacity Plan (after Finance updates Operating plan)
	3	Customer Success Book of Business Update
	4	Customer Success Manager Capacity Planning Updates
	5	Review compensation changes with management
	6	Finalize resegmentation changes
	7	Finalize compensation changes
	8	Finalize territory/book of business changes
Partner	1	Review current Partner Rules of Engagement for any proposed changes
	2	Draft updates to Partner Rules of Engagement
	3	Review changes with sales, operations, and finance
	4	Draft Partner plans/goals
	5	Finalize Rules of Engagement and Partner Plan

	6	Create Partner Agreements
	7	Finalize Partner Agreements and start sharing externally
FY Planning: Finance/ Operating Plan	1	Create FP&A version of new fiscal year Quota File for prelim budgeting
	2	Iterate on Ops. Model and update Quota File accordingly
	3	Incorporate updates to segmentation/verticals/quotas/ assumptions
	4	Alignment on initial pass of bookings/headcount/capacity
	5	Iterate on Ops. Model/Quota File based on management feedback
	6	Final alignment on bookings/headcount/capacity
Fiscal Year Flip Script	1	Stamp Prior Fiscal Year Fields in Prod
	2	Update formula fields in Prod
	3	Prepare Day 1 Field Change Sheet (employee count, type, owners)
	4	Prepare Day 2 Territory Sheet (Account ID, Account Owner-UserID, SDR Owner-UserID)
	5	Update role names in CRM
	6	Audit Holdover Expirations
	7	Prepare Customer Success Owner upload sheet
	8	Audit accounts owned by inactive users
	9	Finalize Quota File
	10	Share Manager Quota Files
	11	Share Rep Quota Files
	12	Upload Quotas into forecast system
	13	Audit Renewal Specialist owners and opportunity owners
	14	Finalize Renewal Specialist books
	15	Update employee count formula and audit overrides
	16	Update assignment groups
	17	Reconfigure all essential reports for updated rules
	18	Update routing rules
	19	Audit hierarchy assignment rules
	20	Audit SDR Assignments
	21	Audit territory alignments
	22	Account and Opp. mismatch corrections
	23	Launch training for new fiscal year
	24	Notify all users of completion and any remaining issues

NOTE Each deliverable should include an owner, due date and show dependencies.

The Beginning of Your Planning Process: The Big Questions

We all want to know the answers to the big questions in life. Finding the answers to your annual planning questions may or may not be easier to tackle. To start your planning process, seek out and document answers to the following questions:

1 What are your strategic levers for the year?

  a. New product/new releases/new features

  b. Geographies

  c. Partners

  d. Pricing

  e. People

  f. Distribution

2 What are the investments you have for the year and what will they affect?

  a. External resources/partners

  b. Systems

  c. Training

  d. Internal resources/new functions

3 What are the external factors you are planning for?

  a. Global markets/economies

  b. Competitors

  c. Industry trends

4 What are the cost constraints you have?

  a. Current cost profile

  b. Required planning cost profile

  c. Company burn rate

When you have the answers to your big questions, you then have direction on what planning models you need to build. As you answer these questions, document them in a shared presentation. This is the draft of your communication presentation that you will use when you launch your new fiscal year. This critical tool will communicate what big bets the business has for the coming year and how they will affect everyone in the company.

Finance's Operating Plan

At the same time as answering the big questions, organizations should be developing and refining their financial operating plan. Finance is generally the owner of the financial operating plan for the next year to three years (and a more detailed version of the plan for the upcoming 12 to 18 months). When the finance department creates their operating plan, this will be the start of what Revenue Operations need to create their supporting plans.

Whether you use planning systems like Workday Planning, Excel, or Google Sheets, the technology doesn't matter as much as whether the plans are aligned. Does Finance's model call for 50 sellers but yours requires 60? Integrated planning is needed to ensure everyone is on the same page to set your company up for success. Technology can make integrating plans easier, but good old-fashioned communication will ensure that you are on the same page.

The financial operating plan will likely provide you with what your top line growth needs to be and a cost profile that you will need to plan within. The best run companies treat this as an iterative process where multiple versions are run between finance and Operations, trading off costs and growth targets as you refine answers to the big questions (strategic levers and investments) for the year. One of Laura's companies had 16 iterations during one year's planning cycle. Version control is critically important during this iterative process. We recommend that you document your trade-offs and key assumptions during this process as well, usually in an accompanying presentation to the plan numbers. While an entire operating plan can be overwhelming, distilling plans down to the key assumptions necessary to hit that plan can make it far more digestible. For example, if the midmarket sales leader knows they need to increase average sales price in their segment by 5 percent in order for the company to achieve its goals, they have a clear objective and ownership to figure out how they hit that objective.

The Power of Cross-Functional Planning

Whether you are entering a new geography, launching a new product, or just maintaining the status quo, don't forget to be cross-functional in your planning. The worst thing that can happen is for your company planning to happen in silos.

Stop us if you have heard this story. Sales puts a rep into a new geography, but then reality hits that the product features can't support users in the new geography or prospects in the new market have never heard of the company, and the rep throws up their hands in frustration.

There should be representatives in your planning process from across the company. For example, in thinking about opening up a new geography, you need to think about:

- **Product:** Language, regulatory requirements, data privacy/protection differences, product changes or needs before you launch in the new region, and if workarounds are possible and for how long.

- **Finance/Legal:** Currency, orders/contracts, typical geography terms and conditions, foreign exchange exposure, legal entity, and revenue and tax implications.

- **Staffing:** Will you hire in region/outsource to an agency/hire as contractor? Consider new employment contracts, tax and employment considerations, and language support.

- **Marketing:** Do you have existing customers? How are existing prospects handled and what will change? Consider local marketing support, marketing agency usage, language considerations, how far in advance of sales does marketing need to lead, brand recognition plan, terminology/language differences between regions (Chevy's Nova sold well in the U.S., but it means "no go" in Spanish).

- **Sales:** What supporting teams does sales need? Local versus centralized, language support, prospecting, technical sales, customer success, longer ramp times and lower quotes, managerial support, and possible outsourcing to partners.

- **Operations:** How to support the new time zone, language, order forms/contracts, pricing, territories, account scoring, and prospect identification.

When one of your levers for the year involves something new, question all of your planning models and bring in all of the functions who will be needed to make that new lever successful. Launching something new requires a different kind of planning than business as usual.

And sometimes the "something new" is economic uncertainty.

REAL WORLD ROLE MODELS

Heidi Thompson is the Vice President of Go to Market Strategy and Revenue Operations at Unqork. Heidi's full interview can be heard on Episode 93 of the *Operations* podcast, "How to Adjust Annual Planning During Economic Uncertainty."[1]

Here are Heidi's key insights on how planning needs to adjust in times of uncertainty:

- It's more important than ever that Ops. supports fast decision making for leaders by providing real-time data, analytics, and insights so that they can move as quickly as possible.

- Conservatively estimate where you can progress. Question all of your assumptions from compensation ratios to ramp times to deal cycle lengths. For sales capacity planning especially, compare your estimates to past performance, particularly focused on the last two years.

- Agree as a company leadership team on the three to five priorities that you're going to execute against and how you're going to do it. Once that alignment is completed, identify what you have to drop off as well. You will have to say no, you have to learn to walk away.

- It is a great time to double down on your customers and make them wildly successful.

- It's not a great time to lose focus of who your ideal customer profile (ICP) is. You shouldn't be distracted by the new shiny object or a hot lead that comes in if they don't fit into your ICP because it's going to reduce productivity.

- Operations can help contribute to efficiency and cost savings by closely evaluating and optimizing the tech stack for any overlaps in functionality.

Reconciling Top Down and Bottom Up Planning Models

When something needs to stand up to scrutiny in science, we use multiple methods to ensure the integrity of the data or results. We triangulate results to increase the credibility and validity of findings. Operating plans are no different: We need credibility, multiple perspectives, and our hypotheses need to be vetted. Great Operators triangulate their operating plans.

Figure 9.3 shows a common planning triangulation method for software businesses. For your business, these three models may not be the perfect fit and that's okay. The goal of triangulation in planning is to ensure that you are thinking of multiple ways to validate and stress test your plan. When you can show your work, quantify your required improvement areas, and communicate to all of your cross-functional partners that your plan is achievable, you align the revenue machine.

Top Down Funnel Plan

Every business generally has a top down funnel. The components, the definition of each step of the funnel, where you start measuring, the conversion rates, the measurements, and the in-betweens may all be different, but at the bottom of every funnel is one outcome: Revenue. A "top down" plan leverages those funnel milestones and conversion rates to predict revenue outcomes.

Depending on your business, you can break that plan down into different components like market segment, business unit, lead source, product, or geographic region. A common problem with top down funnel planning is that the results may not be at the level of detail that you would want or need to track your business. This requires allocating the goals down to a further level of granularity. For example, you can plan for an entire year and then spread it by month/ quarter or even monthly/weekly seasonality if your business needs that. We encourage you to do that allocation during the planning process so that you can compare growth rates year over year.

The top down funnel plan is the first of the RevOps models to validate whether the financial operating plan is achievable. It starts to highlight the implications of revenue goals that were fairly easy to set

FIGURE 9.3 Planning triangulation methods

Top Down Funnel

Bottom Up
Sales Capacity

Bottom Up
Sales Math

in a finance setting (e.g., grow X percent) on the rest of the business. For example, growing revenue by X percent means that you need to grow your top-of-funnel leads by Y percent. Does marketing have a plan for that type of lead growth?

We have provided a simplified example in Figure 9.4 for a recurring software business that has four business units, about $89 million in annual recurring revenue, and $2 million in services revenue. This type of planning model provides goals you can cascade to different organizations; for example, leads for marketing, new business meetings for sales, net new sales in dollars and counts for sales and services, and retention and expansion goals for customer success. Ultimately, these goals or targets (and their corresponding conversion rates) are your guideposts for determining whether you are on track or off track to your financial plan. The operating rhythms we outlined in Chapter 4 provide great forums throughout the year to monitor your actual results against these targets and course-correct along the way.

We would like to offer a word of caution in our Operator zeal to create beautiful planning models. It is very easy to create plans that get you to your desired totals—after all, it is just a spreadsheet. Resist the urge to assume your team will be able to drastically change any of your conversion rates year over year. Use historical conversion rates as your starting point where you can and highlight your assumptions if you assume improvements. With your answers to the big questions, you should be able to identify what support the company is investing in to drive the expected results. For example, if one of your big bets for the year is an investment in customer success tools, processes, and strategy, you would expect to see planned improvements in retention and expansion.

FIGURE 9.4 Top down funnel plan example

Funnel Model	Business Unit 1	Business Unit 2	Business Unit 3	Business Unit 4
NEW BUSINESS				
Marketing Qualified Leads	4000	1000	1500	2000
Conversion of M.Q.L. to S.Q.L.	25%	30%	20%	22%
Sales Qualified Leads	1000	300	300	440
Conversion of S.Q.L. to Meetings	55%	50%	40%	45%
Meetings	550	150	120	198
Conversion of Meetings to Opportunities	45%	50%	55%	40%
Sales Qualified Opportunities	248	75	66	79
Conversion of S.Q.O.s to Sales Wins	42%	40%	35%	36%
Sales Wins/New Customers	104	30	23	29
Average Sales Price	$60,000	$50,000	$42,000	$40,000
Net New Revenue	$6,237,000	$11,500,000	$970,200	$1,140,480
RECURRING BUSINESS				
Existing Customers (Count)	550	400	300	250
Existing Customers (Recurring $)	$33,000,000	$20,000,000	$112,600,000	$10,000,000
Customer Attrition % ($ based)	97%	95%	94%	96%
Customer Attrition $	-$990,000	-$1,000,000	-$756,000	-$400,000
Customer Attrition % (Count)	99%	98%	97%	99%
Customer Attrition Count	-5.5	-8	-9	-2.5
Customer Expansion %	110%	108%	105%	109%
Customer Expansion $	$3,300,000	$1,600,000	$630,000	$900,000
TOTAL SOFTWARE REVENUE				
End of Period Customer (Count)	648	422	314	276
End of Period Customer ($)	$41,547,000	$22,100,000	$13,444,200	$11,640,480
SERVICES BUSINESS				
Attach Rate to New Customers (%)	30%	40%	20%	22%
New Services Customers (Count)	31	12	5	6

New Average Services Price	$30,000	$25,000	$20,000	$25,000
New Customer Services Revenue	$935,550	$300,000	$92,400	$156,816
Attach Rate to Existing Customers (%)	7%	6%	5%	8%
Existing Services Customers (Count)	39	24	15	20
Existing Average Services Price	$8,000	$6,000	$7,000	$8,000
Existing Customer Services Revenue	$308,000	$144,000	$105,000	$160,000
Total Services Revenue	$1,243,550	$444,000	$197,400	$316,816

Bottom Up Sales Capacity Plan

A complementary approach to your top down plan is the "bottom up capacity plan," and your first effort at this plan is truly a monster one. Again, you can buy planning tools or use spreadsheets to create this plan, but either way it will require a significant investment. The objective for creating this plan is to take your existing teams and estimate the expected results in both revenue and required headcount.

It sounds so easy, doesn't it?

The urge to keep things simple in planning is not misplaced. Keep it as simple as you can, but still provide the detailed outputs that you will need to support your plan and ultimately run your business. You want a detailed hiring plan for your entire go-to-market organization and the ability to understand how much quota you have deployed (versus what you planned you needed) at any point in your year. The capacity plan provides one of the most important validations of how achievable your top line objectives are.

The simplest place to start your process is with sales quotas and ramps. Ramp time refers to how long it takes for a newly hired team member to go from their first day to a fully productive member of the team.

As with all things in Operations, your assumptions for ramp times need to be rooted in data. When looking at historical ramp achievements, you can include all historical sellers, but we believe the best sample excludes sellers who were involuntarily let go. Data from successful sellers should drive what your expectations are. Reviewing averages is helpful, but using scatterplots can help you spot outliers and design better ramp schedules. Figure 9.5 shows an example of how you can time neutralize the data series and evaluate sellers ability to ramp to a full quota.

Sometimes, you don't have enough data to find trends. In those cases, review your average deal cycle time, average deal size, and composition of closed deals (smaller expansions versus larger new deals) to construct your ramp. The first months usually have $0 quota expectations and align roughly with the average deal cycle plus training time for a seller.

Once you have completed your analysis, you will have a quota and ramp table that looks something like the following Figure 9.6.

FIGURE 9.5 Ramp attainment example

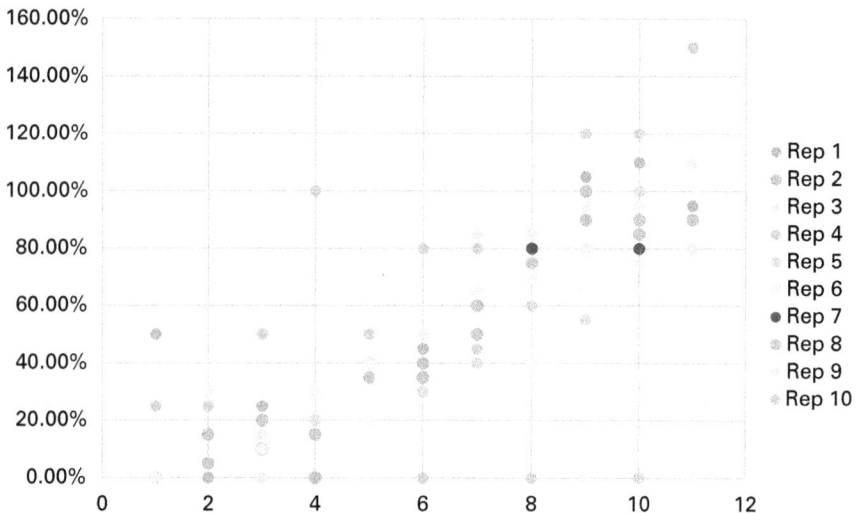

FIGURE 9.6 Quota and ramp table example

	Quota	Ramp M1	Ramp M2	Ramp M3	Ramp M4	Ramp M5	Ramp M10	Ramp M11	Ramp M12
Rep Type 1	$500,000	0%	25%	25%	50%	50%	100%	100%	100%
Rep Type 2	$600,000	0%	0%	25%	40%	50%	100%	100%	100%
Rep Type 3	$750,000	0%	0%	0%	25%	25%	100%	100%	100%
Rep Type 4	$1,000,000	0%	0%	0%	0%	25%	75%	80%	100%

Once you have your quotas and ramps, then you can start on the meaty part of the capacity plan. Input your existing sellers, your planned sellers, quotas, ramps, and then build in assumptions for attrition, productivity, and quota over-assignment (Figure 9.7).

ATTRITION PLANNING

You'll notice that Figure 9.7 takes into consideration some attrition assumptions. The reason for this is that when a rep gets promoted or leaves the business, not only do you lose that person's productivity, but you also need to properly account for the amount of time it will take for that person's replacement to ramp up to the equivalent of the fully productive sales rep you just lost. There are a few different ways you can plan attrition. The illustrative example we have here takes a percentage off of your deployed quota. This is the simplest model and can work well for many organizations. Another option for planning attrition can be actually putting in planned departures and backfills; this allows you to account for the approximately 60 days it takes most organizations to backfill a departure. The advantage of planning in more detail is the ability to track your actual movement in deployed quota and attrition costs (this is our personal favorite way to plan). A third way to plan attrition is to lump it into the expected average productivity. This third way is simple to model but hides the detail of where shortfalls come from.

EXPECTED PRODUCTIVITY/QUOTA OVER-ASSIGNMENT

When you think about how much quota you need to deploy to achieve your company's revenue target, those two numbers should not be the same. The space between the deployed quota and what you are expecting to achieve is labeled as "expected productivity %" in Figure 9.7. This should be shaped by the achievement that you have historically seen from your sellers and also allows for the unplanned to happen. Based on your company's maturity and grasp of all of these different factors, you want this over-allocation of quota to be 20 to 30 percent higher than the company's targets (closer to 20 percent if you're a well-instrumented, predictable revenue machine and closer to 30 percent if you don't have much to go on at all).

FIGURE 9.7 Sales capacity plan example

Plan for RepType 1	Month 1	Month 2	Month 3	Month 4	Month 5	Month 6	Month 7	Month 8	Month 9	Month 10	Month 11	Month 12
Existing Reps (Count)	5	5	7	7	7	7	7	7	7	7	8	8
Ramping Reps (Count)	2	2	0	0	1	1	1	1	1	1	0	1
Existing Reps (Deployed Quota)	$208,333	$208,333	$291,667	$291,667	$291,667	$291,667	$291,667	$291,667	$291,667	$291,667	$333,333	$333,333
Ramping Reps (Deployed Quota)	$41,667	$62,500	$0	$0	$0	$10,417	$10,417	$20,833	$20,833	$31,250	$0	$0
Total Deployed Quota	$250,000	$270,833	$291,667	$291,667	$291,667	$302,083	$302,083	$312,500	$312,500	$322,917	$333,333	$333,333
Attrition Assumption (%)	10%	10%	10%	10%	10%	10%	10%	10%	10%	10%	10%	10%
Attrition Assumption ($)	-$25,000	-$27,083	-$29,167	-$29,167	-$29,167	-$30,208	-$30,208	-$31,250	-$31,250	-$32,292	-$33,333	-$33,333
Expected Productivity (%)	88%	88%	88%	88%	88%	88%	88%	88%	88%	88%	88%	88%
Planned Sales Capacity	$198,000	$214,500	$231,000	$231,000	$231,000	$239,250	$239,250	$247,500	$247,500	$255,750	$264,000	$264,000
Overassignment (%)	5%	5%	5%	5%	5%	5%	5%	5%	5%	5%	5%	5%
Revenue Goal	$188,100	$203,775	$219,450	$219,450	$219,450	$227,288	$227,288	$235,125	$235,125	$242,963	$250,800	$250,800

While it is highly unusual to plan without quota over-assignment, there does need to be moderation in this. If you have too much over-assignment, the company can achieve its numbers without having success at the management or individual rep level. Even when some individuals or specific teams are successful, too much distance between the company's numbers and the deployed quota can generate resentment that the quotas were set too high to be achievable.

Some organizations also plan for buffers or over-assignment of quotas at each level of management. For example, a manager's team has a deployed quota of $1m, but that manager's personal quota is $900k. If you do that, our recommendation is to lock in the manager targets (and how they are calculated) at the beginning of the year with management. If you blindly provide the same discounted manager quota based on that manager's current deployed quota on their team, you can end up with a perverse incentive to not rehire when they have an attrition.

In the next chapter on variable compensation, we will discuss useful benchmarks to ensure that you have healthy quota expectations. And in the final triangulation model, bottom up sales math, you'll learn how to ensure the quotas are achievable in a tangible way for sellers.

HEADCOUNT PLAN

The end result of your capacity plan should be a headcount plan. You have already determined how many salespeople you need, now is the time to build out the rest of your supporting characters. Start with management and construct your org structure (this will also become part of your communication presentation).

Span of control (how many individual contributors per manager) is an important decision to align on with your leadership team. We have seen a range of 5 to 10 for the span of control for first line managers. The low end can be helpful for less experienced teams but has the downside of being so small that any fluctuations on the team negatively impact the manager's ability to succeed. The high end can be cost efficient and appropriate for experienced sellers and managers, but it usually means one or two members of the team will be neglected. Keeping a team of 10 fully staffed is going to be overwhelming and difficult for most managers. Our experience is that somewhere around seven is ideal.

Once you have your management structure in place, it's time for all of the other supporting roles. Your company will have its own unique types of roles, but a few to consider include: Technical or pre-sales, overlays (e.g. specialty experts), customer success, service delivery consultants, SDRs, partnership/distribution, enablement, management levels for all of those departments, and of course, Operations.

Let's spend a little time on SDRs. Typically, SDR headcount is planned as a ratio to sellers—anywhere from 1:1 to 4:1 is normal to see depending on a company's go-to-market approach (inbound vs. outbound), sales cycle, and average sale price. This role, however, has an industry standard time in the role of about 18 months. This is difficult to plan for and manage.

One way to lean into this constant change is through the use of what's called a "ranger rep." This role is described in Trish Bertuzzi's *The Sales Development Playbook: Build Repeatable Pipeline and Accelerate Growth with Inside Sales*.[2] Trish calls for overstaffing your SDR organization above your planned ratios to provide for continuity when you inevitably have an SDR get promoted or leave the organization. You place your more senior SDRs in an elevated "ranger rep" role and drop them in vacant SDR spots or give a needy seller more support for a period of time. Lean into the change. Don't be caught off guard by it.

Lead times for supporting staff can also be important to account for in planning. For example, you may want an SDR fully trained and effective before you hire a new seller, otherwise the seller's ramp could be affected. Additional factors to consider for SDRs or any other supporting type role are geographic region, language, or new product lines. These factors can break your plan ratios and should be planned thoughtfully.

While we focused on sales reps and SDRs in this chapter, these same principles can be applied for any other headcount planning in your organization. Your implementation team's required headcount will be dictated by new logo volume and detailed capacity planning. A customer success team plan needs to take into account factors like service levels and install base revenue.

The end result of your headcount plan draft should be delivered to finance so they can then account for the cost of the operational plan. The reconciliation between the financial operating plan and the Revenue Operations capacity plan will include negotiating the cost trade-offs of pursuing different strategies. For example, entering a new market has a lot of up-front costs that don't see immediate revenue results. The downstream internal stakeholders of the headcount plan include recruiting, facilities, IIT, enablement, and critically, hiring managers. The power of Revenue Operations and integrated planning can help those teams be better prepared for their roles and help your organization predictably scale.

Bottom Up Sales Math

Our final triangulation model is what we call sales math. This is where you pressure test your planned quotas and books of business by showing how to achieve and overachieve the individual goals set for the year. We believe the best Operators produce this for each of their types of sellers, for their SDRs, and other direct quota-carrying individual contributors in the organization (Laura has even taught sales math sessions in some of her companies' sales bootcamps).

Our example in Figure 9.8 is for a direct seller that has four sources of pipeline: Expansion at customers, channel partners, SDRs and self-generated pipeline. The milestone similarity between sales math and the top down funnel model is not an accident. A table like this is not just for a Revenue Operations team. You should provide these directly to sellers to demonstrate a clear path on how to achieve their goals. While the starting point might be historical averages or the ideal path to goal, sellers can then input their own values to show them how they can affect their outcome. The more they understand the levers inside of sales math, the more ownership they have over their success.

FIGURE 9.8   Sales math example

Example Sources	Customers	Channel	SDRs/ Marketing	Self- Generated
Leads (Interest)		35	143	25
Lead Conversion to First Meeting		60%	40%	50%
First Meetings/Demo/ Presentation		21	57	12.5
First Meeting Conversion to Opportunity		50%	30%	40%
Qualified Sales Opportunities	12	10.5	17	5
Opportunities Conversion to Sale	75%	50%	45%	45%
Sales	9	5.25	8	2.25
Average Sales Price	$10,000	$50,000	$50,000	$50,000
Contribution by Source	11%	31%	45%	13%
Sales by Source	$90,000	$262,500	$385,000	$112,500
Total Sales		**$850,000**		

If a seller has four channels to generate revenue, then the sales management team should focus on skill building in each of these areas. Leaders can facilitate best practice sharing on finding expansion opportunities at existing customers, how to work with channel partners, structured check-in meetings with their SDRs and how much time they need to spend prospecting for their self-generated pipeline. Each one of these cells represents a lever that can be pulled to affect the outcome. Sales math provides an important reality check on your quotas as well as a great communication tool to your individual quota carriers as to what avenues are available to them.

Bottom up sales math provides you with key figures like how many wins you need per month, how many meetings per week, or how many active opportunities during a quarter. Validate these expectations against your current performance and the capacity of an individual to manage the expected volume of activity. You can use this technique in a similar way to ensure that the books of business for customer success are appropriately sized for what you expect them to complete: Customer reviews, renewals, surveys, etc.

Territory Planning

There is no such thing as the "perfect territory." And as soon as you think you've got one, something will inevitably change in your business that will quickly render your flawless plan stale and obsolete. Territory planning is something that you will likely do all throughout the year, but big shifts should take place at the beginning of fiscal years. Establish territory goals as part of your initial planning and communication process. Typical goals include:

- fair and equitable territories with quantifiable supporting data for each account
- minimal disruption to existing customers (both internal and external).

Balancing territories is hard, especially if you're building from scratch. Here are some specific tips to help with your territory planning exercise:

1 Assign a specific analyst to own territory planning and run it as its own project.

2 Decide upon your account data's source of truth knowing no source is perfect.

3 Clean your data as part of your annual process.

4 Make all firmographic and demographic traits quantifiable and create numeric scores for each account.

5 Validate your scores against your ideal customer profile and existing customers. This is where knowing what your company sells will pay off.

6 Involve trusted partners to verify samples of your scoring.

7 Balance your territories not just in sum total, but across multiple dimensions, such as across account grades, customer vs. prospect, prior interest, or other firmographic groupings of your accounts.

8 When looking at existing customers, consider the role and responsibilities of your customer-facing teams, the tenure of existing sellers, length of customer relationships, renewal date distribution, and cross-functional staffing alignment.

9   Show your work and involve managers in balancing territories. How you execute this will depend on the maturity of your managers and, in some cases, your territory planning technology. Prepare managers to be the first line of response when sellers have questions.

10 Clearly communicate (and document) the expectations of holdovers, account transitions, and when the changes will take place.

11 Be ready to adjust slightly upon launch, and have clear guidelines on what you change and why.

What Else Needs to Be Planned?

There are a few more specialty items that you will need to ensure you have planned adequately for the year, depending on your organization's maturity and specific business model. Compensation planning is the focus of the next chapter, and will involve other functions including finance, legal, human resources, company leadership, and potentially your board of directors' compensation committee. Services will need its own capacity modeling that will focus on resource utilization, outsourcing levers, and headcount plan. Customer success will need their books of business, keeping in mind counts of customers, complexity, renewal dates, consistency, and service levels. If you have a physical product, there is a whole slew of supply chain planning that is needed.

Communications Strategy and Plan: The Gift that Keeps Giving

We started out this chapter describing that the Fiscal Year Flip is a deliberate approach. One of the critical ingredients of this approach is having a communications strategy built into your entire planning process. When you answer the "big questions," you then need to reiterate those answers all through the planning process. When you have a territory planning session with managers, refer back to the investments the company is making that affect territories and the new products that will impact account scoring. When you review the sales capacity plan with leadership, outline the improved opportunity win rates expected as a result of sales methodology training investments. When you roll out your compensation plan (in the first week of the new year of course), highlight the parts of the plan that amplify your company's strategic goals. Communicate the "what" and the "why" throughout your process.

An additional communication strategy we have hinted at a few times in this chapter is cascaded communications. Starting early allows you to seek input from various levels of the organization and to articulate the strategies of the company. When the flip happens, ensure the first line and second line managers are ready to answer the "why" questions by including them in the process along the way. Hold preview meetings with managers right before the launch of the new year to ensure they had seen the presentation and had their questions answered first. This way, when a seller asks why an account was highly scored, why a policy changed, what's new with their compensation plan or how they can overachieve on their quota, the managers are armed with knowledgeable answers because they were part of the process and they can be your representatives when you're not there.

As a result, when it comes time to actually roll out the Fiscal Year Flip to the broader organization, every level of leadership is aligned on the key ingredients to a successful year. As you carefully craft your positioning for the new year, think about what you want your audience to take away:

- Am I set up for success this year?
- Do I understand the big bets that the company is making and the rationale behind them?
- Do I have a compensation plan that I can understand and achieve?

They don't care about the weeks you spent meticulously merging duplicate account records or auditing data enrichment vendors. They won't appreciate the five rounds you had to go with the CFO before you got that accelerator rate just a little higher than last year. Don't dwell on these things. As we've talked about in the previous chapters, your internal customers care about outcomes. So focus on those.

Lastly, you can't expect anyone to know this information as well as you do, nor can you expect audiences hearing all of this information for the first time to leave having digested everything they need to know. Any live sessions you schedule to present Fiscal Year Flip information should be complemented by follow-up meetings with individual teams, office hour Q&A sessions, and links to relevant supporting resources and documentation.

Are We Done Yet?

Planning is a verb for a reason—well technically, it is the present participle form. It is an ongoing process that Operators employ to build predictable businesses. It is also an exercise that should be viewed across a very long-time horizon. The more annual planning cycles you are part of at a single company, the better you will get at them. You're not going to have a world-class planning motion in your first year in a new organization.

And let us save you the suspense: Things will not go according to your spreadsheet. You will need to be nimble in the middle of the year when a seller leaves or the economy changes or you have a strategic shift in direction. When you have followed this type of comprehensive planning model though, you understand where your levers of growth are, where your opportunities and dependencies are, and how to effectively react when change inevitably comes.

Chapter Takeaways

1 **Execute a timely Fiscal Year Flip:** Avoid operational uncertainties by executing the Fiscal Year Flip promptly. Delays can hinder business execution and lead to challenges.

2 **Start the process early:** Initiate the planning process as early as Q3 to make informed decisions for the upcoming fiscal year. Early planning allows for in-depth discussions, identification of dependencies, and effective communication within the organization.

3 **Embrace cross-functional collaboration:** Collaboration among all relevant departments is essential, particularly when introducing something new, like entering a new market. Ensure that all aspects, including product support, market awareness, and financial or legal considerations, are thoroughly assessed to prevent potential issues.

4 **Triangulate for credibility:** Enhance the credibility of your planning by taking a comprehensive approach and considering multiple perspectives. Stress-testing assumptions can lead to more robust plans.

5 **Prioritize communication:** A well-thought-out communication strategy not only conveys information but also fosters alignment, understanding, and support within the organization throughout the year.

6 **Recognize planning as an ongoing process:** While comprehensive planning is crucial, organizations must remain adaptable, as circumstances can change. Regular monitoring and adjustments are necessary to maintain the plan's relevance and effectiveness.

Endnotes

1 *Operations* with Sean Lane (2022) How to Adjust Annual Planning During Economic Uncertainty, with Unqork's Heidi Thompson, Episode 93 [podcast]
2 T. Bertuzzi (2016) *The Sales Development Playbook: Build Repeatable Pipeline and Accelerate Growth with Inside Sales*, Moore-Lake, Boston

10

Why Variable Compensation Design is Key to Incentivizing the Right Behavior

Have any of these compensation nightmares ever happened to you?

- A sales rep closes the largest deal in the company's history and the comp plan doesn't have any governors in it, and so, the commission check exceeds the CEO's annual salary.

- A brand-new rep closes a large deal one month into their tenure (that their manager mostly closed before they even started), and given their ramping commission rate, they made three months' salary on a single deal.

- A special performance incentive fund (SPIF) gets released in a Slack message to the entire field without any terms and conditions or being cleared by finance that the funds are available.

- Plan participants don't know how their incentives are calculated.

- Rumors swirl about how SDRs make money on things that don't matter to the sales reps they support.

- Account managers believe the customer success managers are incentivized in ways that are in direct conflict with the account managers' plan.

- Your compensation analyst is struggling with calculating commissions because HR allowed mid-month variable compensation changes.

- It is three months into the new year and your participants still don't have plans to sign.

We hope you haven't come across these yourself, but even if you have, this chapter will help you set up your compensation plan design to avoid them.

Incentive compensation design is an exercise in optimization for two parties. The company wants to maximize the revenue impact of an incentive dollar. The individuals on the incentive plan want to maximize their incentive dollars for their work. All of your incentive design work needs to ensure alignment across multiple perspectives and, of course, to look around corners for accidental misalignments.

We recommend a pretty simple framework when it comes to the building blocks of a successful incentive plan:

1 Start with guiding principles.

2 Identify the desired behaviors you want to incentivize.

3 Specify the levers available.

4 Use game theory to look around the corners.

Start with Guiding Principles

In Chapter 9, we discussed the need to include a number of different stakeholders in your compensation planning team. Depending on your company, it may include representatives from Operations, finance, human resources, legal, and leadership from functions on variable incentive plans. It's no surprise we believe that Revenue Operations is ideally suited to lead this process. We like to begin this process with a brainstorm of the guiding principles for the year from all of these interested parties. It should include a clear look at what is not working in the current plans and which goals for next year should be addressed in the compensation plan designs.

Think of guiding principles as how you want to represent your compensation plan to everyone in the company. First, you want principles that will guide your design team in their choices. When you find yourself deep in the weeds on a nuanced commission decision, these are principles you'll lean on to provide guidance and perspective for your decision. Some examples of what some of those principles might be are:

- **Simplicity**: The plan is easy to understand.

- **Transparency**: Everyone knows where they're at against their goals at all times. There are no secrets on what each group's goals are.

- **Ability to impact**: Participants have the ability to impact what they're compensated on and believe they can achieve.

Benchmarks can also be a helpful input in the guiding principles process. An example benchmark in B2B software is the quota to on target earnings (OTE) ratio. Industry best practice would put this at 4x to 5x. If you are earlier in your company's maturity, it may be closer to 3x. A counter metric to balance your quota: OTE ratio is attainment—aim for 75 percent of your reps hitting 75 percent or more of their quota and 50 percent of your reps hitting or exceeding 100 percent of their quota. Use your annual planning sales math, your reps' historical achievement, quota to OTE ratios, and any other benchmarks for your industry to support your quota-setting process (there is much more about setting quotas in Chapter 9). And of course, if you do decide to change quotas, include the reasons why in your compensation rollout.

Identify the Desired Behaviors You Want to Incentivize

Before you start deciding what details to put in your plan or even considering any numbers that might make up the plan, spend time with your stakeholders deciding which behaviors you want to incentivize with your compensation plans. These should be directly tied to the company's objectives for the year. For the behaviors your team decides it wants to incentivize, answer the why: What does it bring to the company? What does it require the individual to do differently? Is it the most important behavior to drive?

For example, if you are looking to increase the length of your contracts in order to increase predictability of your revenue and reduce opportunities for churn, you may want to create additional incentives for longer-term contracts. You will also need to align your contract language, update your discounting policy, and educate your customer-facing teams on how to sell and service longer term lengths. Behaviors can be incentivized through compensation plans and are best supported if your operational processes also support the desired behaviors.

Several other examples you may want to incentivize:

- Overachievement for top performing sales reps
- Increased retention and customer health for customer success
- Reduction of discounting
- New logo acquisition
- Expansion for account managers
- Selling newly developed products/services
- Opportunities that result in closed business from SDR-generated meetings.

Being explicit about **what** you want to see from your incentive programs and why you want that behavior will help you determine **how** you will realize those outcomes through your design. It's easy to make a list of 12 different behaviors you want to incentivize. What's critical is to narrow that list down to the most important two to three priorities. This way, you're living up to the "simplicity" guiding principle (we hope you picked that one), and it makes the plan more digestible when the time comes to deliver it to the team. Each behavior should directly align with a key strategic bet from a company-wide initiative or from your annual plan.

Another important distinction when you're evaluating what goes on this list is which behaviors are best managed through the comp plan and which behaviors are best managed by managers. Comp plans cannot, and should not, be used to drive every single behavior you need for a company to be successful. For example, if you're trying to incentivize pipeline creation, but you're worried that a SPIF or comp plan component around pipeline creation might lead to a bunch of "false" pipeline to satisfy that part of the comp plan, that's where the managers should be stepping in and holding teams accountable. Even in a sales environment where typically 50 percent of an individual's OTE is subject to a variable compensation plan, there should be other foundational expectations included in the base salary that makes up the other 50 percent.

You might not always have a perfect timeline during which you can bring all interested parties together to align on these behaviors. One year, we undertook a significant overhaul of the existing plans, but we didn't have a lot of capacity to meet live to regularly discuss these proposed changes with our finance partners. We created an asynchronous planning process using a shared document. We started with guiding principles, written from each function's perspective, then moved onto the behaviors. Operations conducted interviews with functional leaders and provided summaries of the findings. The shared document then went into the next level of detail outlining the components of each role's plans (sales rep, SDR, CSM, etc.). We created a column for Operations to capture what they thought should be changed, a column to show what finance thought should be changed, and a final column on the negotiated outcome. The transparency of the negotiation process in this documentation helped bring all of the stakeholders to a shared understanding of the results, even without everyone being able to talk through them live. This document also served as a great resource for comparing the prior year and current year plans side-by-side to show exactly what was changed.

Specify the Levers Available

This is where the rubber hits the road for compensation: How you translate ideas into execution. Levers are the mechanisms through which you can incentivize the behaviors from the previous step. We will look at a sample of levers available here, but your company may have others available to them based on what you sell and how you sell it.

Percentage of Variable Compensation to Total Compensation (Pay Ratio)

Your first lever is an important one. It is how much of a participant's compensation is "at risk." Some roles have a standard for an industry; others will require you to think through the role and how much control they have over their outcomes. Direct sales reps often have a 50/50 split of their base salary and variable compensation. Customer success roles have closer to 80/20 or 70/30 splits, similar to technical sales. SDRs usually start in this range as well, and when they "graduate" into direct sales roles, the promotion increases are directed disproportionately to their variable.

Components: What Numbers To Pay On

Determine what the measurements are, how many of them for each of your plans, and what the weightings will be. It can be as simple as a single quota for closed business. It can also get a lot more complex. This is where you can lean on your guiding principles. For example, if one of your principles is simplicity, then you should have a limited number of components (two or maybe three) and all of them should be easy to understand and calculate. Regardless of whether simplicity is one of your principles, never have a component that is worth less than 10 percent of a participant's variable (this is particularly relevant in customer success or services roles where they have a lower percentage of their OTE tied to variable). It will not change behavior. To make this real, calculate the average potential annual value of each component you design for a reality check: Whether people will do the activity you are incentivizing for that amount of money.

Designing your plan's components means taking into consideration every role that has a variable structure, especially where you may have inherent conflicts or opportunities for complementary objectives, such as customer success and account management. So you should attempt to cross connect their plans, to ensure you are balancing your plan components and desired behaviors.

As a part of components, you will have to determine whether a goal is "shared" as a team target or tied to individual performance.

For example, you may have difficulty identifying or measuring an individual's contribution to closing a deal if they are part of a shared service or multiple participants are required to execute a transaction. In the software world, the role of a solution consultant is often difficult to assign or measure on individual goals, and so, they usually have "team" goals tied to the shared service territory or product line they support. The use of shared goals is common in variable compensation for specific roles, but it is also usually accompanied by lower variable ratios.

This may sound obvious, but all of your measurements need to be reliably available on the payout frequency. For example, you may not be able to accurately measure retention on a monthly basis; so, your retention component should be paid quarterly. If you want to provide something to participants on a monthly basis, you can pay a partial advance on a monthly basis, then true up at the end of the quarter.

The other important point is that you must provide a target of what you expect that can be backed up with data. Reduce the administrative burden, manual exceptions, or one-off calculations in this data. Customer health scores, for example, are excellent component measures to use for a customer success organization, but you will need to have some history for your scores with appropriate targets to have enough confidence to put a participant's compensation at risk.

Commission Rates, Accelerators, Decelerators, Caps and Gates

Once you know the components, the targets, and the weighting of those components, you have what you need to calculate commission rates. The commission rate is commonly referred to as the base commission rate (BCR), which is calculated as variable target divided by the quota target (for example, if you have a $100k variable and $1m quota, your BCR is 10 percent).

One word of caution: Sometimes participants can get attached to a specific commission rate, which will change if their quota or variable target changes. Laura once had to have a number of conversations with an SDR manager who was upset after their commission rate per opportunity dropped after they received a raise. If you do show the commission rate on their incentive plan statements, show the calculation for how it is derived.

Accelerators are an exciting lever available to you! Not every company uses them, but if you do use them, they are compelling for compensation plan participants. Where to set your accelerators is a tough call. Your industry and your company's stage (not to mention your finance department) will likely play a part in how high your accelerator is going to be, how many tiers you include, whether you offer them quarterly or annually, and which plans should include accelerators. It is fairly standard to express it as a percentage of the BCR For example, for quota attainment from 100 percent to 125 percent, the accelerator could be 125 percent of the BCR; above 125 percent attainment, the accelerator could be 150 percent of the BCR Be explicit in your documentation about how this is calculated so that it cannot be misunderstood (for example, since most accelerated rates only apply to specific attainment tiers, show examples to your plan participants like we have below).

EXAMPLE ACCELERATOR CALCULATION

If quota is 200,000 and attainment is 280,000 (140%)

Variable Compensation =
BCR * 200,000 (Quota Up To 100%) +
125% * BCR * 50,000 (Quota Attainment between 100% and 125%) +
150% * BCR * 30,000 (Quota Attainment over 125%)

Accelerators can be used to encourage the behaviors you are looking for and reward top performers, but also might be leveraged to counter any foreseeable pricing scenarios. For example, let's say a company wants to sell more three-year deals instead of one-year deals, but they also offer a pricing discount for longer term commitments. You don't want reps worried about getting paid less money on those longer-term deals; so, you can design an accelerator on three-year deals to exceed the commission a rep would receive if they sold a one year deal at the higher price point.

Not all plans need to have accelerators, nor do accelerators need to be the same in each plan across a company. The less control that a participant has over the outcome of their measure, the lower the accelerators should be. For example, participants with a shared team goal should have lower accelerator rates because they are less directly involved in overall achievement. Historical performance data should guide accelerator rates and help model potential financial commitments. You don't want to find yourself in a difficult conversation with Finance about headcount because unbudgeted accelerator payments got out of control.

Decelerators, on the other hand, are when you reduce the BCR These can be helpful if you don't want to reward lower than expected performance. We have seen decelerators used for customer retention components where a decelerated rate is used if the retention is below the minimum acceptable level. The decelerator would be 50 or 75 percent of the BCR if the retention results fall below the minimum target. Decelerators are definitely not exciting, but they are better than caps.

Caps can limit anything in a variable plan from total compensation down to an individual deal payout. Caps should be approached with caution. Even the concept of a cap can be demotivating for a sales force, even if no one has ever actually hit the cap. If your company has a wide range in potential deal sizes, lower quotas, and not a lot of history to understand what overachievement could be possible, an alternative to a cap is putting clauses in your compensation plan to review bluebirds (unexpected, excessively profitable deals). Executive review of deals over a certain size may also make sense.

Gates or cliffs are something that must be true before a component will pay out. An example in a corporate level plan might be that a minimum operating margin must be met before individual executive objectives are paid out. This might make sense in a situation where a minimum level of profitability is desired to be able to afford paying on individual goals. Another example is when you have a gate of a

minimum level of customer retention before paying out a component. Gates can be useful in specific situations, but they should be
used with care and transparency, and set at reasonable levels.
Participants can view gates with mistrust and as a signal that the
company wants to manipulate the plan to avoid paying out.

REAL WORLD ROLE MODELS

Meghan Gill is the SVP Sales Operations and Sales Development at MongoDB. On
Episode 66 of the *Operations* podcast, Meghan discusses how compensation
incentives need to be designed to align desired behaviors with natural
inclinations to pursue the path of least resistance:

> We give the sales leaders the opportunity to flag accounts that they think
> have potential, that they think have what we call "smoke" as in, "where
> there's smoke, there's fire." They tag those accounts as smoky and they're
> actually contributing to the data that we're using to decide how to build
> territories.

> Ideally, sales territories have a blend of some existing customers that you can
> have some opportunity to upsell, some smoky accounts, and some greenfield
> accounts. The other thing that I think about is the incentives because if I'm a
> rep, it's always easier for me to go and expand or milk my existing accounts
> or go after the lower-hanging fruit. Salespeople are like water, right? They
> flow to the path of least resistance, which is the right thing to do.

> But if we really want to try to expand market share, you have to make sure
> we have the right incentives in place. So, in addition to finding them the right
> accounts, we also have incentives around new logos, whether it's bonuses,
> SPIFs, gates to accelerate, or things like that, to make sure that we're not
> neglecting the accounts that could have potential, but don't necessarily have
> signals at this exact moment.[1]

New Hire Compensation

Several of our nightmare scenario examples at the front of this chapter had to do with new hire or ramping rep compensation. This is an
area that can trip up the most experienced compensation designers.
The factors that you will need to consider as you design your ramping

rep plans are: 1) How long your reps take to attain productivity, 2) the length of your sales cycle, and 3) the amount of time it takes a new rep to learn their role.

Draws are a tool you might consider for new reps. Draws are when you pay a rep their variable pay before they have achieved attainment against their quota. Draws come in two flavors: Recoverable (similar to an advance, paid back to the company out of commission from the rep's future attainment) and non-recoverable (guaranteed amount regardless of performance). You will want to have your legal and HR departments assist with the contracts to outline what is expected and what can be recovered from plan participants. Some organizations use management by objectives (MBOs) for ramping periods where managers assess the ramping rep's attainment of either quantitative or qualitative measures.

Ramping BCRs can be very tricky and we recommend modeling out what is appropriate using historical data. Because you have lower expected quotas during the ramping period, the ramping BCR is much higher than the fully ramped BCR This can cause excessive payments for larger early deals. You can protect against this by writing your plan to switch to the fully ramped BCR after exceeding the ramping quota. This isn't a "cap" but it does protect against excessive payouts.

The longer the sales cycle of your product, the longer ramp time you likely need to accommodate. For example, for enterprise sellers where bookings might not come for nearly a year (or more), craft ramp plans to include leading indicators of future success. Rather than having 100 percent of their variable compensation tied to bookings or some kind of draw, assign targets for new customer meetings and pipeline creation. These targets not only incentivize behavior that lead to the individual's future success, it also cements for the individual what "good" looks like higher in the funnel prior to the ultimate outcome: Bookings.

In a customer success or account management scenario, you also need to consider the state of the book of business you're handing someone on Day 1. If there are customer renewals soon after the person is starting in their role, some of which are likely already known customer churn, you need to account for those scenarios in your ramp plans.

Sales Performance Incentive Funds (SPIFs)

Short-term SPIFs can be a fun lever to pull to create excitement and drive specific behavior. If you have outlined what behavior you want to incentivize and your current compensation plans don't emphasize it enough, you can use SPIFs to be explicit about what you want to achieve as an organization. SPIFs should run for a specific period of time and need to have Terms and Conditions outlined as they are released. Typically you will have a budgeted amount for SPIFs with Finance; so, an estimate on the financial exposure of a SPIF needs to be done before it is released. SPIFs should be tracked and celebrated publicly so that you achieve the excitement and encouragement of the behaviors you want.

Use Game Theory to Look Around the Corners

In the early 1900s, the city of Delhi was infested with cobras. To enlist help in eradicating the snakes, officials offered a bounty on cobra skins. Enterprising individuals started raising cobras to make an income. The bounty just encouraged more cobras and cost the government a lot of money. This became known as the "cobra effect"—unintended perverse consequences to incentives. This is exactly what we want to avoid when we set up incentive plans.

When you evaluate your compensation plans, you must look around corners to consider what might go wrong or what participants might do to maximize their commissions. You may not have to worry about cobra farms, but you may be incentivizing the wrong behaviors.

CONFESSION CORNER

The company I joined was trying to move up-market, selling to more enterprise companies with higher price points. They had a history of "land and expand," selling into a small division and then working across divisions to increase their footprint. They were looking to change their selling motion to selling larger initial deals. They had hired enterprise sellers and experienced enterprise managers, and had even launched new differentiated pricing packages to target the enterprise market's needs.

This sales team loved SPIFs (sales performance incentive funds). In fact, one executive used to call it "SPIF nation." SPIFs are a fantastic tool in any sales organization to create excitement, drive new behavior, and be explicit about the company's goals, all without having to commit to permanently changing the annual incentive plan.

The problem was they had a SPIF that rewarded logo captures—$X for Y number of new logos in a quarter. That SPIF was in direct conflict with the strategic direction of selling larger initial deals. It undermined everything that the management team was saying to the sellers.

The one truth about incentives is you will get what you pay for—and the company paid for lots of smaller deals. Smaller deals close faster and as a seller, you would get an extra incentive to close a high number of deals? It was a no brainer.

The problem was so easy to see in retrospect. But because that SPIF was a favorite and had become such a staple of the team, it was put forward without considering, "What could go wrong if our team actually did what we were incentivizing them to do?" Luckily, the SPIFs were only a quarter long so we could re-orient the next quarter.

We recommend brainstorming with your incentive design team on what could go wrong with your plan and to do as much analysis as you can on the proposed plans. Sometimes this is possible, sometimes it isn't possible with real data because you may be introducing new products. When evaluating the previous year plan's effectiveness, look at scatterplots of achievement versus payouts. Analyze the outliers to evaluate what in the plan caused the two to not be in alignment. Review new hire achievement and payouts as a separate analysis to ensure your new hire and ramping plans are meeting your objectives. You may also want to perform a specific analysis of regrettable and non-regrettable attrition to find any patterns.

We have mentioned legal as part of the incentive design team. This is a great time to have them review the terms and conditions for the incentive plans to help you look around any corners. In many of our companies, we required a signature on the terms and conditions paperwork before commission checks were issued. There should be a robust process in place to ensure that new hires understand their plans before they start. Oftentimes this is accomplished by managers, but sometimes the compensation team fills this need.

The last recommendation we have on looking around corners is how you educate your variable plan participants. In Chapter 9, we talked about the Fiscal Year Flip and the importance of communicating your company's objectives, initiatives, and the things to be excited about for the year. Hopefully, your compensation plan is one of the items for your teams to be excited about. If you do have significant changes to your compensation plans, make sure to communicate them as part of your rollout.

Treat any communication about comp plans as a launch with the appropriate amount of pomp and circumstance. Include in your launch communication at least a summary of the first three steps of our framework: Guiding principles, desired behaviors, and levers available. We also believe providing example calculations of how participants can exceed their plan can help drive the behaviors the company is looking for and generate excitement within the team. Keep the transparency going throughout the year with dynamic, ever-present leaderboards and celebrations when plan participants exceed their targets.

The responsibility of designing someone's variable compensation plan is a significant one. Any time your decisions can impact the livelihoods of your colleagues and their families, you need to treat that work with the seriousness it deserves. When done well, variable compensation planning can be a critical lever in driving needle-moving behavior and outcomes for your company.

Chapter Takeaways

1 **Establish clear guiding principles**: Define guiding principles that reflect the company's values and goals, such as simplicity,

transparency, and the ability for participants to impact their compensation. These principles should guide the design team and serve as benchmarks for evaluating plan success.

2 **Identify and align desired behaviors:** Clearly identify the behaviors the company wants to incentivize, aligning them with overall company objectives. For example, if aiming to increase contract length, design compensation plans that provide additional incentives for securing longer-term contracts, and ensure alignment with operational processes.

3 **Specify levers and components:** Determine the levers available for compensation design, such as the percentage of variable compensation, components, commission rates, accelerators, decelerators, caps, and gates. Ensure simplicity in measurements, align components across roles, and carefully consider the impact of levers on participant behavior.

4 **Address new hire compensation challenges:** Pay special attention to new hire and ramping rep compensation. Consider factors such as draws (recoverable or non-recoverable), ramping BCRs and MBOs to support the learning curve and productivity of new hires.

5 **Anticipate unintended consequences:** Use all of your design team to try to anticipate unintended consequences and perverse incentives. Evaluate the potential impact of compensation plans on participant behavior, ensuring they align with the company's strategic direction. Regularly review and analyze plan effectiveness, considering scatterplots of achievement versus payouts, and involve legal in reviewing terms and conditions in order to mitigate risks.

Endnote

1 *Operations* with Sean Lane (2021) Building MongoDB's Complex Go-To-Market Motion, with Meghan Gill, Episode 66 [podcast]

11

Goal Setting in RevOps

Does the phrase "it's time to set our goals" make you break out in hives?

We hope not. We hope it gets you excited and gives you a little pep in your step to start your day, month, and quarter. If it doesn't yet, we hope this chapter will help you get there.

We aren't going to debate the pros and cons of the various goal setting methodologies out there. Whether you use Objectives and Key Results (OKR), Vision, Value, Methods, Obstacles, and Measures (V2MOM), Big Hairy Audacious Goal (BHAG), or the oldie but goodie Specific, Measurable, Achievable, Relevant, and Time-Bound (SMART) methodology, it doesn't really matter. Your organization will likely have a preferred methodology and you can follow along. The real magic is in the actual act of setting, communicating, and executing goals.

Revenue Operations needs to be a leader in goal setting at any organization. Sometimes that means you may run the company's goal-setting process; in other cases, you may just be an excellent example of how to set your departmental goals. We recommend the following process for goal setting:

1 Connect to the company's goals.

2 Check your cross-functional dependencies.

3 Outline your big rocks and involve your team.

4 Make it measurable.

5 Communicate.

6 Monitor.

7 Score and repeat.

Connect to the Company's Goals

In a more formal goal methodology, this step may be as simple as receiving the cascaded goals from your company's executive team. In the absence of that, the annual planning process is a great source of what needs to happen to achieve the company's goals and how the Operations department can support them.

If your company has a quarterly goal-setting process, then align your team to the company's goal-setting cadence. If it doesn't, you have a choice to make on how frequently you go through this process. We believe quarterly is likely the right frequency for most organizations. Twice a year is fairly common for more mature organizations, but we recommend at least a quarterly check-in on whether the goals still make sense or whether adjustments need to take place to better support the business. Annual goals can provide the outline of what needs to be accomplished each quarter, but are often too large, vague, or lofty to provide the guidance and drive needed to execute expeditiously.

It can be tempting to think of goal setting as wasted time—time spent away from just getting the work done. This couldn't be further from the truth. Just getting the work done can mean getting the wrong work done. The old saying of "measure twice, cut once" can be applied to setting goals. When you set goals that will be measured, you identify what needs doing. Then you can cut once and execute the right work once, instead of duplicating efforts or throwing away work because it wasn't conducive to moving the organization forward.

Laura and Sean have had a number of good hearty discussions on what should go in the RevOps goals versus what should go in the marketing, sales, customer success, or services' goals (and so should you with your Operations teammates!). The key is to keep a group's goals within its own primary sphere of influence and control. What can you commit to and take ownership over to drive to completion? For example, if a key assumption in the annual plan is to increase the productivity per rep (PPR), the RevOps goal associated with that should be related to operational efficiency, funnel conversion improvements, or enhancements to rep training and onboarding. Sales should take the primary PPR measurement goal with its supporting objectives. The most important thing is that your goals connect to the key "big bets" of the annual plan.

Check Your Cross-Functional Dependencies

Early on in your goal-setting process, identify any cross-functional dependencies and set your goals together with the teams you'll rely on to complete your objectives. In the example of increasing PPR, perhaps multiple teams will need to be involved: RevOps, training/enablement, sales, and perhaps even recruiting.

There are a number of ways that range from informal to methodical to cross-functionally connect your goals. You can leverage the operating rhythms discussed in Chapter 4 or set specific time to discuss goals. Some organizations might have a robust goal-setting process through which to identify dependencies. No matter the method, though, Revenue Operations should lead the way for what "good" looks like in goal setting. Think of your team as a center of excellence that other functions can look to for both setting goals and identifying any dependencies. What you'll find over time is that your organization will become more skilled at identifying and collaborating on these dependencies, and more importantly, you'll get more done.

REAL WORLD ROLE MODELS

Karen Borchert is founder and CEO of Alpaca and the former COO at Flywheel. On Episode 19 of the *Operations* podcast, Karen discussed what she learned about goal setting with cross-functional partners:

> One of our big areas of learning the first year or so of goal setting was around the idea of dependencies and interdepartmental dependencies.

> We would have people who would set extraordinary goals, but they were completely dependent on product launching a certain thing by a certain day or sales selling a certain amount. And then when those dependencies didn't happen, it was really frustrating and disappointing to the people who would set these goals that have those dependencies.

But rather than saying, "Okay, nobody set any goals with any dependencies," which basically gives everybody permission to operate in a silo, we said, "For each of these goals that are at the company level, we're going to assign an owner."

That owner might not be the person who runs that department or who leads that effort overall. It might be; but sometimes it's going to be somebody who is really passionate and excited about it, and who works on it in some way, but isn't necessarily the owner of that department.

It gives permission to each company owner to really bring those dependencies together and to say, "Okay, if we're going to move the needle on this goal, I'm going to need marketing to do this, sales to do this, product to do this and finance to do this." It gives that owner permission to enlist that cross departmental work. It gives a framework for those dependencies rather than trying to make goals a dependency-free environment.[1]

Even if your company doesn't have company-level goal owners, Operations can help identify dependencies and tie together what it will take to accomplish something important.

Outline Your Big Rocks and Involve Your Team

We believe it is important for you, the RevOps leaders, to set the stage for the rest of your team and outline the broad themes of your goals, but not to outline all the details. Your job is to translate the **"what"** RevOps needs to do to support the company goals. Involve your team to detail the **"how."**

A technique that we've used to do this was at the start of the goal-setting process, we would outline the "big rocks" for RevOps in a shared presentation, tying those big rocks to the company objectives or the "why." Then we would send the draft around to our team for them to assign owners, revise the goals if needed, suggest additional ones, and add in measurable outcomes and interim steps. As part of this process, we allowed everyone including leadership to put in comments to ask questions, clarify, or suggest edits. Then, we would review the overall document together to discuss team capacity, identify where dependencies existed, assign ownership, and ensure that everyone on the team understood all of the goals.

Allowing your team to have input into the goal-setting process fosters ownership, exposes more detail on what it will take to accomplish something, and ultimately, transforms department goals into "our shared goals."

When you're drafting your goals, it's important to also look inward within Operations for initiatives that will improve both the team and the company as a whole. Every organization has technical or operational debt: The workflow that's been broken for a while and just needs concentrated time to fix, the automation of drudgery tasks, or overhauling that nightmare report. Not everything that Operations does can be splashy or obvious like the launch of a new tool. How do you balance the noticeable outcomes with the "under the hood" maintenance?

If you have a lot of debt, we recommend attacking that debt with a dedicated project and measurable goals that result in benefits to the organization. Perhaps you need a CRM relaunch or a tune-up. This type of work will certainly affect all of your stakeholders, so market that project with "what's in it for me" (WIIFM) statements and tangible outcomes. One "under the hood" project of Laura's reduced the clicks for processing leads from 25 to 10. There was no new functionality, just streamlining the existing tools to match the workflow of the users. The key was to describe the outcome of the project as a benefit to the organization. Even automation projects that reduce your Operations team's workload can provide benefits to the larger organization (maybe now you can take on that new project you didn't think you had the bandwidth to complete!). Quantifying these types of projects will help you assess whether it is worth the investment.

Make It Measurable

We can't emphasize enough the importance of measurable outcomes. In Chapter 7, we discussed the use of KPIs in making successful internal changes. All of your goals should be measurable with explicit targets. If you are tackling something that doesn't have a current measurement, your first goal can be to create a baseline against which to measure future progress.

When you're drafting your goals, picture yourself at the end of the quarter. If you can't tell whether you hit your goal or not in less than 30 seconds, you didn't do a good job of crafting your goal. It is tempting to have goals written in ways that are binary—it was done or it wasn't. Push yourself to find ways to measure the desired impact of a goal beyond merely accomplishing a task. For example, the first draft of a goal could be to launch a new tool. A better goal is to have a target adoption percentage or a specific reduction in the amount of time a task takes that the tool is being implemented to improve.

It can also be difficult to break down complex, intricate projects that span across multiple quarters. Don't set yourself up for failure by saying, "We need a new ideal customer profile by the end of the year." Instead, break that goal down into its most bite-sized chunks and create measurable checkpoints along the way. See Table 11.1, which does just that.

TABLE 11.1 ICP goal example

Category	Objective Description	Measurement
"Big Rock" Theme	Increase Win Rate to 45% by Next Fiscal Year	Win Rate% measured quarterly moves from 40% to 45%
Operations Annual Goal	Implementation of New Ideal Customer Profile by end of year	Territories scored and within 10% variation of scoring; ICP score is 80% predictive of win; new customers have 90% fit of new ICP definition
Q1 Ops. Goal	Predictive analytic models of existing customers; identification of new sources of data (if needed, Q2 goal to implement)	Existing customers fit 80+% of draft models; new sources of data evaluated and scored on Vendor Evaluation Template
Q2 Ops. Goal	Creation of multiple predictive scoring models (at least two options); pilot group testing of accounts by internal stakeholders	Predictive Scoring Models show 80+% fit; pilot Sales Group provides feedback on 20 accounts by each data point
Q3 Ops. Goal	Apply scoring model to Y.T.D. wins and evaluate accuracy; finalize scoring model and socialize with all internal stakeholders; obtain management buy in on new model	Y.T.D. wins show 90+% fit to models; formal sign off by marketing, product, sales, and customer success

(continued)

TABLE 11.1 (Continued)

Category	Objective Description	Measurement
Q4 Ops. Goal	New predictive scoring model applied to territory planning for next year; training material prepared for Q1 kickoff	Pilot Sales Group shows 10% higher win rate than control group; next year territories scored and within 10% variation of scoring; ICP score is 80% predictive of win; training material completed and signed off by internal stakeholders

We in Operations are in the business of outcomes; our goals should reflect that.

Communicate

Identifying how goals connect throughout the organization and highlighting dependencies are just the start of goal communication. Look for multiple opportunities to communicate your goals among your stakeholders, teams, and cross-functional partners. Utilize the operating rhythms from Chapter 4 to communicate your goals, and if you don't have those rhythms yet, this can be a great time to initiate them.

If your organization has company-wide initiatives, the communication process should include how your team's goals are tied into the top-level goals. Employees are more engaged when they understand how their day-to-day work connects with the broader organization. Even if you don't have top-level formal goals, you can communicate the "why" behind your goals and how they contribute to achieving the company's desired results.

Communication also helps with something that is guaranteed to happen: A new goal crops up outside of the goal-setting process. Life and business keep happening and priorities can shift in between planning cycles. Documenting and communicating goals allows you to have trade-off discussions if needed when a new goal crops up. Check out Chapter 23 for additional tips and techniques on managing expectations and priorities.

Monitor

Ever set a goal at the beginning of a quarter and completely forget about it until the quarter is over and it's time to measure your results? You wouldn't be alone. So, how do you avoid this? You make your goals visible and monitor them along the way.

Build monitoring goals into your routines. You should host a team-wide monthly check-in to review goal progress. Rate each goal monthly with red, yellow, or green color-coding to communicate the current likelihood of accomplishing the goal by the end of the quarter, offer a status update on progress, and raise any blockers or risk areas where the team needed help. These monthly checkpoints should also serve as an honest assessment of new work that has come up, and if any reprioritization or re-allocation of team resources is required.

Operations can be a very demanding function with daily firefighting. Find your own ways to keep your eye on what's important, but not urgent. In Laura's case, she has a whiteboard that serves as a constant reminder of her quarterly goals. At the end of each week on Friday afternoons, she reviews her whiteboard and writes down the four to five things that need to be done the following week to stay on track for the quarterly goals.

One of our companies used the application 15Five (a performance management platform) for weekly check-ins where each employee identified what they had done that week and what their goals were for the following week. This can be a great way to ensure your team is balancing day-to-day responsibilities with the high-impact work towards the goals, and a helpful medium through which team members can give each other feedback. Whatever method you use, visibility of your goals and progress towards those outcomes are critical components of driving a high-performing and engaged organization.

Score and Repeat

Because you have done a great job in creating measurable outcomes, the scoring should be pretty easy. Score your goals as soon as you can after the due date and review the results as a team. Transparency and accountability create trust. Each company will have their own culture of where to set targets and what are acceptable levels of accomplishment. Some methodologies stress stretch goals BHAG, some stress achievability (SMART).

Scoring is the start of your next cycle of goal setting, and the entire beautiful cycle begins anew. Look back at your learnings from the previous quarter or goals that might not have made the list previously to help get you started.

When you set your goals well, and you find the right method for holding yourself and your teammates accountable to those goals, the impact that the Revenue Operations function will have on your company will be undeniable. Seek out opportunities to drive needle-moving change and ruthlessly prioritize those opportunities above all else.

Chapter Takeaways

1 **Motivate through goal setting:** Set clear and meaningful goals to motivate individuals and teams. Revenue Operations should take a leadership role in the goal-setting process.

2 **Focus on effective execution, not methodology:** The specific goal-setting methodology matters less than the actual process of setting, communicating, and executing goals effectively. Choose a method that suits your organization but focus on execution.

3 **Collaborate across functions and within your team:** Identify cross-functional dependencies early and collaborate with multiple teams to ensure alignment and successful goal achievement. Involve your team in determining the detailed "how" of achieving the goals, fostering ownership, and turning department goals into shared goals.

4 **Measure and communicate goals:** Goals should be measurable with explicit targets, moving beyond binary success criteria and focusing on the impact of goals on the organization. Effective

communication of goals within teams and across the organization is essential to ensure everyone understands how their work contributes to the larger objectives.

5 **Monitor, score, and continuously improve:** Regularly monitor goal progress as a part of your regular routines. The scoring process marks the beginning of the next cycle of goal setting.

Endnote

1 *Operations* with Sean Lane (2019) Imperfection is Commitment's Secret Weapon, with Karen Borchert, Episode 19 [podcast]

12

Data, Data, and More Data: The Evolution from Reporting to Insight to Prediction

"We are moving to a place where, if you want to be successful as a company, everyone, literally, in my opinion, everyone, has to have some level of comfort with using data. They don't have to be an analyst, but they really have to understand how to use it to inform their work. I think that that will be the deciding factor of what company comes out on top in different industries."[1]

Take it from Bridget Zingale, former Global Director of Analytics at Hubspot. She's seen this truth first-hand. If everyone has to use data to inform their work, the Revenue Operator's responsibility to be the single source of truth for all go-to-market data carries some serious repercussions. But we must go beyond just data. We have to strive for predictable and scalable systems that generate insights.

We think of this journey in four milestones, each building upon the previous one:

- Data
- Reporting
- Insight
- Prediction.

We had a quarterly practice of evaluating where we as a collective team stood on this spectrum. We would discuss as a team what progress we had made and what specific projects were pushing us in

FIGURE 12.1 Data to prediction continuum

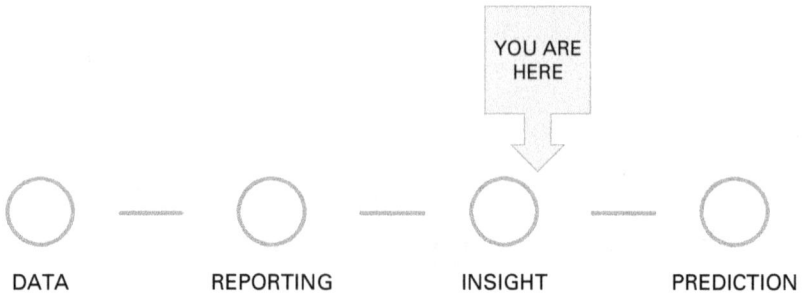

either direction. It gave us a signpost against which to measure our progress and keep our eyes on always advancing to the next milestone.

Data is the Foundation

Data is the starting point of Figure 12.1. It is the foundation of everything. So it's common to want to jump into action when faced with data issues: Start a de-duplication project, clean the data, fix the problem. But the Revenue Operations Mindset tells us to focus on outcomes, and to be strategic and tactical.

Kyle Morris, former Gigya Operations Director and founder of SifData and Kicksaw, has an excellent analogy to help us here:

> Consider your CRM as a polluted lake. Most people's solution is often the obvious one: Filter all the water to clean out the contamination. But that solution won't do you any good if there's a stream dumping polluted water into the lake. You can filter the water all you want, but you'll never make any progress. The right thing to do to clean a messy CRM is to first stop the influx of bad data. Before you clean anything, you have to get at the source of the problem.[2]

Once you stop the sources of your data pollution, the most meaningful next step to improve the quality of your data is to expose it. Data gets better when it is visible. Laura once joined an organization where they ran their forecast meetings from spreadsheets. The night before the meeting, the Operations team would run the reports from the CRM and send reports to each manager. The manager then edited the opportunities they wished to present in the meeting and provided their forecast call back to Operations in time for the meeting. How many times do you think there was confusion on what the correct numbers were? Or questions on where that opportunity from last week's meeting went? Or whether the right version of the spreadsheet was even being displayed? There was no source of truth. The first few meetings where the CRM was used as the single source of truth for opportunities were painful—really painful—but trust in the system started to rise with each meeting and the data got better.

Our top recommendations to improve your data:

1 Fix the sources/causes of bad data.

2 De-duplicate proactively where possible, retroactively where necessary.

3 Automate data collection where it makes sense.

4 Pick a source of truth for enriching your data (knowing nothing is perfect).

5 Don't mask the quality of the data: Provide visibility to improve it.

The Importance of Reporting (and Doing More Than Just Reporting)

Reporting usually tops the list of responsibilities for Revenue Operations teams. This book advocates to expand your role beyond just reporting, but make no mistake, this responsibility is one of the most critical ones you have. Your team must be reporting experts, and, more importantly, they need to be the teachers (and champions) of data literacy within your organization. The old adage of "Provide a fish, you feed someone for a day. Teach someone to fish, you feed them for a lifetime" applies to reporting more than any other area for Operations.

Territorial Operators will try to hold onto the "power" that comes with access to data, and put themselves between that data and their internal stakeholders. This is a mistake. Instrument your business with reporting, and widely share that reporting (and documentation) within your organization. Teach your internal customers where to go. Create reports with the filters and segmentation that your audiences need to understand their business. If you don't, they'll create their own, and it will create multiple sources of the truth, causing even more problems for you down the road.

We recommend creating a "reporting essentials" folder in your CRM that provides the foundational reports for everyone in the organization to use. Teach every new hire where to go to find these reports and what they mean. This way, everyone starts their own reporting work from a validated source of truth (e.g. reports for meetings held, activity, pipeline, bookings, and customers). Then, when you're asked for a report, you can point your colleagues to a report in this folder, saving you both time and reinforcing the right behavior for the next time around.

Now, this is obviously only true for the simplest reporting needs. We also recommend instrumenting DITL reporting folders and dashboards for each of the various roles of individual contributors and managers in the go-to-market organization. The needs of one level of seniority are different from those above and below them in your org chart. These DITL dashboards (which we covered in Chapter 6) and accompanying reports should be designed to provide end users with what they need to run their individual businesses. Reporting is your key to operationalize the company processes for your audiences.

REAL WORLD ROLE MODELS

Sylvia Kainz, former Vice President of Global Revenue Operations at Eventbrite, discussed how to make that journey from reporting to insights and beyond on Episode 9 of the *Operations* podcast:

> If you have good business ops. people, the RevOps team starts to become a really smooth engine, which is really the ultimate goal. But that's not the

whole story. There's my analytics team and these are the people who are coming in once the system is in place, once the processes are in place, and projects are rolled out. They actually look with a very critical eye at the performances of the different teams. They are the owners of saying, "Are we all aligned when we measure how successful we are with the business?" When you look at a large company such as Eventbrite, which is in many, many countries around the world, and has many sales and marketing teams in different geographies, you need to have a very standardized approach in managing them. The analytics team is strongly focused on creating that set of KPIs, and visibility allows everybody around the world to know how we perform.

Now, what's really critical is they can't do one-offs. And when I say one-offs, this is how most smaller companies still operate. They ask the analytics team, "Oh, can you run me a report so I know where I am because I have a board meeting," or "I need to report out to my CRO" And when you grow and you grow fast, you start understanding that it's not scalable because you need to throw a lot of resources at the analytics team.

The analytics team's key big project is not just keeping everybody informed, but doing it in a very smart, automated, and transparent way by making this available to everybody in your organization 24/7. And then there is availability of these resources or team members to do deep dives into really specific questions that the CRO or CFO or somebody else might have. And that's where they should spend their time because that's what they like doing and that's what they're really good at. You suddenly start understanding that you can use these very expensive resources to actually do some really interesting analytical deep dives.[3]

Insights: Understanding the Why of Your Reporting Findings

Reporting can tell you what happened, but if you just stay in the reporter mode of outlining the facts, you miss the power of insights to help you answer why and what next. Insights provide potential opportunities for the business. The transition to insights is a hard one.

Where do you start? If you have built your knowledge of your business from Part One of this book, then you can begin with your operating rhythms from Chapter 4. There will be specific rhythms that are natural to begin with such as the pipeline generation routine or QBRs. Turn the reporting into a narrative commentary as a start. Doing this will make you better at stating explicitly what the numbers are and the reasons why they changed.

Just showing up to these routines and "reporting the news" isn't enough, though. Spending time with your data, understanding how it has changed, and combining those quantitative findings with your business context is where you'll uncover your hypotheses. Review your insights as drafts with leaders of an area. Show your work. Remain curious, collaborate with your internal customers, and be open to other explanations you may not have seen in your initial view. Recognize that initial forays into insights can uncover trust issues with data (or processes). It can also reveal actual data quality issues that require you to initiate a clean-up effort. (If this is the case, don't hold onto your insight just because you spent time on it; you have to re-validate your data and try again.)

If this process sounds iterative and somewhat slow, it is! Proceed with intention and a longer-term view of where you want to be, but know that this journey is not a linear one (just like that of building a world-class RevOps team). The impact of Revenue Operations can be incredibly powerful when you begin to provide insights to your organization. It is an earned right, though, and requires a solid foundation of business knowledge, data, and reporting. Achieving insights usually needs specialization in your Operations team. Find the team members who want to understand why and what next.

Predictable Revenue Machines

In Chapter 8, we explored the forecasting process and how to start becoming a predictable business. The journey from data to prediction is more than just forecasting bookings, though. It is about finding the key ingredients that make your overall business work.

REAL WORLD ROLE MODELS

Kyle Poyar, Operating Partner at OpenView, describes how critical product event information is to predicting conversion to revenue:

> What's fascinating to me is that third party product analytics platforms are still actually not the most widely adopted. What you want to be able to do is

take all of the product event information that you're getting, and be able to send that through one of these platforms that allow you to get self-service access to the reports, insights, and dashboards that you need, and to be able to open up that access to all the teams that need the information for their decision making or their day-to-day workflow.

As a starting point, investing in those kinds of tools can make your life a lot easier, and everyone's life a lot easier. Next, the thing that I look for is an analysis-intensive project re-architecting the journey that folks have gone through in the past to say, "What activities did someone do in their first day, first week, first month, that were leading indicators that they were ultimately going to buy or renew?"

If you have any sort of free trial motion, you probably can start looking at this retrospective analysis, and then you're looking for essentially a product activation metric where someone did X in their first week, which means they're much, much more likely to buy. Then you also start identifying these product qualified lead indicators where they took these really high value actions that increased their conversion likelihood from 30 percent to 50 percent or 60 percent or 70 percent.

With activation, while it can be a really intense data project, it tends to be simple at the end of the day. Imagine a tool like SurveyMonkey. It's going to be someone who fills out their first survey and gets a minimum viable number of responses back from it. Not over complicating it, not looking to see if they set up a HubSpot integration yet or if they deployed with three or more team members. It's that bare bones moment of, they did the thing that the product told them that they should be trying to do, which means we can now start to have a deeper, more commercial conversation at this point.[4]

Revenue Operations teams that have reached the prediction milestone in the continuum can begin to provide their organizations with proactive signals of critical business drivers: Potential customer churn, high quality lead or account scoring, the deal ingredients that are more likely to result in a win, predictive upsell opportunities, and more. The technologies that support this part of the continuum are exploding by the minute. If you haven't reached the prediction stage just yet, each day presents an opportunity to get incrementally better. Ensure that your data foundations are solid, and evangelize the merits of data literacy and data-driven decision making to move your business forward.

Chapter Takeaways

1 **Start with a strong data foundation**: Address sources of bad data before cleaning. Use visibility to improve data quality.

2 **Reporting mastery**: While reporting is a crucial responsibility for Revenue Operations teams, it's essential to go beyond simply generating reports and become champions of data literacy within the organization. Share standardized reports widely to avoid multiple truths. Operationalize processes with public reporting folders for different roles.

3 **Transition from reporting to insights**: Understand that reporting can tell what happened, but insights provide the "why" and suggest potential opportunities for the business. Turn reporting into a narrative commentary to explicitly state the reasons behind changes in numbers. Collaborate, remain curious, and address trust and data quality issues.

4 **Build predictable revenue machines**: Prediction is not just about forecasting bookings but understanding the key ingredients that make the overall business work. Ensure solid foundations and a deep understanding of the business for teams providing predictions.

Endnotes

1 *Operations* with Sean Lane (2019) Building a More Data-Centric Company, with Hubspot's Bridget Zingale, Episode 30 [podcast]
2 *Operations* with Sean Lane (2019) Why Ops Pros Should Learn to Code, with SifData's Kyle Morris, Episode 8 [podcast]
3 *Operations* with Sean Lane (2019) How to Build a RevOps Team from Scratch, with Eventbrite's Sylvia Kainz, Episode 9 [podcast]
4 *Operations* with Sean Lane (2021) Under the Hood of Product-Led Growth, with Openview's Kyle Poyar, Episode 65 [podcast]

13

What Happens When Things Break: How to Look Around Corners and Plan for Your Own Mistakes

When you were a kid, when your parents asked you to go clean your room, were you one of those kids who just stuffed everything inside the closet and closed the door and then just marveled at how clean the room looked? It's okay if you were… no judgment here!

But, as everybody knows, hiding a mess inside the closet doesn't make the mess go away. You open the door the next day and an avalanche of all your stuff comes sprawling out, right?

If you're in Revenue Operations at a growing company, you are scrambling to keep your metaphorical room clean every single day. And let's face it, some days it's cleaner than others. Sometimes it's spotless and other times you're scrambling just to keep the closet door from busting back open with everything that's inside it. And sometimes, you just plain forgot about that thing that you threw in the back of the closet six months ago.

As you scale an Operations team and an organization as a whole, you are constantly building new systems, introducing new workflows, launching new campaigns, adding more tools to your tech stack… the list of changes is endless. No matter how great of a planner you are, no matter how much testing you do in a sandbox, things are going to go wrong and things are going to break. We're not ashamed to say it's happened to us, and if it hasn't happened to you yet, it will.

Once you acknowledge that things are going to break, the next question is what can you do about it? How can you put systems in place so that when things do break, you're not caught off guard, or even worse, you don't notice at all?

What's the key to keeping your Ops. closet clean? As always, sunlight is the best disinfectant.

The Danger Dash

Product and engineering teams have long had a variety of tools available to them for proactive alerting when things break in their code or their products go down. Companies like DataDog, Dynatrace, and PagerDuty are all incredibly successful through solving this problem. They do two things: 1) Increase observability, and 2) decrease unwanted surprises.

In recent years, companies like Sonar, Metaplane, and LeanData have started to address similar pain points specifically for the Revenue Operations persona. If you have the budget to invest in software like this, amazing. But that's not always the case and, quite frankly, not always the right solution. Like any other problem that can be solved by technology, you need to have a thorough understanding of all of the ways things can go wrong before you can leverage technology to solve it.

In the past, we created something we affectionately referred to as the "danger dash." As you might expect from the name, it's a dashboard that, you guessed it, detects danger.

Here's how it works: Every single morning when we got to work, there was an email waiting for us with the danger dash inside of it. Put simply, it's a selection of individual reports compiled in a dashboard that monitors all the different places where a system, a lead capture process, a tool, a workflow, or any key technology-driven conversion point in the customer journey could break.

The most beautiful sight any Operator could see in the morning is an empty danger dash.

But that dashboard doesn't just show up magically empty, and it certainly isn't empty due to sheer luck. There are a few key steps to building your own danger dash in a thoughtful way that will give you and your colleagues the peace of mind that you're not blind to a business-threatening issue.

Anticipating Breaks

First, you need to identify your possible points of failure. The easiest way to do this is to follow your customer journey from beginning to end (see Figure 13.1). Look at all the different conversion points or hand-offs that you might have. Those could be hand-offs between humans or they could be between systems—don't assume either one is impervious to breaking.

A good example might be to look at how contact information is captured early in the customer journey. You need to ask yourself all of the following questions:

- How do leads get captured?
- Do you have a form on a landing page? Do you capture that information through a marketing automation tool like HubSpot or Marketo? Or, do you use a conversation tool like Drift, where someone might give their email inside of a widget or a chat box?
- What happens next to that lead? Do you enrich that contact or the company they work at with third party information?
- How does that information get captured inside of your CRM?
- How do you know where it came from? What was the source? What stamps that information?
- Which leads make it to your sales team?
- How are those leads distributed? By region? By product? By grade? What rules govern this process and who manages them?

Every single one of those hand-offs is an opportunity for something to go wrong. Take the time to think through each possible break

FIGURE 13.1 Customer journey map

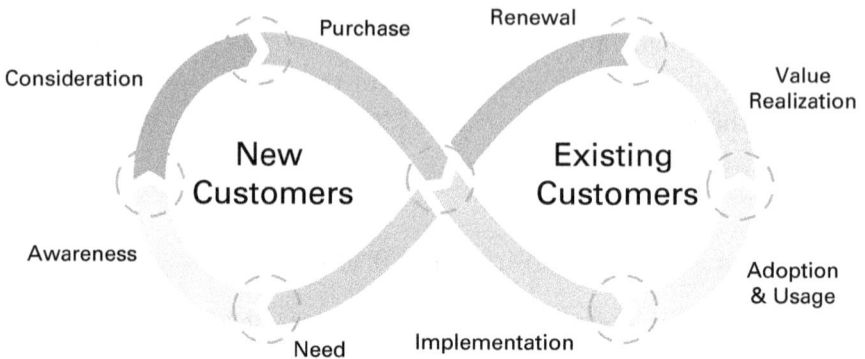

point in your processes. This doesn't just apply to the sales and marketing funnels. If you work with implementation or customer success teams, you might have breakpoints when a new customer is assigned post-sale resources, or in the way product usage data is captured and surfaced to your team. In these scenarios, you need to ask yourself the following questions:

- What happens when a brand-new customer is signed?
- How are post-sale resources (onboarding, customer success, account management) assigned?
- What triggers that assignment? Are the rules different by region? By product?
- In what period of time do you expect the first customer engagement post-sale to take place? How is that engagement tracked?
- How is product usage information passed from the product into your CRM or to a place where customer-facing teams can see it?
- How do you know that product information is accurate and up-to-date?

Accountability and Ownership

Once you have identified each possible point of failure, the next step is to create measurable reporting for every single one. Don't take even the simplest automations for granted. The more you break down the customer journey into its smallest components, the easier it will be for you to identify, troubleshoot, and resolve problems as they come up.

For example, if you have a workflow that distributes leads once they exhibit a specific behavior, you would create a report that shows you every single lead that has exhibited that behavior, but not been distributed. If you expect every brand-new customer to receive a welcome email upon user creation, you would create a report of all recently created users who have not received that email. You get the idea.

Once you have thoroughly identified and instrumented all of your potential breakpoints, the second step is to assign clear ownership within your team for who is responsible for each component of the danger dash.

That doesn't mean the sales ops. team collectively owns one component and the marketing ops. team collectively owns another. It's one of those things that if everybody owns it, nobody owns it. For every single component that you're going to put inside of your danger dash, you need to assign a single person as the directly responsible individual (DRI).

This way, when the danger dash email goes out in the morning, the name of the person responsible for each report on that dashboard is literally written below the corresponding component of the dashboard. So, if you see that you didn't stamp your lead sources properly yesterday, you can go to the DRI for lead source stamping and say, "Hey, what happened here?" Or better yet, the DRI can see it themselves and take action.

Another important accountability step with the danger dash is that you don't just send it to the Operations teammates who own the different components. You also want to send this to your internal customers, especially if those internal customers are Operationally-minded themselves.

Yes, there will be CROs who don't care about that beautiful workflow you built or the fact that you caught something they expect to "just work" in the first place. But there are other leaders who monitor these critical funnel conversions every single day. Their job performance depends on these systems working; so, they absolutely want to see your danger dash, and they will take comfort in the knowledge that systems aren't getting in the way of the business.

This extra step of sharing with your internal customers will create not only transparency and accountability, but a valuable lens for the VP of marketing or the CRO who just wants to know things are working (and an easy source report to point to when you need to clearly communicate that something isn't!). If you can give them confidence that the systems aren't hindering outcomes, that type of quiet efficiency is wildly valuable and reassuring to them. This is also a great way of showing your work in a way that makes the business better.

Troubleshooting and Resolution

Once you have instrumented all of your breakpoints and assigned owners to each one, then it comes time to actually do something about what breaks.

If you broke your customer journey down into its smallest pieces, you'll thank yourself when it comes time for troubleshooting. Let's take the lead stamping example again: In your business, you might have a requirement that every single lead in your CRM needs to have a lead source (the channel it came from), the lead source detail (the campaign in that channel), and the timestamp at which the lead performed this particular action. For anything that shows up on the danger dash missing those pieces of information, the DRI won't have a clean report until they've addressed those gaps. So if you have five leads missing information, you're not done until all five are resolved.

A few things are important to keep in mind when addressing issues surfaced by your danger dash:

1   **Review the components you're responsible for *daily*.**
    If all of your danger dash reports are actionable, you should be able to address any issues and "zero out" any components on a daily basis. This way, small problems don't become big ones overnight. Otherwise, troubleshooting and finding the root cause

of the issue gets more challenging with each passing day that a break goes unaddressed. Also, an added benefit of this daily review is that you'll very quickly learn the "normal" rhythms of the business. *How many meetings do we normally have in a day? What does our typical daily active user count look like?* You'll be amazed how quickly you'll be able to tell when something is broken in the business.

2 **Don't just fix the problem in front of your face.**
Our natural instinct is to solve the problem right in front of our face, check it off our to-do list, and move on. When we say you should "zero out" the danger dash each day, that doesn't mean you should just manually fill in the missing information or fix the broken step, and then come back and do the exact same thing the next day. Each problem you find, each break you encounter, is likely starting somewhere upstream in your process. Seek out the true root cause of the issue, and solve that once, rather than solving the same problem in front of your face every single day.

3 **The dashboard is a living, breathing thing.**
The first version of the danger dash is not going to be a comprehensive compilation of everything you need to run the business; it's a work in progress. Think of it as a living, breathing thing. Just like the way you isolated components to add to your dashboard in the first place, when the next thing inevitably breaks, be ready to identify it, build a new report to instrument that issue, and add it into the dashboard. The danger dash should not be a static thing that never changes. You and your team should always be looking around corners, anticipating what could go wrong, and proactively planning for when it does. And when you launch that new product or enter that new international market, guess what? It's time for another danger dash.

CONFESSION CORNER

My team was leading an ambitious project to replace an existing CRM system while the airplane (the business) was still flying. We chose a phased approach and had decided upon a lower risk initial deployment that focused on just the beginning of the opportunity cycle. We had a risk-averse user base who were skeptical about the new system and didn't want to give up their known, nine-year-old system. We sold the benefits and did the "what's in it for me." Users were involved in the design. Super users were already trained before the rollout. The testing team was banging away at the system for weeks before the launch. We had such high hopes.

When it came to launch, we nearly destroyed all of the goodwill we had been building. The users nearly revolted. Our downfall? There was a simultaneous project underway to cleanse and create a new customer master database. We had weekly updates and status reports, and in those, all was going according to plan. BUT we had neglected to confirm exactly what we would see; we didn't have their data in our test database. We didn't dig into the data to ensure that things were as we expected. The customer master team had done a great job with what they were trying to do with data and reduced duplicates beyond their target metrics. We just hadn't done the detailed work to verify how it would affect our data and our users. We neglected to consider what could go wrong in our launch in projects external to us. Launch day came with loads of user complaints. *"I can't find my customer account." "I can't figure out which of the six accounts that come up is the right one." "You changed my customer account name." "Your team swore it would be better, this is a hundred times worse."*

Oof. Not what we wanted at all. The only saving grace was we launched with a smaller audience with a non-critical process. We reacted fast and came up with a good plan to recover. We rolled back the customer master for our system to match the existing CRM system so that at least we didn't make the data worse. We created tons of new reporting to monitor the new customer master data and did error clean up. Most importantly, we communicated to all of the parties involved what happened, what we did to fix it, and what to do if they encountered other problems. We nearly tanked the implementation by not looking around the corner.

If you follow these steps (ok, you don't have to call it a danger dash, but we think you should), you'll have a very bright spotlight to shine on every part of your customer journey, and you'll feel much more in control of your business as opposed to your business controlling you.

When Sean worked at Upserve, they had a sign on the door that employees walked by as they left the office each day. The sign read, "Let's make better mistakes tomorrow."

And that's really what the danger dash is all about. You are never going to be able to predict every single scenario or look around every corner, but operating discipline stems from learning from our mistakes. Shine a spotlight on them and move on to what will inevitably be the next mistake. At the very least, your next mistake won't be the same as your last.

Chapter Takeaways

1 **Anticipate breaks:** Acknowledge that systems will break and mistakes will happen in scaling operations within a growing company.

2 **The importance of visibility:** Enhance observability and reduce unwanted surprises by creating a proactive monitoring system like the "danger dash" to identify potential breakdowns in customer journey conversion points.

3 **Identify points of failure:** Thoroughly map out the customer journey and identify possible points of failure in lead capture, enrichment, CRM integration, sales lead distribution, and more.

4 **Accountability and ownership:** Assign a directly responsible individual (DRI) for each identified point of failure, ensuring clear ownership, and accountability for troubleshooting and resolution.

5 **Continuous improvement and learning from mistakes:** View the monitoring system as a dynamic, evolving tool. Learn from mistakes, iterate the dashboard, and continuously improve processes to mitigate future risks and handle unforeseen issues effectively.

PART THREE

Build Your Partnerships

14

Strategic Partner vs. Support Function: The Choice is Yours

Sean once had a candidate interview debrief that he'll never forget. He was looking to hire a new member of his Revenue Operations team, and they had found a stellar candidate. The feedback was positive from every member of the hiring team. But one piece of feedback from an interviewer caught Sean off guard.

"You know what I really like about her?" the teammate asked the room. "She actually likes salespeople."

Sean was floored by this. It's not that the feedback wasn't true (she genuinely did like salespeople), but that the interviewer viewed this as a trait unique enough among Operators to comment on it. How did that happen? How did that become the norm?

The very first tenet of the Revenue Operations Mindset is, "Operators are strategic partners, not a support function." Let's make something perfectly clear: The quality of your cross-functional relationships will make or break your Revenue Operations team. If you don't appreciate and respect the work that your internal customers do, the rest of this chapter (or this book for that matter) can't help you. They are your customers. Treat them as such.

The comment by the interviewer on Sean's team was the first time he had heard someone insinuate that a level of steady disdain existed between Operations teams and their counterparts, but it wouldn't be the last. Sure, you can get frustrated. You might feel slighted sometimes. But find us a role or a function that doesn't feel that way.

Every Operator says that they want to be a strategic partner, and not a support function, but before you set out to make that a reality, ask yourself, are you willing to be a collaborative partner as well?

With that foundation, now you can set about fulfilling your goal of becoming a strategic partner. There are three critical ingredients to earning and keeping your "seat at the table" as a revenue leader at your company:

1 Creating value.

2 Communicating your value.

3 Maintaining alignment on work worth doing.

Creating Value

The truth about "having a seat at the table" is that you have to earn that seat in the first place. The easiest path to doing that: Creating value. Create value for your internal customers, for your partners, for your team, and for your company.

If you are new to a company, you have the enviable opportunity to set the standard early for what Revenue Operations can offer to the business. Take advantage of that opportunity! Whether you're an individual contributor coming into the business as the very first Revenue Operations hire, or a VP brought in to take over an existing team, you have a small window of time when you first start to show people exactly why having you on the team is going to be good for them.

You can do this by asking a lot of questions, attacking low-hanging fruit (obvious problems you can solve with little effort), and shipping valuable solutions quickly. And when we say quickly, we mean in the first 30 to 60 days in your role. If you do this effectively, you'll lay the foundation for a really strong relationship. Additionally, if you ship meaningful work early, it makes your internal customers' lives better; you're also banking some goodwill for when (not if) things inevitably go wrong or you find yourself in contentious situations with your internal partners.

The best way to identify this early work is by directly observing your internal customers in the work they do. Sit with them (physically or virtually), see how they organize their day, take note of the places that they get stuck or find painful, and seek out solutions to them. If you just sit behind your spreadsheets, or glean all of your information from dashboards (or even if your internal customers perceive that to be the case), you're not taking advantage of the best way available to you to build trust with your internal stakeholders. We'll talk more about designing processes with your end users in mind in Chapter 17, but nothing can replace actually shadowing the work that your internal customers do.

If you're not new to your role, laying this foundation and earning this seat at the table is not impossible, but it can be more difficult. In either situation, if you are redefining what Revenue Operations means for the company, you have to battle the ingrained perceptions that others within your organization have of you, or of the Revenue Operations role itself. And don't forget: Some of these perceptions might have absolutely nothing to do with you personally. Maybe they didn't have a strong RevOps team at their last company. Maybe they aren't used to a partnership like this one. Maybe the last person in the role damaged the relationship that you now need to repair. Or maybe someone once told them that, "Operations folks don't like salespeople."

In these situations, it's even more critical to identify opportunities to help your internal customers be better at their jobs, and ruthlessly prioritize that work. You don't have the benefit of having just started, but that doesn't mean the recipe for success is any different. Ask lots of questions and ship valuable solutions to the pain points you uncover.

Communicating Your Value

In Chapter 4, we introduced the idea that you can apply a different definition of "managing up" for Revenue Operations.

While most advice on "managing up" is about giving and receiving feedback with your boss, or managing expectations on projects and goals, Operators need to expand the definition of managing up. "Managing up" as a RevOps Team is about managing the perception that others have of you, the work you do, and the routine you're running. How people perceive you, your team, and the value you add to the organization is all a product of managing up.

Now, don't confuse perception with politics. This isn't about misrepresenting data or offering rose-colored glasses to make yourself look good. It's about taking advantage of the opportunity that these routines present to you to secure your position as a strategic partner in the business.

In Chapter 4, we were applying that definition to the routines you run in your business, but it's true of all work you do as a Revenue Operations team.

The truth is that many Operators aren't good at this. Learning to communicate your work is just as (if not more) important than the work itself. Jake Randall, the COO of Common Room and long-time Operations leader at Okta, explained, "I think a lot of what makes people successful in the role is empathy for the different people that they support, and the ability to communicate hard things, either that are very technical or very analytical. It's the ability to take that analytical mindset and translate it into an empathetic conversation with your business partners—with the head of sales, with the head of marketing—and ultimately bring about change."[1]

We want to believe that everyone knows exactly what we do, the value it provides, and that the work speaks for itself. Why would anyone question the utility of what we do and what we bring to the business when it's so clear to us?

You may be asking yourself right about now, well what about sales? What about marketing? No one questions why they exist. We actually believe it's quite the opposite, and that our go-to-market partners are held to consistently high and well-understood standards when it comes to their performance.

REAL WORLD ROLE MODELS

On Episode 108 of the *Operations* podcast, LinkSquares Chief Legal Officer, Tim Parilla, posed this hypothetical:

> Imagine a new Chief Marketing Officer coming to a quarterly business review, and just providing some anecdote, "Hey, we made this commercial and it aired a bunch and like, people thought it was really funny."
>
> No, that's never going to fly. So why is it that some of these other functions (like legal and Operations) can get away with walking in and saying, "I talked to a couple of people who are major consumers of what we provide to the organization and they're happy."
>
> That's just one part. The other is, how do I know if you're any good at what you're doing? Just because the people you work with are happy doesn't mean you're doing your job well. It doesn't mean that your core competencies are strong. It doesn't mean that you're holding your work to a particular standard of care.
>
> Every executive needs to demand data from anybody who reports into that executive. If you are managing a function, you have to bring data to show how you contribute. If you're not doing that, it's a huge mess, and nothing else that you're doing really matters.[2]

So, instead of assuming people just inherently understand and appreciate the value of the Revenue Operations function, take it upon yourself to articulate that value. Again and again and again.

At every company we've been at, we have created some form of a Revenue Operations charter. Most commonly, this takes the form of a slide deck that explains who our team is, why we exist, the type of work we do, and how we can help the audience to which the charter is being presented. There are a few key components to this charter:

- **Your team's North star:** Write a mission statement for why you exist. This will not only help when you present to other internal stakeholders, but it will also serve as a touchstone for you and your team when you're trying to prioritize the work you do. For example, your North star might be, "Create a high-achieving, understood, and predictable revenue engine."

- **The type of work your team does:** Whether you have fully adopted a Revenue Operations model or not, clearly articulate what your team is responsible for and provide examples of the type of work you've done in the past. This is your opportunity to set clear expectations of what your team owns and, just as importantly, what you don't!

- **How your team is structured:** Whether your team has two people or twenty, leave your audience with a clear understanding of how your team is structured, who is responsible for what, and who they can go to for help on the topics most relevant to them. "Oh, anyone can help you with that" or "Just come to me for everything" aren't helpful responses for your internal customers or for you.

Once you have crafted this charter, test it out with your team first. Ask for their feedback. Do they believe in what is being communicated here? Is this the type of team they want to be on? Then, once you've incorporated their feedback, it's time to take that charter on a "road show" internally to every function at your company.

This road show applies whether you've had a Revenue Operations function at your company for years or you're starting one for the very first time. At Upserve, when Sean was building the company's first RevOps function, he not only had to communicate what the team was going to be doing, but also convince his various internal stakeholders across sales, marketing, and customer success that the team should even exist. Figures 14.1 and 14.2 show sample slides from that first roadshow deck he presented.

The investment to craft a deck is not a small one, and you could easily justify deprioritizing something like this in place of other, more "business-critical" projects. But don't put this off. Once you nail your messaging, this deck will serve as a critical resource for your existing internal customers, and for every single new hire at the company.

FIGURE 14.1 RevOps road show, previous state

One of Sean's favorite responsibilities in RevOps is spending time with new team members that join the company. This is another amazing opportunity to communicate the role of RevOps early in someone's tenure and to begin building important relationships with your stakeholders.

"My job is to make you better at your job," he would say. "I want you to find all of the things that suck, and tell me about them." (Laura admittedly didn't love when he did that because it set some dangerous expectations for what Operations could impact, but that was Sean's way of communicating the team's value. Find what works for you and make sure you can back it up.)

The other goal of meeting with customer-facing colleagues when they first join the company is to turn the page from whatever flavor of Operations—good, bad, or non-existent—that they had experienced at their previous company. As we established in the Introduction, Operations can be a broad spectrum of work; so, clarify for your new teammates what Revenue Operations means at your company.

FIGURE 14.2   RevOps road show, future state

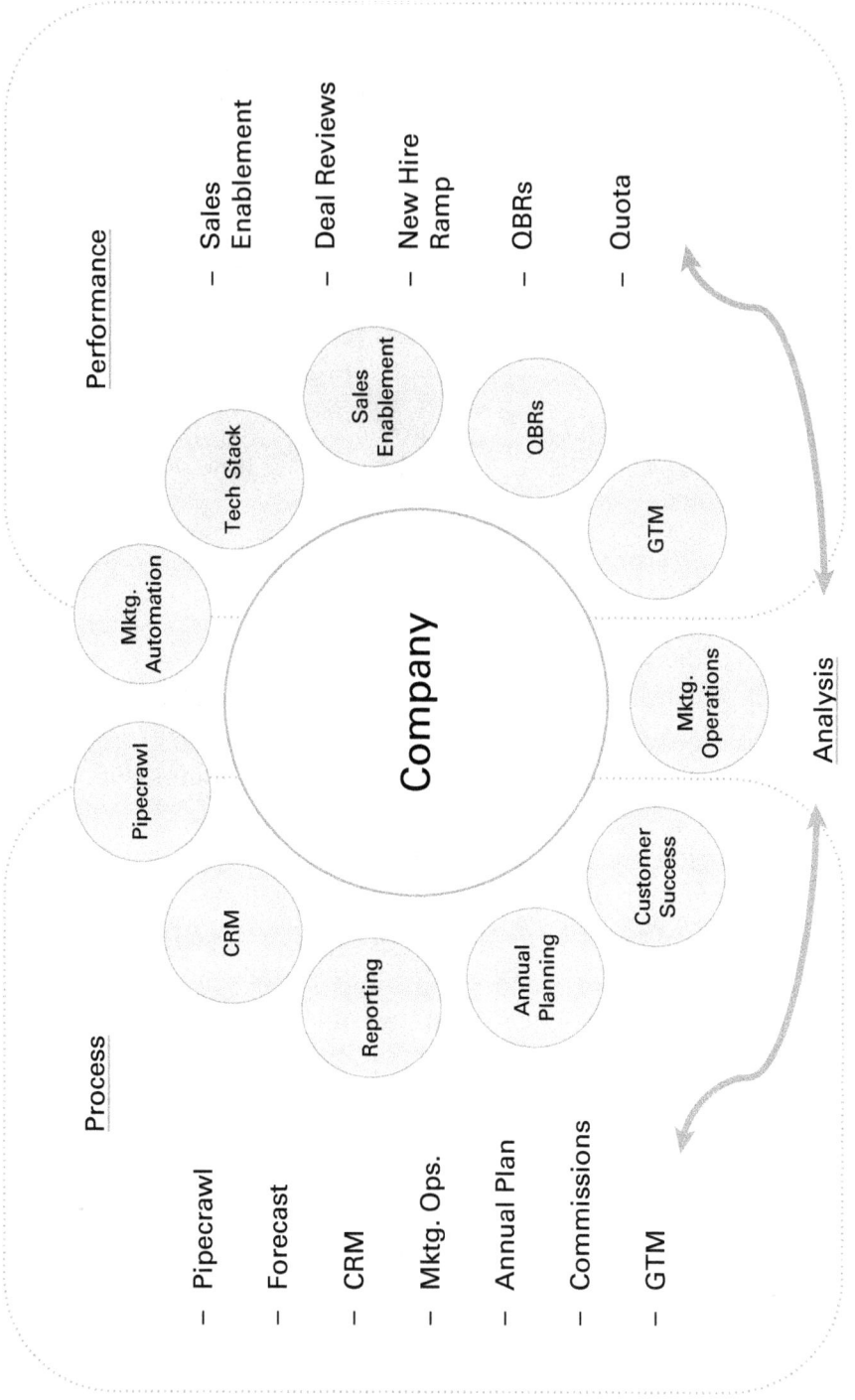

Process

– Pipecrawl

– Forecast

– CRM

– Mktg. Ops.

– Annual Plan

– Commissions

– GTM

Performance

– Sales Enablement

– Deal Reviews

– New Hire Ramp

– QBRs

– Quota

Analysis

Company

Pipecrawl

CRM

Reporting

Mktg. Automation

Tech Stack

Sales Enablement

QBRs

GTM

Mktg. Operations

Customer Success

Annual Planning

A quick word of caution here: If you've followed all of the advice in this book and created a world-class Revenue Operations function at your company, your new teammates might be floored by what you show them in that first meeting, excited even. *This will not last.* Like anything, we get used to what we have and your internal customers will inevitably come to expect the things they used to find exceptional. This is normal, and it's *good*. This dynamic will challenge you to continue to raise the bar for yourself, for your team, and for what Revenue Operations can be at your company.

CONFESSION CORNER

Even if you take great care in crafting a Revenue Operations charter and do a great job of sharing that charter on a road show within your company, you're still going to face difficult situations and difficult conversations.

I once received a tough call from a leader my team supported. When I picked up, he was already mid-conversation, irate.

"I don't report to your team! I don't know who [teammate] thinks he is, but I'm not taking orders from him."

This wasn't the first time that tense conversations had happened between these two colleagues, but it was certainly the most explosive. My teammate, while likely with good intentions and highlighting processes I had asked him to enforce, was clearly not a trusted partner to this leader. This is also not all that rare when junior Operations team members are tasked with holding more senior revenue leaders accountable for certain processes or pipeline management expectations.

Without careful messaging, clear expectations from senior leadership, or a carefully crafted foundation of trust, Ops. can take on a weird "policing" role with its internal customers. This is not a place you want to be. Not only are you not creating value in this type of role, but it's probably not the job you signed up for in the first place. With some coaching, we adjusted some of the language my teammate used in these types of situations and also coached the leader on the intention behind them. Leverage technology, systems, and documented rules of engagement to help you with policies and protocols; then you can get back to the fulfilling work of a trusted Operator.

Maintaining Alignment on Work Worth Doing

Once you've started to create meaningful value and clearly articulated that value as a Revenue Operations team, congratulations, you've reached the hard part.

Not what you were expecting? It's true. What you've done so far is lay an incredibly strong foundation upon which to now run your business. You can't skip the previous steps we've outlined in this chapter, but you also can't expect them to be the only ingredients to being a strategic partner.

Now that you've earned your seat at the table, you keep it by continuously providing value quarter after quarter after quarter. This requires discipline, over-communication with your internal customers, and a constant search to make things incrementally better tomorrow than they were yesterday.

It also requires alignment with your stakeholders on the work that is going to drive needle-moving outcomes for the business. The routines we outlined in Chapter 4 and the goal-setting methodologies from Chapter 11 are the ultimate combination to maintaining this alignment. When goals are set well and then progress against those goals is regularly reviewed, you'll be an invaluable partner to your internal customers.

This focus on constant alignment will also assuage the concerns of any Revenue leaders who might be skeptical of the Revenue Operations model. People like having their own "go-to" resources that they don't have to share with anyone else, so when RevOps is built with the entire customer journey in mind, individual functions might feel like their biggest priorities will be left behind. And in fairness, that *might* happen. Sylvia Kainz, a former RevOps leader at both Airbnb and Eventbrite, explains:

> It's a very common occurrence that leaders gravitate to people they've worked with before, or they believe is the expert in a particular area. And there's nothing wrong with that. It's just not scalable because that's just one person, and how much work can that person do? People will question, are they still servicing me? Are they still helping me when I am in need?

I think the reputation of Revenue Operations has to build over time. You need to build trust very clearly with your key stakeholders. It requires a lot of communication, clarification and time. But once we got there, everybody said, "Oh, this is awesome, now I don't just have one person. I actually have a whole team I can rely on."[3]

That doesn't just mean taking what someone else asks of you and blindly making it a reality. An important byproduct of the Revenue Operations Mindset is you will start to develop your own point of view about what would improve the business, and inject your position into these alignment conversations. Kainz offered this perspective:

I don't like to talk about a support function. We aren't just here to make sure that the systems are aligned and the processes are fixed. A RevOps leader should have a vision of the biggest impact RevOps can have on top-line growth. Our focus should be on making sure that our vision, along with that of the Chief Revenue Officer, actually gets executed. Aligning all these teams and making sure they're focused, ensuring they have the same objective that they all collectively go after.[3]

Developing your own point of view and regularly checking in with your stakeholders also means that you will need to be nimble as a team. Business conditions change, new priorities emerge, and to be a strategic partner, you need to be able to adapt. Nothing will sour the partnership faster than an entrenched Operations group with no openness to deviate from the plan (conversely, leaders who change their priorities every week are just as detrimental).

You'll know that you have reached a "flow" state in your internal partnerships when you're experiencing the following things:

- Revenue leaders turn to you for advice and input before making a key decision.
- Everyone understands and can articulate the value of your team.
- Goal setting and operating routines aren't chores; they're collaborative, iterative processes to make the business better.
- The work you're doing has clear value to everyone involved, not just one party.

FIGURE 14.3 Tom Wentworth: Ops appreciation tweet

Tom Wentworth ✓
@twentworth12   ...

To all my marketing/sales ops pros working deep in the trenches.

I know automation work isn't glamorous. No one seems to care about your Process Builder hack or that clever Marketo lead routing program you created.

But without you, there are no hypergrowth companies #respect

5:44 PM · Oct 17, 2018

And in some rare cases, you'll come across leaders who not only appreciate the outcomes, but who have also developed an appreciation and an admiration for the work it takes for Revenue Operations to truly excel. Hold onto those leaders. Tom Wentworth, CMO at Recorded Future, and former Marketing Executive at companies like Acquia and Rapidminer, put it best in this tweet (Figure 14.3).[4]

Every Operator says they want to be a strategic partner, and not a support function. Now go be one.

Chapter Takeaways

1 **Operators as strategic partners:** The Revenue Operations Mindset emphasizes that Revenue Operations teams should be viewed as strategic partners rather than mere support functions. Building strong cross-functional relationships is crucial, and respecting internal customers' work is fundamental to success.

2 **Earn a "seat at the table":** To become a strategic partner, Operators must focus on creating value for internal customers, partners, teams, and the company as a whole. This involves asking questions, addressing low-hanging fruit, and delivering impactful solutions within the first 30 to 60 days in a new role.

3 Communicate value: Effective communication of the value provided by Revenue Operations is as important as the work itself. Crafting a Revenue Operations charter that outlines the team's mission, responsibilities, and structure helps manage perceptions and secures a strategic position within the organization.

4 Overcome challenges in alignment: Maintaining alignment on work that drives meaningful outcomes requires discipline, constant communication, and a commitment to continuous improvement. Regularly reviewing progress against goals ensures ongoing collaboration and helps dispel skepticism about the Revenue Operations model.

5 Become a trusted strategic partner: Successful Revenue Operations teams are distinguished by their ability to offer valuable insights, adapt to changing business conditions, and develop a collaborative, iterative approach to goal-setting. When done well, you will become a sought-after advisor and a key contributor to overall business performance.

Endnotes

1 *Operations* with Sean Lane (2019) What Ops Pros Can Learn from This $9 Billion Company, with Okta's Jake Randall, Episode 2 [podcast]
2 *Operations* with Sean Lane (2023) Navigating from Start-up to Scale-up, with LinkSquares' Tim Parilla, Episode 108 [podcast]
3 *Operations* with Sean Lane (2019) How to Build a RevOps Team from Scratch, with Eventbrite's Sylvia Kainz, Episode 9 [podcast]
4 T. Wentworth. To all my marketing/sales ops pros working deep in the trenches. I know automation work isn't glamorous. No one seems to care about your Process Builder hack or that clever Marketo lead routing program you created. But without you, there are no hypergrowth companies #respect 🫡 [Twitter] 17 October 2018, https://twitter.com/twentworth12/status/1052676694128189440 (archived at https://perma.cc/DH62-47K9)

15

Go Beyond Sales: The Importance of Cross-Functional Relationships

Stephen Hallowell is the VP Professional Services at HighSpot and he has held sales enablement and Operations leadership roles at massively successful companies like MulseSoft and Snowflake. As a guest on the *Operations* podcast, Stephen recalled:

> I've been fortunate to have been a part of a few pretty interesting companies, and I've observed that many companies struggle in the same places. For leadership teams, many of these issues are cross-functional, and I've found that leadership teams tend not to have clear focus on the most important places that their cross-functional group needs to dig in and mature how they operate.[1]

Revenue Operations is often viewed as the silver bullet to siloed decision-making and inconsistent data sources, but you can't expect a perfectly cohesive operation simply by investing in an organizational structure. If anything, we've found that sometimes Revenue Operations can just be sales operations in disguise, with some added responsibilities to other internal stakeholders. If sales is still the dominant voice in your go-to-market planning and execution, you're missing out on the potential benefits of a truly cross-functional Revenue Operations group.

Teams often don't achieve this ambitious cross-functional state because it's *hard*. When you have multiple internal customers, it's harder to prioritize work across all of them. It's harder to move fast when you have to stop to consider what a decision in marketing will mean for sales, or the ripple effects of a new sales process in customer success.

But it's worth it.

Hallowell confirmed it:

> I think there are a wide variety of org structures that can work. What I think matters, though, is that somebody is willing to take on a leadership role in driving this sort of conversation. I think especially Ops. and enablement are really in a unique spot to step into that leadership role when they want to. You're not beholden to one slice of the business, you're not optimizing on just new opportunities generated or number of leads. You're a bit more strategic and able to step back and look at the bigger picture, and you have access to the data around what's happening.
>
> I think it's a really interesting opportunity to say, "Are we doing the right things? Where do we have the opportunity to sharpen up?" While you're going to be leading through influence and not through ownership, I think that can still be a very powerful place to lead from.[1]

REAL WORLD ROLE MODELS

Todd Abbott, the former CEO of InsightSquared and a multi-time sales leader, explained on Episode 60 of the *Operations* podcast his approach to bringing his cross-functional leaders together through data:

> As an ex-CRO myself for many years, I always struggled with executive business reviews where every function comes with their own data and their interpretation of that data. One of the biggest friction points tends to be between marketing and sales.
>
> Marketing says, "I've got all these website hits, all these downloads, all these leads I've created, your guys aren't responding to them quickly and you've got to respond on leads. You're not meeting your SLA" Meanwhile sales says, "Yeah, but you know X percent of them are crap and they're not converting."

Another example is with product. Product says, "I've got the best product, you should never be losing. Why are you losing?" And then sales says, "Stop telling me how great your product is and help me win against this competitor, because when this competitor gets engaged by this stage, the win rate drops by 20 percent."

This friction goes on in every company to some degree. And so what you're really looking for is to get out of the siloed data with your own interpretation and get one data set for the company. Then, you can bring cross-functional teams together to one view, grounded in facts and data, and use that to drive cross-functional execution.

This is a real struggle for CEOs because no one is aligned. CEOs know they aren't optimized cross-functionally because they've never had the data, everybody's got their own tech stack with their own analytics, and their own interpretation of the analytics.

True revenue analytics breaks down those silos and brings everybody to the table. Leverage data to help you execute better by understanding the friction points in your sales process and removing them."[2]

We as Operators are uniquely positioned in our organizations to build, strengthen, and maintain these cross-functional relationships. As we learned in the Introduction, we are the "central connectors" of our companies. So, how do you develop the right types of relationships beyond sales to pull this off? Let's go function by function with some key partners to find out.

Marketing

There are so many unique opportunities in RevOps to partner with marketing. CMOs turn to Operators more and more now as a trusted advisor to help them run their teams, and not just as a reactive resource, but a proactive partner.

Karen Steele, a former marketing executive at companies like LeanData, Marketo, and VMware, explained the data-driven foundation of this relationship:

It starts with, *"Show me the data."* I think that every CMO today wants to see the real data behind the story. It's not ideal for a CMO or a Head of Demand Gen to always be asking for the data, or trying to tweak reports. Come to me proactively and show me the data. Give me your hypothesis of different things you believe may be happening that we're not paying attention to.[3]

Not every leader thinks this way right away in their career. Dave Gerhardt, a former marketing executive at Drift and Privy, acknowledged his perspective on the marketing operations function evolved as his career progressed:

> I used to be more biased towards other stuff. *"Let's just keep doing more, faster."* People are showing up at our store, let's not worry so much about where they came from, as opposed to the fact that they're here. What I learned is that my job as the marketing leader is so much harder for hiring, budgeting, planning, forecasting, and modeling without good data. If you have good data, good analytics, strong operational foundation, relatively speaking, it all gets easier. Plus a lot of smart CMOs I talked to were telling me the first thing they do is hire Ops. Build that foundation first and then build from there. I think the combination of all those things is why I've changed my opinion on that.[4]

Marketing is often the closest partner to sales when it comes to go-to-market execution, so Revenue Operations teams must be trusted liaisons between the two groups. When sales comes to the table with one version of the truth and marketing with another, RevOps must act as the unbiased, objective party.

It's also important to help marketing strengthen its own relationships with groups outside of sales. You can't just be focused on acquiring new customers. Functions like customer marketing or digital customer experience require extensive cross-functional support, and oftentimes, RevOps can demonstrate the art of the possible to these groups. Point out ways that a marketer might be able to use a customer's action in an app to trigger a targeted campaign specifically for that role. Just showing people the options available to them can be the catalyst they need.

A few sample projects or responsibilities a RevOps team might work on with marketing include the following:

- Defining your ideal customer profile.
- Firmographic scoring (what traits are common of companies that buy our product?).
- Behavioral scoring (what intent signals are common for prospects that buy our product?).
- Lead distribution and speed to lead (SLA).
- Campaign planning, forecasting, and execution.
- Marketing automation platform design and administration.
- Marketing spend budgeting.

Customer Success/Professional Services

While the standard Revenue Operations definition usually includes customer success as an internal customer for RevOps to serve, post-sale teams frequently get the least attention compared to their sales and marketing counterparts. It's understandable—growing companies tend to focus on securing revenue first before spending time and resources figuring out how to keep that revenue.

Caitlin Quinlan, former General Manager and Operations Executive at Gainsight, saw this same story in her career. She explained on the *Operations* podcast,

> I laugh because my title has gone from plain Operations to Sales
> Operations, to Business Operations, to Sales Strategy, and then RevOps
> for pre-sales, and now RevOps for the entire go-to-market. And
> specifically, in customer success, we've seen it rapidly develop over the
> last few years in tech as these new teams emerged to address a newer
> part of the post-sales motion. You have a business model where a
> customer can leave you at every turn, versus staying in your install base
> forever. And so, as we've seen that role expand, there's also a mandate to
> ensure that you have the entire customer journey tied together. I resource
> C.S. Ops. the same way you would sales Ops.; it's not a part-time thing.
> It's analytics, enablement, process and systems, just like sales.[5]

Leaders like Caitlin can't make their visions a reality without the Revenue Operations Mindset. Don't make the mistake of prioritizing your sales and marketing partners over all post-sale teams. From onboarding to customer success to professional services, Ops. partners can drive enormous value.

A few sample projects or responsibilities a RevOps team might work on with customer success include:

- Designing the customer journey: Hand-offs, communication, roles, and responsibilities.
- Customer health scoring.
- Renewal and retention analysis.
- Voice of the customer design and analysis.
- Capacity planning and utilization.
- Book of business design.

Product

How many times have you been part of an important meeting with strategic go-to-market ramifications and a representative from the product team isn't even in the room? You might not have ever even stopped to question it before, but looking back at it now, it seems kind of absurd, doesn't it?

Even if from an organizational design standpoint your team doesn't formally support the product team at your company, it's critical you build strong relationships with that group. First and foremost, there is so much that we as Operators can learn from our colleagues in product and engineering. Operations teams are the product managers of the company itself; so, anything we borrow from how they run their teams can only help us improve.

Also, this partnership is critical both to maintain alignment between product and go-to-market and to leverage the vast amount of data available to revenue teams from the product itself.

On the *Operations* podcast, Sean interviewed a pair of colleagues from Drift's data engineering team (Arun Venkateswaran) and business intelligence and analytics team (Kyle Thelemann) about the "two-way highway" of their partnership. Kyle explained:

> My role is to take all the hard work and data processing that Arun and his team do to get data from the product, flow that into a data warehouse, and then make that data readily accessible for our business teams, like marketing, customer success, sales and product, so they can take action off of that data. I need to be able to speak Arun's language from an S.Q.L. standpoint, and Arun can speak my language from a business intelligence tools standpoint."[6]

This is especially true in any sort of product-led growth environment. If your company relies on its product to drive initial adoption, there is a treasure trove of data available to you to help your revenue teams succeed – your job is to make sure it's accessible, relevant, and actionable.

If you do find yourself in a situation where interactions between Revenue Ops and product have not been the norm, seek out creative ways to get in front of that audience. For example, every Friday at Drift we held a company-wide "show and tell" meeting, where each function presented something they had recently shipped. We knew this was an opportunity to get in front of our product team and we were always thoughtful about the message we presented to them. Take advantage of any time you can get!

Lastly, if you work at a company where you are a customer of your own product, you have a unique opportunity to shape the future product development itself. You are customer #1. Provide feedback, offer suggestions, and hold your product team accountable to making things better.

A few sample projects or responsibilities a RevOps team might work on with the product team include:

- Product-led growth motions.
- Surfacing product usage data to customer-facing teams.
- Matching role-specific users (and their actions) to specialized campaigns.
- Providing feedback as a user of your own company's product.

Finance

Finance is undoubtedly one of the closest cross-functional partners for RevOps. For everything from annual planning to compensation design to budgeting, it's important you go out of your way to form a trusted partnership with your finance counterparts.

Some organizations have their RevOps team reporting into the CFO or as part of the general and administrative (G&A) department, and so, the relationship between the teams might be inherently built into the reporting structure. When this is not the case, that makes it all the more important to seek out opportunities for a collaborative relationship. You can do this by including finance in some of the routines we mentioned in Chapter 4, allocating budget properly for the tech stack from Chapter 6, leaning on them as a sounding board for business forecasting in Chapter 8, and being in lockstep for every single step of variable compensation planning from Chapter 10. You simply can't run your business if finance and Ops. aren't on the same page.

A few sample projects or responsibilities a RevOps team might work on with finance include:

- Building your company's operating plan.
- Capacity and hiring planning.
- Designing compensation plans.
- Tech stack budgeting.
- Deal desk.
- Bookings policies and rules of engagement.
- Order forms, billing, and subscription management.

HR/Talent

When you're looking around your organization for other teams that are faced with as broad a charter of responsibilities as RevOps, look no further than your human resources (HR) and talent partners. Due to the nature of our work, Operations and HR teams are often the first ones to know sensitive information, working behind the scenes to ensure a good experience for all other employees. HR also has the same internal customers we do, so spend time with them.

When a sales rep that is struggling is about to go on a performance plan, you and the HR business partner need to be in lockstep on how that plan will be delivered and measured. When you are about to make a big hiring push, being aligned with your recruiting team about every single hire is critical.

Jeremey Donovan, EVP Revenue Operations and Strategy at Insight Partners and former Operations executive at Salesloft, illustrated this well:

> During my time at Salesloft, we were worried we were going to miss plan at one point a few years back. And our biggest challenge was we couldn't hire fast enough. We didn't have enough capacity, we didn't have a good capacity plan, and we hired this brilliant recruiter named Carly Jones. If I think of single people who added some of the most value to the companies that I've worked for, she's hands down one of those people. She aligned the capacity plan with the finance team and sales and Revenue Operations, and then she built an organization that was just world class at recruiting to make sure we met the capacity plans.[7]

A few sample projects or responsibilities a RevOps team might work on with HR/talent include:

- Hiring planning.
- Performance management.
- New hire onboarding/offboarding.
- Performance review frameworks.
- Succession planning.

You could argue that everything in the "Build Your Partnerships" section of this book is outside the core job description of Revenue Operations roles, and you might have a fair argument, if you only want to be an *average* Operator. Everything in this section is about setting your team apart and setting your company up for the incremental success that inevitably follows.

We do worry sometimes that the charter for Revenue Operations might be too broad, that we're setting Operators up for an impossibly tall task. But instead of thinking about managing an overwhelming laundry list of individual relationships, consider this alternate perspective. RevOps teams aren't there simply to seek out new efficiencies on the path to revenue; we exist to serve as a center of excellence—a role model—for all varieties of operational efficiency. Each cross-functional interaction you have is an opportunity to be an ambassador of that efficiency to the rest of your company. Every team in the company (not to mention your customers) benefits as a result.

Chapter Takeaways

1 **Cross-functional collaboration is crucial:** Cross-functional challenges are common in leadership teams, and addressing them is vital for operational maturity. Revenue Operations offers a truly cross-functional approach necessary for success.

2 **Leadership role in driving cross-functional conversations:** Revenue Operations leaders have a unique opportunity to drive cross-functional collaboration. They are strategically positioned to lead conversations beyond individual business slices.

3 **Data-driven cross-functional alignment:** Effective cross-functional collaboration requires breaking down silos and establishing a shared data set from which to drive action. Executive leadership teams often face friction due to disparate data interpretations.

4 **Function-by-function relationship development:**
   - **Marketing:** Establishing a data-driven foundation is crucial for the RevOps-marketing partnership. RevOps serves as a liaison between sales and marketing, ensuring unbiased, objective collaboration.
   - **Customer success/professional services:** Post-sale teams are equally important, and RevOps can drive significant value by

partnering with these teams for consistency, scalability, and value realization.

- **Product:** Building strong relationships with the product team is critical for alignment and leveraging data for revenue teams. Understanding their language and integrating data streams can enhance collaboration.
- **Finance:** A close partnership with the finance team is essential for budgeting, compensation design, and overall alignment. Collaboration ensures smooth operations and optimized cross-functional performance.
- **HR/Talent:** Human resources and talent teams share a broad charter and face similar challenges. RevOps collaboration with HR is crucial for effective hiring planning, performance management, and overall success.

5 **Ambassadors of efficiency:** Revenue Operations teams, with their broad charter, serve as a center of excellence for operational efficiency. Each cross-functional interaction is an opportunity to showcase and cultivate efficiency, benefiting the entire company.

Endnotes

1 *Operations* with Sean Lane (2020) The Go-to-Market Maturity Model Part I, with Highspot's Stephen Hallowell, Episode 31 [podcast]

2 *Operations* with Sean Lane (2021) Get Reps Out of the Data Entry Business, with InsightSquared CEO Todd Abbott, Episode 60 [podcast]

3 *Operations* with Sean Lane (2020) How to Maximize the Partnership with your CMO and Accelerate Revenue, with Karen Steele, Episode 35 [podcast]

4 *Operations* with Sean Lane (2021) Why Drift's Dave Gerhardt Changed His Mind About Marketing Ops, Episode 63 [podcast]

5 *Operations* with Sean Lane (2021) Designing the Post-Sales Customer Journey, with Gainsight's Caitlin Quinlan, Episode 55 [podcast]

6 *Operations* with Sean Lane (2020) The Two-Way Highway of Drift's Data Engineering and Data Analytics Teams, with Arun Venkateswaran and Kyle Thelemann, Episode 40 [podcast]

7 *Operations* with Sean Lane (2023) Separating Practices from Best Practices, with Insight Partners' Jeremey Donovan, Episode 96 [podcast]

16

Get Your Partners Involved: Make Sure You Have Them "Crack an Egg"

When packet cake mixes first came out in the 1950s, they didn't sell as well as expected though the convenience was off the charts because all you had to add was water. The cake-mix makers commissioned a consumer input study to find out why the mixes weren't selling well. In interview after interview they heard, "Well, I just added water so I can't really say this is homemade."

The product developers came up with a new version of the mixes that required their customers to add an egg—and miracles of miracles, the sales skyrocketed!

Laura first heard this story in the midst of a CRM rebuild project earlier in her career. The moral for a CRM rebuild project (and Operators everywhere!)?

Always ensure your internal customers (the users of the system) get to crack an egg. Give them input into the design. Provide them with mock-ups of the screens, review policies with key representatives, give them choices for how things can work. Let them crack an egg to ensure they have ownership and can call it their own.

As with the best stories, this one actually glossed over some realities. The cake mixes were selling perfectly well in the late 1940s; only in the late 1950s did they stall. The companies did want to increase sales after stalling; so, they did a consumer study. And they did find that only adding water made the customers feel like they really didn't do much. But here is the key finding: When the real egg was added to the mix, it actually increased the quality of the cake outcome.[1]

Making the mix with a fresh egg not only made the consumer feel better about using the mix, but the *outcome* was also better tasting and higher-selling. Giving input to the design of what Operators are implementing may make people feel better about the outcome, but more importantly, you actually get a higher quality outcome as well.

As Operators, we often believe that we know best. It is an easy trap to fall into and getting input takes time you may feel you don't have with tight deadlines. It can be easier to just design the forecast system without having to take the time to get input from the sales managers, the sellers, customer success, or executives. They often have conflicting input anyway, right?

Getting our stakeholders' input on anything we are designing as Operators is our number one recommendation for "building your partnerships." Not only will you end up getting support when you eventually roll it out (as we learned in Chapter 7), but most importantly, the outcome of what you end up rolling out will be better for having gotten the input.

Operations is a team sport. You need to work with many partners throughout the organization. How wonderful is it to know that you can get higher quality outcomes by involving your partners in the process.

Get Real Input

In preparing for a feedback session, the most common mistake we see Operations teams make is having all of the questions already answered. They come in with a deck that shows the project they are working on and what the plans are for the implementation. Even if they say they want feedback, the only input they are really looking for is a simple "thumbs up." The review meeting goes sideways because the review team asks questions like, "What else can we do?", "What about …?", "I want to see XYZ in there," and the Ops. team ends up frustrated and feeling like they went backwards, further confirming their biases that asking for feedback just delays projects.

People being asked for feedback want to feel like they are adding value. They want to earn their keep, help the process, and see that their needs are being addressed. If you ignore the value they bring to the table or don't harness their valuable input, you are missing out on a very tasty egg to add to the mix.

The best Operators ensure there are very specific questions they want feedback on when they seek input. They are up front about the problems they are trying to solve and what pain they have heard about from their users. They provide options to help answer the "What else can we do?" question. They ask questions of their review committee to help shape the outcome. They provide visuals, screenshots, or examples where possible. They leave an egg to be cracked by their review team.

Some of our best practice tips on how to get your partners involved:

1 Provide context for the feedback session. Explain what is possible/not possible and what is wanted from the reviewers.

2 Provide an agenda for the feedback session.

3 Establish your guiding principles or boundaries on whatever it is that you are seeking feedback on.

4 Communicate who from their teams you interviewed and got feedback from as part of this process.

5 Give real choices to your stakeholders. Don't just ask for superficial input.

6 Be transparent about how you established the choice order so that reviewers don't feel manipulated into making the decision you want.

7 Be curious. Ask questions. Pause for input. Ask for the "why" behind the feedback.

8 Be specific in responding to why something can't or shouldn't be done.

9 Establish how you are going to summarize their feedback and report back how you incorporated it (or didn't) into the final solution.

In one of our prior companies, we did an overhaul of the rules of engagement policy. The project manager met with each of the VPs for their biggest concerns for the current policy, talked with the Ops. leadership about the current stickiest areas of contention, and evaluated our rules against a couple other companies' policies.

In a weekly staff meeting, the project manager walked the VPs through a series of questions and options for different sections of the policy, with example scenarios wherever she could provide them. Each week, she documented the results of the discussions and the outcomes that would be created in the policy. More importantly, she showed the work that had been done and the decisions that had been reached so that we didn't have to keep having the same debates.

It took us a couple of months to complete the entire policy overhaul, but in the end, all of the VPs understood the decisions the management team made together on each item so that when the policy was rolled out, every VPs could answer why each decision was made. In the end, it was the entire leadership team's policy, not the Operations team's policy. When you involve those who are going to have to live with the consequences of something in its creation, the effort of enforcing it becomes everyone's job, not just the Operations team.

Diversity and Inclusion

The "cracking an egg" philosophy isn't about adding a step just to make people feel good. It's about the powerful impact you get with diversity of thought. You create processes, systems, policies, and operating mechanisms that work across the entire company, not just for a select few.

Some examples of including diversity in your design processes include:

- **Hierarchy:** Have you asked individual contributors, managers, and senior leaders for input?

- **Geographic locations:** Does the UK sales office need to quote in GBP and euros?

- **Departments:** What are the marketing and product departments' usage of opportunity loss reason codes?

- **Experience:** Will your first-year sellers understand how to pick the right products in the new quoting tool?

- **Time zones:** Are the forecast deadlines thoughtful to all territories and time zones?

Even if you can't satisfy all of your constituents' desires, you can make a better decision and have a better communication strategy if you are more aware of the diversity of inputs.

REAL WORLD ROLE MODELS

Kyle Bastien was the Vice President of Sales Readiness at Drift. In Episode 85 of the *Operations* podcast, Kyle talked about the genesis of something called Sales Lab.

The CRO asked me what I am learning about the sales process. I started building a list of what should change and how we want to change it. I was trying to tackle one big thing in particular. But as I was working through what the solution was to this part of the process I wanted to fix, it occurred to me that I needed more help on this. For this to happen, sales leaders would need to say yes and buy into it. Reps would have to help me validate and adopt this. I would need to try this because it represented a fairly big change to a certain part of our process.

But the way we work at Drift is we don't sit on these huge ideas, work on them in private, and then reveal them. It's a very collaborative way that we work here. You basically share your idea early, you build upon it, get feedback, and ideally you get to the desired solution faster. And so that's why the Sales Lab was formed.

I had to recruit allies. I wanted to get a leader from each of the sales units. I asked folks in Operations, sales enablement, the solutions consulting team, product marketing, and marketing. And we pretty quickly got a group of about 10 to 12 people that all just said yes.

I first said, *"Everybody, for the first meeting, just write down everything that you think is broken or that you want to fix."* You could only say a problem if you had some notion of what the solution looked like. And then you put your name on it.

The next meeting was awesome. It was basically *Shark Tank*. Everyone who submitted an idea had two minutes to pitch the group on the merits of the idea. Then people were able to vote on five things. We decided that we were going to do the top three. My idea wasn't even one of them!

We sent the people who had proposed the top three away to turn their line item into a brief and basically just add another layer of detail of what they were proposing. I gave them a one-page template: What problem are we trying to solve? What should happen if this goes really well? And then what could go wrong along the way?[2]

Seek Feedback, Not Consensus

It can be difficult to reconcile all of that feedback you receive, and realistically, you can't (and shouldn't) always act on all of the feedback that you receive. Sometimes the feedback conflicts and frankly, some ideas just aren't that good. We recommend that you first establish your guiding principles/objectives for whatever project you are seeking feedback for. This creates a measuring stick against which you can evaluate feedback and allows you to redirect input quickly if it starts to move away from the principles.

One of Drift's leadership principles was "seek feedback, not consensus." This is an important philosophy to lead with, especially as you seek feedback across various groups. The goal of seeking feedback is to get to the best idea, the best outcome, the tastiest cake—not to please everyone. It's also about seeking feedback from the right people, not everyone. If you lead with this principle when you ask for feedback, you can set the expectation right there that just because someone gives you feedback does not automatically mean that you execute on it. Once you do make decisions, follow back up with your feedback groups on what the final decision was and why you made it, especially if it wasn't in line with their input.

There are also times when you may seek feedback not necessarily on the content of a project, but perhaps on the communication of the content. For example, seek feedback on your compensation rollout presentation from first line managers by providing a preview of the presentation before the individual contributors see it. We recommend you also include a few first line managers in your early-stage information gathering for compensation planning, but by previewing the launch with all of them, they can provide you with valuable input on how and what information is presented to the people they work with every day. They will also be more familiar with the details and support you in answering questions on the actual rollout day instead of processing the information at the same time as their reports.

Getting input and involvement from your customers creates joint ownership, reduces surprises, and creates higher quality outcomes. That sounds exactly like what Operators are in the business of producing.

Chapter Takeaways

1 **Involve users and stakeholders:** In any operational project, ensure that the end-users and stakeholders have a say in the design and decision-making process. This involvement will lead to ownership, stronger partnerships across your organization, and most importantly, better outcomes.

2 **Ask specific questions:** When seeking feedback, avoid presenting a fully formed plan. Instead, ask specific questions and provide options.

3 **Embrace diversity and inclusion:** Seek input from different roles, geographic locations, departments, experience levels, and time zones.

4 **Seek feedback, not consensus:** Establish clear guiding principles for your projects, and make decisions based on the best ideas.

5 **Communicate decision-making:** After making decisions, circle back to your feedback groups to explain the final choices and why they were made. This transparency builds trust and understanding.

Endnotes

1 L. Shapiro (2004) *Something from the Oven: Reinventing Dinner in 1950s America*, Viking, New York

2 *Operations* with Sean Lane (2022) The Genesis of Drift's Sales Lab, with Kyle Bastien, Episode 85 [podcast]

17

Designing Your Processes with the End User in Mind

Once, when Sean first accepted a new job, a colleague invited him to a team outing at a bar before his first day. At first he was a little nervous to meet his new teammates, but Sean went anyway because he thought it'd be a good opportunity to get to know people ahead of his start date. When he arrived and was being introduced around as the new "Sales Ops guy," one of the reps jumped forward and hugged him. "We need you so much," he said.

Sean laughed, and also took a mental note that he probably had his work cut out for him.

In Operations, we have to think about the experience of both our internal customers (our colleagues) and our external customers (our company's actual customers). We covered the importance of a frictionless customer journey for both of these groups in Chapter 5, but this chapter is all about those internal customers and the professional environment we design for them.

Maybe you haven't literally been embraced by one of your end users expressing their gratitude for your existence, but if you haven't, you should be. As Operators, we have to take our role seriously as the ones responsible for crafting the end user experience for all of our internal customers.

Understanding Your End Users

In Chapter 1, we posited that if your company is the product, your Operations teammates are the product managers of that product. By extension, all of your colleagues are your users. As you approach the problems that you're solving every day in your business, every solution you propose should keep those end users in mind. How will a change impact their DITL? Will it add friction? What type of enablement is required for even the smallest of changes?

The most important first step toward designing with your end users in mind is developing a comprehensive understanding of those users. What do they care about? What motivates them? How do they spend their time today? What's painful for them?

To develop this understanding, you need to spend time with them. Operators are frequently designing systems and processes in spreadsheets and in the admin views of their powerful tools, without investing in the first-party research to actually understand what the system or process will mean for the end user. Get out from behind your spreadsheets! As we called out in Chapter 3, there is no better substitute than to sit, literally or virtually, with your internal customers to see how they do their job.

Michelle Pietsch, a Founding Partner at BeaconGTM and a former Sales Executive at Datadog and Drift, says that this approach applies for all go-to-market leaders, not just Ops:

> I've learned that it's best to get on the reps' level before putting out a process or dictating something that they're supposed to do. You have to understand what their day is like and what's getting in their way. I've rolled out a process before and just expected it to work, but it doesn't because it may not make sense for the reps' day-in-the-life. I'd host town hall meetings with my team to ask them what's working, what's not, and hear directly from them about the hurdles in their day. Just sit back and listen, and you'll start to hear themes and you figure out what is truly a pain for everyone on the team.[1]

A very common example of an internal process that Operators design is opportunity management. Whether it's for new business or an upgrade or renewal motion, Operators have to design how our internal sales and customer team members manage and ultimately close their opportunities.

This is a chance for you to meticulously craft their experience. First, go through the experience yourself with these questions in mind:

- How many fields are required from opportunity creation to closed won?

- Is every one of those fields necessary?

- What will the rest of the company do with the information we require?

- Does the process we've designed serve either the external customer or other teams within the organization?

- Which of these processes or values might be better completed via systems or automation instead of a human?

- How many clicks does it take to close an opportunity?

After you've designed the process for the first time, inevitably there will be changes to the business or internal people will want you to add or tweak something. It's easy to just say yes to those requests and tack them on to existing workflows. But you'll wake up in six months with Frankenstein processes and systems all over your company. It's important to revisit earlier decisions you made because the context will change, new technologies will become available, and the rationale for your previous decisions (however well executed in the past) will no longer hold up.

You have to ask yourself these questions for every new field, every new workflow, every new piece of information that you or someone at the company wants to capture. When in doubt, consider, "Is this piece of information something that will improve the customer's experience?"

If the answer is no, communicate your reasoning back to the requester and move on.

REAL WORLD ROLE MODELS

In Episode 60 of the *Operations* podcast, Todd Abbott, the former CEO of InsightSquared, talked about the evolution he has seen when it comes to capturing key information from the sales process, and the transition from human-entered values to system-captured ones:

> We've grown up in a world where every sales leader or revenue leader looks at the same things going into a month or quarter, whatever the forecast period is. You know how many reps you have, you know what to expect from each rep, you know what the typical conversion rates have been. What is my funnel based upon those three data points? We spend the first few weeks of a quarter doing a lot of interrogation of reps to be able to validate what's real in that funnel and what's not. It's probably the least stimulating aspect of the engagement for both the rep and the manager, but it goes on in every company.
>
> It's crazy, right? Because that time should be spent on coaching and helping the rep execute; instead, it's an interrogation. Who cares what the funnel coverage is? I want to know what the funnel is going to deliver.
>
> What's fundamentally changing is that we can get reps out of the data entry business and get the rep out of needing to be interrogated by leveraging data to be able to assess the health of a deal. That health comes from how a customer is engaging with your team. If your value prop is resonating, customers will engage, they will respond to emails, they will schedule the next meeting, they will look at your attachment.
>
> But let's stop relying on a rep to tell us what it is in the system. Let's get the data. The "digital footprint" of the sales process is the data that we've never had, because we've relied on what the rep puts into the CRM and reps will give you the least amount possible. They want to be spending time out selling, not updating systems.
>
> The digital footprint of how a customer is engaging through the sales process is what's fundamentally changed in this game. And if you can get that data into your system, and have it on a deal-by-deal basis, then you can combine all that data and tell you the health of your funnel to give you a predictive forecast.
>
> It's also now a much more enriching, engaging discussion that's helping a rep execute. Your best reps will say, "Wow, this is really good because I'm actually getting insights now about benchmarking every one of my deals relative to this activity profile. So I'm actually managing my territory and

engagements much more effectively." And your lesser performing reps can't hide. They're going to get the coaching they need earlier.

If I'm a first line manager, that's how I should be coaching. I can validate a high confidence deal in 10 seconds. I don't need the 5 or 10 minutes to interrogate a rep. It's done.[2]

Scalability and Documentation

Once you've determined what your end users need to do their job and crafted an experience tailored to them, it's time to think about two more important ingredients in the end user experience: Scalability and documentation.

Scalability is tough in a fast-growing company. You have to look around corners and anticipate where processes are going to break and what new challenges might arise. But your end users don't care about that added complexity; they just want the outcome they're looking for as painlessly as possible.

Zubin Teherani, co-founder and COO of Leagueside, recognized that it wasn't enough for his Operations team to just solve problems. They needed to think through every step of the process. He explained:

> A realization for us is that Operations might be solving problems, but you have to do all these steps to make it work perfectly right, and it's really hard for our internal users to follow all those steps.

> So we started reimagining the UI/UX of Operations internally. We were defining within the interface of a salesperson the one action or maybe even no action that a salesperson should do. And then all this magic happens behind the scenes, and the salesperson just gets the output that they're expecting and they want. Meanwhile, Operations handles all the plumbing behind the scenes. As we scaled those systems, we thought a lot about how to avoid institutional knowledge in a way where you could just press a button, and then magic happens.[3]

One way to ensure that magic is understood and continues to work is through documentation. Yes, documentation. It's not sexy, it's not flashy, but it's required.

On an episode of the *Operations* podcast, Crissy Vetere-Saunders, CEO of CS2, made the case for documentation:

> Documentation is key and there are different types of documentation. There's operational documentation, or how something is set up. Then there's internal user-facing documentation. For example, what's going to be documentation that your SDR team can look at to do their job? It's important to keep them up-to-date and to figure out which format is best for your end users. Be creative, build it into people's workflow and their process. Ops. teams are always getting all these questions and I think it really could be deflected if they just had better documentation.[4]

If you design your processes with the end user in mind, make them scalable, and document them—maybe you'll find yourself on the receiving end of an end user's hug, too.

Chapter Takeaways

1 **Prioritize end user experience:** Designing processes requires a deep understanding of internal users, ensuring that every decision considers their needs, motivations, and daily challenges. Operators, and all go-to-market leaders, must invest time with internal customers, observing their tasks firsthand and actively listening to feedback to create tailored experiences.

2 **Emphasize scalability and documentation:** While creating user-centric processes is crucial, it's equally essential to ensure they scale efficiently, anticipating challenges in a growing organization. Additionally, comprehensive documentation, both operational and user-facing, streamlines operations, reduces user questions, and maintains consistency across the board.

3 **Leverage technology and seek opportunities for continuous improvement:** Adopt technology to gather data-driven insights, reducing manual data entry and providing reps with actionable insights. Regularly revisit and refine processes to accommodate changing contexts, new technologies, and evolving organizational needs, ensuring that solutions remain relevant and effective.

Endnotes

1 *Operations* with Sean Lane (2021) Solving for the Reps' Day in the Life, with Dooly's Michelle Pietsch, Episode 59 [podcast]

2 *Operations* with Sean Lane (2021) Get Reps Out of the Data Entry Business, with InsightSquared CEO Todd Abbott, Episode 60 [podcast]

3 *Operations* with Sean Lane (2022) Make Operations your Start-up's Incubator, with LeagueSide's Zubin Teherani, Episode 78 [podcast]

4 *Operations* with Sean Lane (2021) Inside a Consultant's Operations Framework, with CS2's Crissy Vetere-Saunders, Episode 69 [podcast]

18

Blurred Lines: Where Does Training and Enablement Fit With a Revenue Operations Team?

Operators are in the business of selling. We have to make things happen that otherwise wouldn't—the very definition of selling. The difference is we sell to internal customers; we sell processes, applications, policies, methodologies, and compensation plans every day.

Laura had an experience a number of years ago after a sales methodology class. She and the sales managers were discussing the topics covered that day in class—asking open-ended and probing questions, and using active listening with paraphrasing. One of the managers, a peer, looked at her and said, "You've been using that technique with me since you met me." And her immediate answer was, "Yes. Yes, I have. It's effective, isn't it?"

Potential Organizational Structures

It's easy to think that Revenue Operations should leave the selling to the salespeople, but we believe that Revenue Operators need to be skilled in selling, at least to internal audiences. This doesn't necessarily mean you must have the training and enablement function within the Revenue Operations structure. That will depend on your organization, the people you have, and the experience of the leaders in different functions.

But dismissing Operators as potential teachers and enablers for customer-facing roles is a mistake. You have the business context, customer exposure, and unique blend of skill sets required to play a critical role in enabling your internal customers.

Here are the different flavors of organizational design that we have seen work:

- Enablement sits under Revenue Operations.
- Enablement reports to the CRO as a peer and critical partner of Revenue Operations.
- Enablement is specialized and sits under each function, e.g. customer success, sales, services.
- Enablement sits under Revenue Operations or the CRO and partners with the HR's training organization to execute specific programs such as onboarding new hires.

There is one additional flavor we have seen, but not seen work well, and that is enablement reporting directly to HR/talent. This model does not have enough specialization or depth of expertise on what it takes to yield higher revenue productivity, which needs to be the ultimate focus of any enablement program.

REAL WORLD ROLE MODELS

Carlos Nouche is a Vice President of Visualize, Inc. and the CEO and founder of Coaching for Success Inc. Carlos shares some of the experiences he has had with enablement functions as part of his work with clients in Episode 122 of the *Operations* podcast:

> The reality is when we think about enablement, if you just purely think of it as a function, you kind of get trapped in some spots. But if you really think about the people you have and what you're trying to do, there's multiple places in an organization that it could work.
>
> The key thing is alignment.
>
> I don't think it should be part of HR as a training function. I hate it when enablement is trying to go through the motions of, *"We did this program, we don't really care if it was successful or not, but we got all fives. People loved it,*

they did nothing with it, but hey, we did our job." That is the last thing I want it to be; that's what I think is the kiss of death.

All you want is for enablement to work in alignment with the rest of the organization. So if that's your focus, it could be under Operations or under sales or under your CRO, if they have enough time to focus on it. But I think the bigger thing is, what are they getting paid to do? And this is where their alignment should be about driving revenue success, not about "training people."

There's not a single person out there who says, "Man, I can't wait to go to sales training." But what they do want to do is to get better at their function. They want to get better at connecting with their buyers and their existing customers to deliver a value outcome.

I really want to change the mindset. I don't want to be in the "selling people" business. I want to be creating a revenue engine where we help people solve really complex problems and create customers for a lifetime.[1]

Enablement Requires Partnerships

Whichever flavor of organizational structure you have, it requires enablement (and Operations) to foster partnerships throughout the entire company to be effective. This chapter's title starts with "blurred lines" because effective enablement programs need input from many organizations. Some include:

- **Specific field organization:** What knowledge is required to be productive? If you are in services, how soon can you be a billable resource? If you are in sales, what do you need to know to execute your first sale? If you are an SDR, what do you need to know how to do to start prospecting?

- **Training:** How do you design programs for adult learners? How do you train participants to be able to find information later when they need to use it? What material is effective live, what is best recorded, what can wait for just-in-time learning within the day-to-day activities?

- **Product:** How do you provide the multiple layers of understanding of the product from beginner to expert, depending on what that learner needs to be productive in their job? Support personnel will need to have more detail than SDRs. Service implementers will need expertise that sellers will not.

- **Marketing:** How to communicate what is differentiated? How to describe the ideal customer profile and why that profile is ideal for your product or service? What language does everyone use to be consistent with the company's messaging and value proposition?

- **Operations:** What are the systems, processes, and policies that each role needs to be effective? How do you embed this information for easy access within each role's day-to-day activities and embed it within the systems and workflows? What are the strategic goals of the organization that need to be embedded within enablement programs? How can Operations use the operating rhythms of the business to perform enablement, reinforce enablement, and inspect adherence?

REAL WORLD ROLE MODELS

Marcela Piñeros, Global Head of Sales Enablement at Stripe, was so full of great tips and suggestions, we had to pick just the highlights from Episode 77 of the *Operations* podcast, "Shifting the Finish Line of Sales Enablement with Stripe's Marcela Piñeros":

Leverage your subject matter experts in the company:
The reality is that you can never have the very latest information if the enablement team is responsible to be subject matter experts. Trying to be the only content creators just sets you up for this endless treadmill of demand. Our job, instead of creating all the content, is to be really savvy about who's who in the organization, who can we go to and do a 30-minute interview, get a recording that we then chop up into a masterclass that people can consume. That is how to be very quick to be able to go to market.

Shift the finish line:
My team is significantly focused on what we call shifting the finish line. It's looking beyond that moment in time to what happens afterwards. What happens after someone is aware of something? What is it that you need to do to ensure that then transfers to their day-to-day and the last mile actually results in the changes that you want to see?

A new way to onboard:
With our program, what happens is that when you join our go-to-market organization, you need to do 20 customer ride-alongs in your first 30 days. From the onset, you're going to be observing what is happening in the wild. We give you the resources so that when you have a question, you have a place to go to get answers. At the end of the ride-along, you have to fill out a form to answer:

1 What was the most surprising thing I saw?

2 What is the most confusing thing I saw?

3 Where will I go to get more information?

The most surprising thing is actually just helping them reflect quickly on everything that they just witnessed, and that reflection helps retain the information. The most confusing thing is actually a data point for us, because if we have a lot of new hires highlighting the fact that there's something that's very confusing, common among all of them, that's an indicator that it is a good place for intervention. And the question on where they're going to go to get more information, sometimes they respond with things that we didn't even know existed, repositories that have happened organically across the organization. So it becomes a great data point for us to be able to source, where is knowledge being shared?

That's the big shift. Instead of having people sitting, observing, and trying to consume content at an incredibly hectic pace, what we're doing is trying to get them into the field, exposed to reality as soon as possible. The old premise of giving somebody the answers before they're asking the question, doesn't give you the same results.[2]

Key Enablement and Operations Crossover Areas

Regardless of whether enablement exists under Operations, we believe there are some critical best practices for you as an Operator to keep in mind when it comes to enabling the revenue machine.

- Have the leaders of Operations attend any methodology training. You will need to understand it well enough to incorporate it into any systems, routines, and processes you run for the organization. You may even pick up tips on how to better sell internally. Some methodologies have introductory courses that you should consider having your entire team take (go back to Chapter 3 for more on this!).

- Use all opportunities you have in your operating rhythms to reinforce enablement. For example, a common operating rhythm is to have monthly sales all-hands meetings. Enablement should be at least one of the objectives for these expensive meetings. Introduce, reinforce, and re-enable the audiences during these times together.

- Seek out experts to enable. If you aren't an expert on selling, negotiations, or whatever topic needs teaching, source an expert to teach it. Sometimes this can mean you find the stars within the organization who do it best to enable the rest of the team. Sometimes you need to find an outside provider. The Operator provides the process, structure, and connection to the strategic needs of the organization.

- Put enablement within the systems you manage. Place information inside the day-to-day activities that your internal customers perform. When you roll out a new system, train the users as they will use it and preferably use your pilot team to assist in the fielding of questions.

Both enablement and Operations are roles in service to others. People who are best at both roles seek out solutions that are best for their customers, and then relentlessly pursue those solutions on their behalf. There's no one-size fits all org structure that we could recommend to work for every company, but if you are constantly striving for alignment and outcomes, you can't go wrong and those lines will get a little less blurry.

Chapter Takeaways

1 **Alignment over function:** Emphasize alignment with the overall organizational goals, particularly driving revenue success. Avoid isolating enablement as a standalone training function within HR. Instead, integrate it with Operations, sales, or the CRO to ensure a focus on creating a revenue engine rather than just providing training programs.

2 **Cultivate partnerships for effective enablement:** Regardless of the organizational structure, foster partnerships across the entire company for effective enablement. Collaborate with different departments like individual field organizations, training, product, marketing, and Operations to tailor enablement programs to specific roles and ensure alignment with organizational goals.

3 **Integrate enablement into operational rhythms and systems:** Integrate enablement into regular operating rhythms, such as monthly sales all-hands meetings, to introduce, reinforce, and re-enable teams. Embed enablement information within the systems and day-to-day activities managed by Operations, ensuring accessibility and relevance for internal customers.

4 **Leverage subject matter experts and shift the finish line:** Tap into subject matter experts within the organization for content creation instead of attempting to be the sole creators. Focus on "shifting the finish line" by considering the long-term impact of enablement beyond initial awareness, ensuring that knowledge transfers to day-to-day activities and leads to desired changes.

Endnotes

1 *Operations* with Sean Lane (2024) Should Enablement Report to RevOps, with Visualize's Carlos Nouche, Episode 122 [podcast]
2 *Operations* with Sean Lane (2022) Shifting the Finish Line of Sales Enablement, with Stripe's Marcela Piñeros, Episode 77 [podcast]

PART FOUR

Build Your Team

19

Staffing Your Team: What Makes a Good Revenue Operator?

Have you ever found yourself in a store analyzing and optimizing the workflows and processes? Maybe even getting a little mad? We would not be surprised if you said yes.

Laura found herself in a pour-over gourmet coffee shop a few years ago with a group of SDRs and Operations analysts. Laura nearly crawled out of her skin standing in line while the group ordered one-by-one. A barista greeted each person in line, took their order, and proceeded to make their order, eventually meeting them at the cash register and taking payment. It sounds great. One continuous customer experience with an expert who is helping you from start to finish.

Except it wasn't continuous. Each kind of order took different lengths of time to complete and since the store was busy, a barista would start another order while previous customers were waiting for theirs to complete. Customers lost sight of who their barista was while they milled around clogging the order line. Payment was slow because baristas kept having to interrupt their workflows of making drinks to struggle with the register and customers couldn't pay until their order was ready. No numbers were used and no names were taken; so, the order type was shouted out when it was ready. Chaos. Utter operational chaos.

After exiting from the shop, Laura interviewed the group she had brought to see what everyone noticed. The Operators in the group had noticed the things she did too. The non-Operators had been (blissfully) unaware. In this chapter, we will talk about how you find the best Operators, without having to take a field trip to your local coffee shop.

The Three Core Traits of Successful Revenue Operators

Let's revisit our definition from the Introduction to remind us of the mindset that we are looking for in staffing a world-class Operations function.

The Revenue Operations Mindset means:

- Operators are **strategic** partners, not a support function.

- Operators focus on **outcomes**, not inputs.

- Operators are the perfect blend of **strategic** and **tactical**.

- Operators are **lifelong learners** and not afraid to be proven wrong.

- Operators champion their work and are proud of the **impact** they create.

- Operators believe in constant, incremental **improvements** and a "better, better, never done" approach.

In the past, Sean asked his Ops. team to brainstorm a list of traits to describe the kind of team they aspired to be, what they saw in each other, and how they wanted others to see the team. The results, shown in Figure 19.1, echo what would become the Revenue Operations Mindset and highlight some key themes.

You could expand the team's list to hundreds of traits, but we believe you can distill any list down to three core traits of the most successful Operators.

FIGURE 19.1 Operator traits

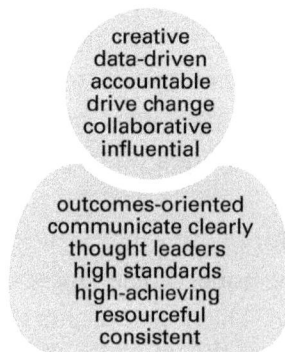

creative
data-driven
accountable
drive change
collaborative
influential

outcomes-oriented
communicate clearly
thought leaders
high standards
high-achieving
resourceful
consistent

1 **Pick a North star**
We highlighted the importance of a team North star in Chapter 14. Whether you run an Operations team or you are the most junior member of the team, this North star is what the team can point to and say: This is why we exist. When things get hectic, or you have to make a tough call, that North star is what your team can use to rally around and it serves as a touchstone for what's most important.

2 **Be adaptively excellent**
Being adaptively excellent means that when you're dropped into any brand-new situation, instead of being overwhelmed or frozen by that situation, you're able to look around, use your previous experiences in the context of that situation to make smart decisions, and ultimately thrive in that situation. That's really what Operators do so well.

Adaptive excellence is not the same as improvisation. In an interview, if someone says "I'm quick on my feet," that really just means, "I'm good at bullsh*!!ing." If someone says, "I'm adaptively excellent," that means "I know my stuff!" And that distinction in an Operator makes all the difference.

3 **Solve problems**
The best Operators solve problems. They seek them out, they identify them, and they make things better. And believe it or not, there are ways to practice building this muscle. The first is to practice extreme ownership. Take ownership of the problems you see around you. Not all of them might be your fault, but as a leader, as an Operator, they're your problem. They're your responsibility. So go fix them. The second way is that you want to be the person who wants to solve the problem, not the one who passes the buck or waits for somebody else to figure it out. Find people like this, surround yourself with them, and be one yourself.

How to Interview to Find Excellent Operators

Now that we know what to look for in Operators, how do we connect this in job interviews? Start by creating excellent job descriptions. Resist the urge to copy and paste from the last time you hired or whatever ChatGPT spits out. In Chapter 20, we will talk about different organizational structures for Operations teams. This will provide clarity on what capabilities you need to hire for and how to split up the work.

To write your job description, go and find at least 10 similar job descriptions for the role you want to hire. Leverage those examples for the core components of the role and then customize your own job description for your company's needs. This will also provide you with excellent market intelligence on what your potential hires are reviewing and reading. Job descriptions are marketing messages; treat them as such.

Then, design your interview team around key themes and provide each interviewer with a focus area that is connected to the job description. At a minimum, have someone on your interview team interview for technical skills, functional skills/experience, team fit/culture, and internal customer/stakeholder relationships. The best interview panels also include an internal customer/stakeholder who will interact with the new hire.

You may even want to seed some interview questions for your interview panel participants. Ask interview questions about the impact of their prior work, how they have solved problems working with stakeholders, how they handle conflict with internal customers, and how they learn new things. You also want to ask them about projects that have failed and what they would do differently given a second chance. This will help you measure not only their coachability, but also self-reflection.

Dig into the details that are critical for success in the role. For example, if someone needs to be really good at using spreadsheets, ensure an interviewer is really diving deep into that skillset. Instead of asking someone to rate their level of expertise in spreadsheets, ask them what their favorite formula is. We have both administered a spreadsheets skills test for analyst roles. One technique Laura has used is to administer a 15 to 20 minute test while she is in the room. This allows you to see if they ask questions or clarify what is wanted. One of her favorite questions an interviewee asked was, "The test asks to summarize quarterly numbers, can you confirm which quarter system you are on—calendar or an alternative fiscal?" It was the epitome of demonstrating adaptive excellence.

Onboarding After You Hire

Set your new hire up for success by creating an onboarding plan. We recommend that each of your new hires have a 30—60—90-day onboarding plan created for them before they start. Start with their job description and work through what information, systems, and people they will need to be successful. By asking how your interviewee learns up front, you can design an onboarding plan that matches their learning style—be it reading, listening, or doing. Set expectations for what you want them to be able to do independently at each of the monthly milestones. This becomes a living document that you'll use in 1-on-1s to ramp your new hires into the team.

REAL WORLD ROLE MODELS

Anu Krishnakumar is the SVP of Global Sales Operations, Enablement, and Development at SmartBear. In Episode 80 of the *Operations* podcast, Anu breaks down the lifecycle of an Operations hire.

Anu's key insights on hiring and ramping Operators include:

- Clearly define the role you want. Think about what problems you're trying to solve. Decide what kind of person you want. Are you looking for someone who would manage your Salesforce? That's an entirely different hire than a sales Ops person who's going to be a strategic part of your organization.

- Look for someone who has an entrepreneurial mindset, is a problem solver, and can be the strategic partner to your internal stakeholders.

- With each incremental hire you make, you have the opportunity to remove some of the less sexy day-to-day mundane tasks from your existing team.

- In a Revenue Ops. organization, ramp time is especially complicated because it's not just someone learning how to do the job. They actually have to learn so much organizational knowledge. Two to three months is where you're basically feeling your way through the dark, six months to kind of know what you're doing, and a full year to be a needle-moving, contributing member of the team.[1]

Diversity in Your Operations Team

In Chapter 16, we spoke about the importance of seeking input from diverse groups throughout your organization to achieve better outcomes. As you form your Operations team, not everyone should be the same kind of Operator. Yes, we believe there are some core traits of Operators, but you also need to bring together different kinds of strengths to form a well-rounded team. As you look for your incremental hires, take stock of the strengths you have in your current team and what strengths could level up your organization.

There are a number of different methodologies you can use to evaluate the styles and aptitudes you have on your team. One of our favorites is the nine Belbin Team Roles®. Glenn M. Parker, DISC®, Myers-Briggs®, and Enneagram are sometimes also used to help understand team members, create empathy, and foster a collaborative environment that leverages the strengths of the group.

As you mature as a Revenue Operations function, you need to think about matching the skillsets of your team with the maturity of your company and you need to supplement the strengths of your existing team members (including your own) with new ones. Early-stage companies, for example, need a lot of creative problem solvers who can handle lack of structure and thrive in autonomous work environments. As companies mature, they need to add Operators who thrive in more structured, specialized settings, and are good at crossing the t's and dotting the i's. Certain roles will also have more natural fits—for example, you want a commissions analyst to be detail-oriented and love process, while you want teammates who work in deal desk to have a rapid response customer service mindset.

Continuous Development of Your Team

Operators are lifelong learners. In Chapter 21, we will review different management philosophies well-suited to leading Revenue Operations, but here we want to emphasize the development of the staff you already have.

It's easy for Operators to feel pigeon-holed in a role that is too specialized. Structuring your team as a comprehensive Revenue Operations group tasked with the entire customer journey is a great way to combat that feeling.

It's not enough, though, to just structure your team in a way that optimizes for growth. You have to facilitate that growth. One exercise to prompt meaningful conversations about an individual's growth is to encourage some self-reflection by each member of your team.

In the RevOps Areas of Focus box, you can see the areas of focus we've used with our teams to outline all of the different disciplines within Revenue Operations. Each individual is responsible for color-coding the areas where their preferences, skills, and desires to learn are. This inventory not only helped us identify development areas for each member of the team, but it also gave us a good idea of which skills were missing in our organization and where we might need to seek external hires. We asked our teams to refresh their lists bi-annually and then regularly referenced those focus areas to seek out relevant projects for each person within our broader RevOps goals.

REVOPS AREAS OF FOCUS

Mark each area of interest:

A   I like doing this type of work, and I think I'm good at it

B   I do not like doing this type of work, but I think I'm good at it

C   I like doing this type of work, and I want to get more exposure/learn more/get better at it

D   I don't like this type of work, and I don't have any interest in it

E   I don't know if I like this type of work; I want to learn more

1   Metrics, reporting, insights, and analytics

   1.1. Regular reporting: Mechanisms, metrics, frequency, and audiences

   1.2. S.F.D.C. (CRM) dashboards: Ownership and maintenance

   1.3. Analytical tools: Business intelligence, access, training, ownership, and approvals

   1.4. Ad hoc reporting: Ownership, process, and review

   1.5. Pricing analytics

   1.6. Analytics, summaries, and recommended actions

2   Tech stack infrastructure

   2.1. Roadmap: Ownership and record of roadmap plan

   2.2. Funding/approvals

   2.3. Requirements

   2.4. Design

   2.5. Testing

   2.6. Approvals for changes/change control

   2.7. Execution of changes into production

   2.8. Notifications to users

   2.9. Training for managers and users

   2.10. User access controls and approvals

3 Compensation and incentives

    3.1. Plan design

    3.2. Plan documentation

    3.3. Plan approval

    3.4. Calculation

    3.5. Review and approval for calcs

    3.6. Training for managers and users

    3.7. Sales performance incentive fund (SPIF)/short-term incentives design

4 Capacity planning

    4.1. Annual operating plan that links with finance's overall top line plan

    4.2. Regular updates (frequency) for sales/customer success/services capacity and monitoring against expectations

    4.3. Hiring plan: Ownership, monitoring, and regular updates

    4.4. Annual process to evaluate what will be required/modeling options/cost target modeling/assumption changes

    4.5. Mid-year changes/updates to the plan

5 Territory/book of business planning

    5.1. Strategy for segmentation

    5.2. Discussion with sales/customer success leadership

    5.3. Account/customer health scoring methodology

    5.4. Account procurement, enrichment, and scoring execution

    5.5. Modeling proposals and visualization of territories

    5.6. Approvals for territories

6 Training and enablement

    6.1. Strategy for training plan for the year

    6.2. New hire/bootcamp

    6.3. Training event content development

    6.4. Sales/customer success/services methodology: Training, reinforcement activities, built into cadence

6.5. Application training

6.6. Process/procedure (e.g. order form) training

6.7. Bid support

6.8. Templates for request for proposals

7   GTM execution, team management, and cadences

7.1. Forecast

7.1.1. Process: Owners, frequency, deadlines, reporting, tools/data

7.1.2. Meetings: Frequency, attendees, topics, tools/data

7.2. Quarterly business review (QBR): Frequency, attendees, topics, tools/data

7.2.1. Facilitation

7.2.2. Data prep

7.2.3. Blending with other training/events/speakers

7.3. Day-in-the-life (DITL) design and supporting processes

7.4. Win/loss reviews

7.5. Deal reviews: Either pricing, go/no go, and/or deal strategy

7.6. Product interlock meetings

7.7. Objective and key results (OKR) meetings/monthly metrics/ quarterly metrics

7.8. Cross-functional interlock meetings

8   Communication strategies and structures

8.1. Intranet/wiki: Ownership, content, maintenance, usage

8.2. All-hands meetings

8.3. Team meetings: Ownership, content, frequency, data

8.4. Communication of goals, leaderboards, win stories: Medium, frequency, audience, authors

8.5. Policies: Bookings guide, account rules of engagement, discounting authority

8.6. Pricing: Ownership/philosophy, discounting authorities between departments, execution of system controls, deal desk structure, financial control verifications

9 Organizational structures and hiring practices

9.1. Strategic ratios: Presales/solution consultants, customer success, account managers, sales development representatives (SDRs), Ops., etc.

9.2. Ratios for Individual Contributor (IC) to Manager

9.3. Hiring practices: Interview structures, presentations, panels, profiles

9.4. Personnel review processes and whether Ops. is involved

9.5. Ops. support structures and coverage of Ops. org.

Sylvia Kainz, the former RevOps leader from Airbnb and Eventbrite, knew that designing her teams with skill-developing growth opportunities in mind was critical to the team's success. She explained:

> The last thing Operators want is to be pigeonholed. They're actually people who like working across the organization. They thrive on that. They like talking to business owners and translating requirements to the technical team. They like to go broad instead of necessarily deep.
>
> And what's really important is that you don't keep them in a typical marketing ops. function if they don't want to be. Part of their career development is to say, "You've done marketing ops. and marketing project management for almost a year. Let's expand your scope." They get super excited about that. They learn.
>
> They're the type of employee who likes to learn, who likes to stretch their mind, they love to better understand the organization and how all those pieces are fitting together. And if you get that right mindset, you can get an awesome team.[2]

How can you read that description and not want to go surround yourself with people like that?

Chapter Takeaways

1 Cultivate the Revenue Operations Mindset: Great Operators seek a North star, are adaptively excellent, and solve problems.

2 **Recruit excellent Operators:** Craft well-defined job descriptions. Build interview panels with a clear focus on key areas such as technical, functional, cultural fit, and relationship skills.

3 **Onboard new hires effectively:** Create personalized 30-60-90-day onboarding plans based on job descriptions and the new hire's learning style.

4 **Seek diversity in your Operations team:** While there are core traits of Operators, seek diversity in strengths and skills within your team. Consider using methodologies like the nine Belbin Team Roles® to evaluate and enhance team dynamics.

5 **Continuous learning and development:** Regularly assess interest and seek to update the skills of your Operators to ensure they remain effective and adaptable in their roles.

Endnotes

1 *Operations* with Sean Lane (2022) The Lifecycle of an Operations Hire, with SmartBear's Anu Krishnakumar, Episode 80 [podcast]
2 *Operations* with Sean Lane (2019) How to Build a RevOps Team from Scratch, with Eventbrite's Sylvia Kainz, Episode 9 [podcast]

20

Choosing the Right Organizational Structure

Operations executive Molly Graham is one of our favorite writers (go Google some of her stuff if you've never read anything by her). In one of her posts, Molly writes about coming across new words and acronyms in your job:

> When you first start out, you feel stupid for not knowing what the word means, so you look it up after the meeting... It ALWAYS turns out that each word has about 10 definitions and no one agrees on what it actually means. In every industry.
>
> Welcome to "black hole words."
>
> To me, these are words that are commonplace in a given industry but everyone has a slightly different definition of them. You can have a whole meeting and if you don't define the word, you just wasted an hour of everyone's time. They suck all the meaning and consensus out of a room, out of a business and out of a company.[1]

Molly cites examples like "culture," "strategy," "growth," and "performance reviews" as black hole words. "Revenue Operations" definitely fits the bill for these black hole words.

In the Introduction, we offered our own definition.

Revenue Operations transforms siloed, unpredictable businesses into high-achieving, predictable, and scalable revenue machines.

We also wrote:

> Just choosing to invest in RevOps is like signing up for a marathon, but never putting on a pair of running shoes.
>
> Choosing to invest in RevOps is not the finish line—it's the beginning.
> You have to commit to running your business in a specific way.
> Otherwise, all you've done is commit to a diagram of an org chart.

So what is the "right" version of that org chart? How should you best design the Revenue Operations function at your company to fulfill our definition and all of the responsibilities we've described in this book?

A lot has been written about the different types of team models and reporting structures in Operations. Understandably, people want to find the "perfect" model that unlocks all of the benefits we've promised this team can deliver. While we agree that it's critically important to be thoughtful and deliberate about how you design your team, we've been part of enough organizations and lived through enough team models ourselves to know that there isn't one perfect answer for every company at every stage of maturity. How you set up your team, how you specialize within that team, who you report to, and what you're ultimately responsible for are often fluid in the multi-year evolution of a RevOps team.

And let's be honest: In the real world, you don't always have a choice. You might get hired into a team where the structure is already set up, or you might be too junior to be able to make these types of decisions just yet in your career. So, whether you're a first-time member of a RevOps team, feeling out how to contribute, or you're a VP setting up your organizational structure from scratch, there are some core principles around which you can build your team.

In this chapter, we'll explore the merits and shortcomings of two different models, and offer some consistent truths we believe should exist within your team regardless of your org structure.

The Centralized Model (a.k.a. "The Hub and Spoke Model")

The first model—and perhaps the one people think of most commonly when talking about a consolidated Revenue Operations function—is the centralized model, a.k.a. "the hub and spoke."

FIGURE 20.1 The centralized model

In this model, the RevOps group (the hub) serves as a centralized resource to a number of different internal partners like sales, marketing, and customer success (the spokes). This model has become increasingly popular largely because it lives up to many of the aspirational outcomes from this book.

The centralized model (Figure 20.1) breaks down silos in your company, with RevOps serving as the source of truth (particularly when it comes to things like systems and reporting), and this consolidated group has a unique, comprehensive view of the entire customer journey, not just a portion of it.

A centralized group might report to a CFO or a CRO if that CRO is responsible for all of revenue, not just sales. Being together on the same team as all of your Operations peers has its benefits, too. You can share learnings, more naturally uncover potential dependencies and pitfalls, and beg, borrow, and steal from what's working in each other's areas of expertise. Not only that, but you create an expectation of operational excellence that can permeate through the organization. In our experience, the earlier you implement the centralized model in a business, the better. This embeds systems-first and data-driven thinking in the DNA of a company for years to come.

But that doesn't mean this model is perfect.

TABLE 20.1 Pros and cons of the centralized model

Pros (+)	Cons (−)
(+) Break down silos between different go-to-market teams	(−) No dedicated resource(s) for each individual function
(+) Single source of truth for all reporting and analytics	(−) Not all internal customers are treated equally
(+) Unique, comprehensive point of view of entire customer journey	(−) Ops. may be overwhelmed and become a bottleneck for the company
(+) Natural sharing of cross-functional learnings and dependencies	(−) Potential for less expertise in specific focus areas

When you have one team serving and partnering with a variety of internal customers, it's inevitable that one internal customer is going to get more support than the others. And as we explored in Chapter 15, this is usually sales. Not having dedicated resources for each go-to-market function can lead to a misalignment of resources or, even worse, Operations can end up becoming a bottleneck, slowing down the entire company.

Also, when you have a centralized team, you run the risk of lacking true functional expertise. If your hub and spoke model leads to a team with knowledge that is a mile wide and an inch deep, that team probably isn't going to be adding a lot of value to those C-level routines and operating rhythms from Chapter 4.

While we're very supportive of the centralized model, it's important to be aware of its shortcomings and put specific measures in place to mitigate those shortcomings (Table 20.1).

The Decentralized Model (a.k.a. "The Function Model")

The second model—and one of the most common alternatives to the hub and spoke approach—is the decentralized model, or "the function model." As you might expect, the function model is where specific Operations teams like sales ops. or marketing ops. are aligned to and report directly into their corresponding function. Instead of having a

FIGURE 20.2   The decentralized model

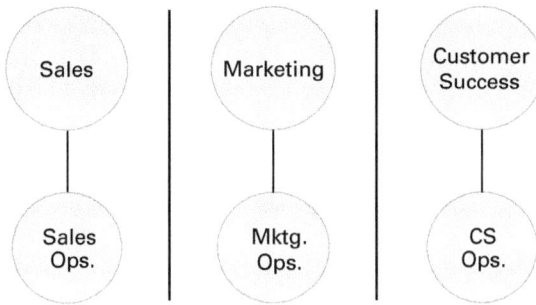

consolidated team acting as your hub, sales ops. reports into sales, marketing ops. into marketing, CS ops into customer success, and so on (Figure 20.2).

The merits of this model are the inverse of the first. Unlike the hub and spoke model, the function model offers dedicated resources for each go-to-market function. You can form deeper relationships with your internal customers, offer the domain expertise that might be lacking in a centralized team, and perhaps most importantly for some Operators, feel like a real member of the team you support. Instead of being this separate, Swiss-like neutral party, a marketing ops. teammate feels fully aligned with their marketing counterparts.

On the flip side, you can imagine that the function model is a breeding ground for silos. Misaligned reporting, selfish decision-making, and narrow-minded views on what's happening in the business can all develop within this model if you're not careful.

But if you're a larger organization with complex needs and an Operations group that can never quite get to everything or is struggling to juggle multiple demanding stakeholders, the function model could be just the antidote to inaction that you need.

Over the course of our careers, we've experienced both of these models, and as we've detailed, neither one of them is perfect (you might even end up with some sort of hybrid of the two). What's most important is to intimately understand the pros and cons of each to get the most yield out of the model you're in (Table 20.2).

TABLE 20.2 Pros and cons of the decentralized model

Pros (+)	Cons (−)
(+) Dedicated resource(s) for each individual function	(−) Potential for silos between different go-to-market teams
(+) Clear alignment between an individual GTM function's priorities and Operations	(−) Potential for reporting discrepancies
(+) Less likely misallocation of resources or bottlenecked projects/deliverables	(−) Narrow, fragmented view of the customer journey
(+) Domain expertise in specific focus areas	(−) Less natural communication and sharing of cross-functional learnings and dependencies between Ops. groups

Three Consistent Truths in Designing Your Operations Team

We believe the RevOps function is built slightly differently for every company that is wise enough to form one. Perhaps it's because we are one of the newest functions in the corporate world. Perhaps it's because RevOps is where every company puts a little of their secret sauce. Perhaps it's because organizational design is often more influenced by who is in a role than business schools would have you believe.

But more than that, we've come to believe that the diagram of the org chart matters less than the Revenue Operations Mindset you bring to your work and three consistent truths about designing your Operations team.

Truth #1: Put the Customer at the Center of Everything You Do

As we've discussed throughout the book, we have two unique sets of customers—external and internal. Our external customers are our company's customers, and our internal ones are the internal stakeholders we partner with to run our go-to-market motions of our companies. In Ops., we have to pay attention to both.

Regardless of the structure of your team, you have to care about what happens across the entire customer journey, not just the part that you're responsible for. If you are in marketing operations, and you approach your work with blinders on, you're not going to be a very valuable Ops teammate. Instead, consider what the work you're doing will mean for your counterparts in sales Ops. It's easy to only solve the problem directly in front of you; it's harder, yet more outcome-oriented, to consider the ripple effects of your solution. If you take the time to consider your approach and look around corners to anticipate those ripple effects, who you report to on an org chart doesn't matter.

Truth #2: The Type of Work You Do Matters More Than the Model

Regardless of which model you're in, regardless of whether you report into a CRO, CFO., or some special dotted line combination, defining the work you're responsible for and how you'll attack that work is far more important.

Remember that we're here to build high-achieving, predictable, and scalable revenue machines. So, the question is, what is the best way to acquire, retain, and grow that revenue?

If you are following the color-coding exercise we recommended in the previous chapter, you might leverage the macro-categories from our "RevOps areas of focus" to define what your team does and design your org structure to assign that work accordingly:

- Metrics, reporting, insights, and analytics.
- Tech stack infrastructure.
- Compensation and incentives.
- Operating plan and capacity planning.
- Territory/book of business planning.
- GTM execution, team management, and cadences.
- Communication strategies and structures.
- Organizational structures and hiring practices.

When we worked together, we took this exercise a step further and used this type of specialization to organize our team and put in place a structure to support the broader company as well.

FIGURE 20.3 RevOps lifecycle

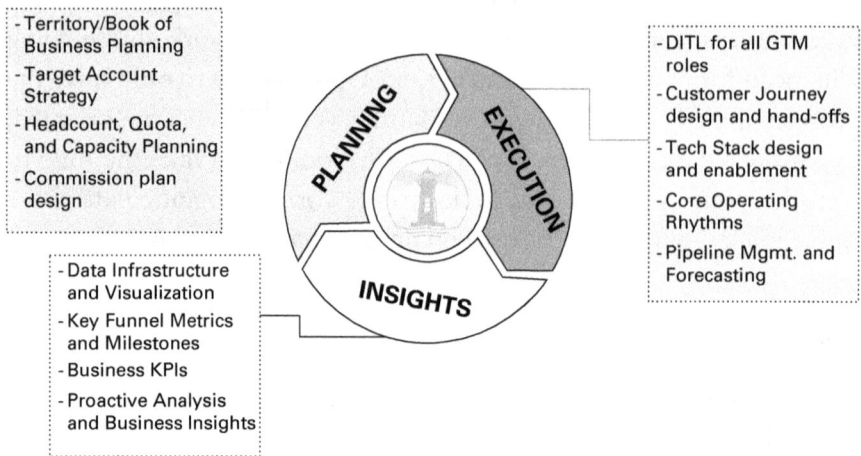

- Territory/Book of
  Business Planning
- Target Account
  Strategy
- Headcount, Quota,
  and Capacity Planning
- Commission plan
  design

- Data Infrastructure
  and Visualization
- Key Funnel Metrics
  and Milestones
- Business KPIs
- Proactive Analysis
  and Business Insights

- DITL for all GTM
  roles
- Customer Journey
  design and hand-offs
- Tech Stack design
  and enablement
- Core Operating
  Rhythms
- Pipeline Mgmt. and
  Forecasting

SOURCE Courtesy of BeaconGTM

Three core functions resulted: Planning, execution, and insights (as detailed in Figure 20.3). Planning referred to everything that happened before our go-to-market counterparts were even in their roles, execution encompassed everything in the DITL of those teammates, and insights was the proactive bridge between the two.

The beauty of this flavor of specialization is that it can be applied to either a centralized or decentralized model. Want to add in professional services ops.? Product ops.? Partner ops.? The "planning, execution, and insights" lifecycle works. With each passing year and new business realities, we stress-tested this model, and each year, it survived the stress test.

The danger here is you take on too much in the stated "work you do." Systems architecture, data engineering, or CRM administration responsibilities are possible areas to carve out for a separate team entirely. While a RevOps group should own anything inside of those DITL workflows, a systems group might more closely align with IT or even engineering.

Max Maeder, CEO of FoundHQ, a platform for hiring pre-vetted Salesforce consultants, feels strongly that RevOps and systems should be separated. He explained on the *Operations* podcast:

> I fundamentally believe that RevOps should not be owning go-to-market tech strategy, and therefore Salesforce strategy. Especially as

companies reach scale, where they have hundreds, if not thousands, of users, they have a dozen systems specialists still reporting into RevOps. Meanwhile, the HR team has started to hire Workday administrators, the Finance team has NetSuite administrators. And it becomes an unbelievably fragmented system strategy, where each individual business unit is charting the course for the tools that they use. I think that that is a poor way to build a scalable enterprise applications infrastructure. If there's one area of RevOps that I see as being a little bit of a runaway train, one that is the easiest to carve out and give to another team, I think it has to be the tech piece.[2]

No matter where you land, name the work your team is going to do and go do it.

REAL WORLD ROLE MODELS

Noah Marks is a serial Operations Executive with a resume that includes Udemy, WalkMe, Okta, and Salesforce. On Episode 123 of the *Operations* podcast, he uniquely articulated how he designs his teams, and the challenges and thrills that come with a broad charter of work within an Operations group:

> Ops. needs to sit with whichever leader owns the strategy and ultimately the overall business. Ops.' role is to provide guidance back to those leaders as to what's going well, what's not going well, what we need to drive, what we want to collectively build out, and then how we get there. Those long-term goals are the things that Ops. needs to be pushing on.
>
> That charter really comes in three parts. One is day-to-day, making sure the business is running. The second is alignment, the ability to align the organization really succinctly to a common point of view and avoid all the drag of misalignment. The third is about scaling.
>
> There are various tiers to scaling. The fundamental tier is around the integrity of the business: Data integrity, system integrity, making sure that you know where you are, before you talk about where you're going to get to. Once you get that built, then you can look at where we are efficient or not efficient. Next, you start building out processes to create repeatability. And if you're repeatable, you can get to predictability, knowing where you're going to be in the future.

Predictability is impressive, but the true nirvana is actually one step above that: Productivity. And for a lot of organizations, this is the one that's the most meaningful for the business. When you look at your teammates, the people in the organization, you have to ask yourself, "How does everybody get better? How does everyone produce more?" But you can only do that once you have those other tiers in place. Then, you're ready to start talking about next quarter, next year, and three years down the road, and you're building an engine that gets there.

That's fundamentally what I feel is my main concern for the business. Get those first two down—the day-to-day execution and the direction alignment—to be able to really focus on scaling to productivity.

That's how you make a truly iconic, long-term success story. That's what drives my passion, building something great. In this role, we're just trying to do whatever is ultimately going to create the best value for the business.[3]

Truth #3: Change is Constant

In RevOps, and in companies as a whole, change is constant. As we mentioned earlier in the chapter, we've worked in a number of different team models and, chances are, we'll find ourselves in a brand new one sometime in the future. If you care more about the model than the work, then you're going to be disappointed and frustrated pretty often. Embrace the reality that things are going to change, and you'll be able to let go of the things that may seem important in the moment, but don't really matter in the long-run.

CONFESSION CORNER

A company I was working at was changing the desk layout on the floor. I was a new manager, and I felt strongly that the new proposed location for my team wasn't the best possible environment for the people on my team.

I felt so strongly about this that I had a one-on-one meeting with our VP of People to voice my concerns and make my objections known in person.

> Looking back now, I'm embarrassed to even recount the exchange. I don't even remember what I was concerned about. I'm guessing the seats probably even changed again within a few months, rendering all of my hand wringing utterly useless.
>
> But this is what happens. Change jars people from their norms, their routines. If you don't learn to expect it and embrace it, the constant shifting will drive your behavior in unexpected (and unproductive) ways.

There's an image (a gif to be more accurate) we often turned to when conveying this point to our teams. It's a pencil spinning on a page, drawing a circle. But the eraser of the pencil follows the same circular path as the tip of the pencil and it immediately erases what was just written down on the paper. It just keeps going round and round, writing and erasing, writing and erasing (see Figure 20.4).

This is a pretty accurate representation of what it feels like to work in Operations, especially in a growing company. Some people love it, some people hate it, but change is the only constant and that truth is not going away.

FIGURE 20.4 Life in RevOps

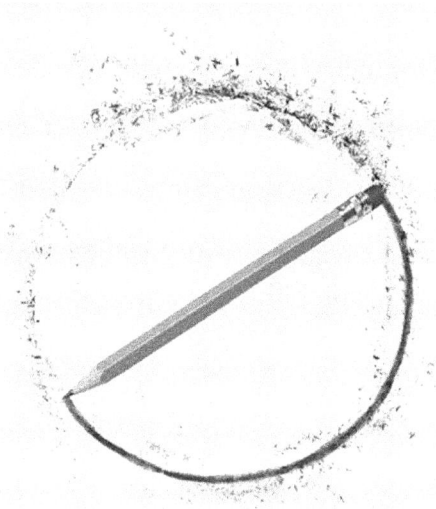

If you bring the Revenue Operations Mindset to your team design and focus on these three truths, neither "RevOps" nor "organizational structure" will be "black hole words" for you or your team.

Chapter Takeaways

1 Avoid black hole words: Provide clear definitions for terms that lack universal definitions within industries and potentially lead to misunderstandings and wasted time in meetings.

2 Centralized vs. decentralized models:

- Centralized model: Known as the "hub and spoke model," it provides a unified, comprehensive view of the entire customer journey but may lead to resource misallocation and potential operational bottlenecks.

- Decentralized model: Also termed the "function model," it aligns specific Operations teams directly with respective functions (e.g. sales ops. with sales) but may lead to silos and sub-optimal company decisions.

3 Core operational principles: Regardless of the organizational structure, there are three consistent truths in RevOps:

- Customer-centric approach: Focus on the entire customer journey, not just individual segments.

- Work definition over model: Prioritize defining the tasks and responsibilities of the team over choosing a specific organizational model.

- Embrace constant change: Recognize that change is inevitable in RevOps and adaptability is crucial for long-term success.

Endnotes

1 Molly Graham. "Black Hole Words" and the power of asking stupid questions [blog] *Lessons*, 26 July 2022, https://mollyg.substack.com/p/black-hole-words-and-the-power-of (archived at https://perma.cc/FQZ2-NA7Y)

2 *Operations* with Sean Lane (2023) Finding the Right Consulting Resources for Your Most Important Projects, with FoundHQ's Max Maeder, Episode 104 [podcast]

3 *Operations* with Sean Lane (2024) The Passion for Building and Scaling Iconic Businesses, with Noah Marks, Episode 123 [podcast]

21

Management Philosophies: It's All About the People, Silly

The Pyramids of Giza. Burj Khalifa. *The Matrix* movies. Queen's 1985 Live Aid performance.

What do all of these things have in common? They all required a lot of individuals to accomplish something that no one individual could ever accomplish alone (we also believe they all required a lot of operational support!).

The achievement of goals together with others is the sweet reward of hard work as a group. To really excel as a group—sustainably—you have to realize that the achievement is only possible with your team, your people, your tribe. That tribe needs leaders who are there to help every member (including themselves) be better. Whether you're in a formal leadership position today, or aspire to be some day, that means you need to be thoughtful about the kind of leader you want to be. We've compiled a list of management guiding principles for Operators like you on that quest to be better.

1 Be human first

2 Be kind and direct

3 Assume good intent and have good intent

4 Be curious and action-oriented

5 Have consistently high expectations

6 Set the vision

Be Human First

Let's face it. Operators deal with a lot of things that require quick responses, are critical needs, and oftentimes, are just plain stressful. Remembering that you, your team, and even your internal and external customers are human first, with all of the grace and imperfection that comes with that, is the heart of this principle. There are many things that can happen outside of the interaction you are having with another party that can affect their (and your) reactions, behaviors, performance, and awareness. Being a leader who embodies this principle allows your team to bring their full selves to work and it promotes psychological safety.

Laura had a team member who loved to say, *"It's not hearts and lungs, people!"* as a way to inject some humor and alleviate the intensity when something in our Operations world didn't go as planned. Now, if you are running an oncology ward, a cardiac unit, or a pulmonary center, please know we didn't write this book for you, and it really is a matter of life or death in your world. The things that aren't a matter of survival can be important, and we can continue to do our best to perform at the highest level, but we can't forget to have that relative sense of perspective.

Be Kind and Direct

This is one of our favorite principles. The two must go together, neither one individually is sufficient for real, sustainable, long-term growth and achievement. Leaders have a responsibility to be both kind and direct.

There are company cultures where directness is prized. We love directness. You know where you stand. You know what people are thinking. You know what the goals are. You know where the minefields are. You know when people are happy, sad, disappointed, or stressed. Directness can take away the mental load of having to guess about all of those things. But directness without kindness just isn't the kind of culture we personally can be in for the long haul.

Prizing directness without the dual requirement of kindness can result in a cut-throat culture, where anything can be said that is direct, without consideration if it is helpful. Kindness considers both whether something is objectively helpful and how you can share something directly so that it will be helpful.

No value or principle should be adopted in a vacuum. When a company/group/department values kindness over everything else, we lose all benefits of directness. Kindness unfettered or unqualified is also a type of culture we personally cannot be in for long. There are too many things that are left unsaid because people worry that they aren't kind. Things get missed; results suffer. Too many young professionals are underdeveloped because their manager didn't give the tough feedback that would make them better out of fear of being unkind.

As a leader, if you can't provide direct feedback to help your team be better, your colleagues plateau, and you both will be limited in what you can achieve. Being kind and direct means thinking about how the recipient can take the feedback to improve the outcomes.

As an Operator, if you aren't direct, your company misses out on the benefits of your holistic perspective. If you aren't kind, you can be dismissed as rigid or judgmental.

Assume Good Intent and Have Good Intent

This principle is a bit of a corollary to "be kind and direct" because it addresses the intentions behind actions. Assuming good intent actually makes processing what happens a bit easier and having good intent checks your own motivations on what and how you put things out into the world. When you receive a critique of something you or your team produced, assuming good intent allows you to search for the learning, the message, potential future improvement based on that critique. It allows you to take criticism without becoming defensive. And in your response to the criticism, having good intent will allow you to be productive and additive to the matter without sounding defensive or striking back.

We've observed founders and CEOs whose superpower is their lack of defensiveness. They embrace any potential improvement someone can find in their business. The feedback could come from a colleague, a junior employee, or a partner; the best founders and CEOs have no sentimental attachment to the way things were or something they personally built. They just want the best possible version of their company to create the best possible outcomes. It's admirable.

This principle can be hard to follow when things are intense and emotions are running high. It takes intention to think before we act, to consider the good intent behind something, and to be deliberate in our actions to demonstrate our good intent. Take this principle to heart when considering your internal relationships with your peers but also for your own long-term stability. Jumping to conclusions about malintent is a fast track to burnout. It can be as simple as considering the best option for delivery of feedback: Is it appropriate for one-on-one or would a group environment be more helpful? What language is used? Can you think of more than one possible reason for an observation? You'll be amazed at how this approach improves every interaction in your day.

Be Curious and Action-Oriented

We believe that one of the key hallmarks of the Operations persona is curiosity. To solve problems, you have to be curious about why they happen. We pair curiosity with action because Operators are, of course, all about the outcomes. Curiosity without action is academic. Action without curiosity is reactive.

Some folks believe Operators need to be truth tellers in the organization. We believe we need to be truth seekers. It's a one-word difference, but it is key to being a good partner to every team within your company. A truth teller can be blunt and narrowly-focused in their explanations. A truth seeker understands there can be more than one reason for what happened in the past and more than one path forward. A truth seeker recognizes that just because something failed the first time doesn't necessarily mean that thing was done well the first time. A truth seeker is direct and kind, curious and action-oriented.

Operators tend to play the role of "fixers"—people send them in when there is a problem to solve. Of course we agree with Operators being driven to action; it's in our make-up. We also believe that whatever the problem, leading with curiosity will get you to the better action. This is true for organizational, system, data, and personnel issues. Being curious about why something has taken place will help you find a better solution.

Have Consistently High Expectations

To power a high-performing revenue machine, you have to develop a high-performing team. People tend to rise to the expectations that you put in place so having high expectations seems to be a natural philosophy. Our addition to this is to be consistent in your high expectations. Consistent means across your team, and for yourself, at different times of year, and in different tasks. This provides clarity for your entire team and creates an environment where people know what to expect.

Something that can happen even in the best teams is to have one member who is not performing well. It is tempting to think that one low performer won't hurt anyone, and that as long as the whole team is performing, it isn't a big deal. It is a big deal. It hurts the rest of your team who don't understand why they should try so hard if someone else doesn't and "gets away with it." It impairs the internal customers of the low-performing individual and damages the reputation of your team. It also hurts the individual because they might not be in the right job. You owe it to them to be curious, kind, and direct about performance.

This doesn't mean that everyone should be the same; they have different roles and are at different levels. We recommend creating competency models to outline what is expected at each level in different skill areas. This allows you to be consistent and to be explicit

TABLE 21.1 Operations competency model excerpt

COMPETENCY/LEVEL	L.1	L.2
CULTURE	Contribute positively to the overall environment by working hard and consistently having a good attitude.	Contribute positively to the overall environment by helping to build and maintain relationships with other divisions.
EXECUTION	Execute clearly defined tasks that come your way. You are detail-oriented, know when to ask questions, and you produce dependable analysis with little or no defects.	Move from one-step work to multiple-step deliverables effectively. Not only know how to use but also manipulate key systems throughout our stack.
COMMUNICATION	Consistently share your work and progress with your manager and the Ops. team on your assigned tasks.	Consistently share your work and progress with your manager and the Ops. team so that people know what you are working on and the status of key projects. Proactively offer feedback to identify areas for improvement throughout the team.
DEVELOPMENT	Work with your manager to come up with your development areas and then you both hold yourself accountable to those development goals.	Set some of your development goals, proactively seek feedback on those goals, and hold yourself accountable to those along with your manager.
AUTONOMY	Rely on others to give you the next task to complete and for guidance along the way when completing those tasks.	Consistently execute repeatable and established tasks with little or no direction but still rely on some help and coaching when deciding/prioritizing larger projects.

SOURCE Courtesy of Will Collins

about what your standards are. We have used these types of models in many work environments. Start by establishing the competency areas that are critical for your environment, then build out the expectations by level (see Table 21.1). Establish regular assessments, both by the individual and the manager. We have found that holding these assessments every other quarter (with the RevOps areas of focus from Chapter 19 exercise in between) was a good cadence to encourage growth, balance, and communication of expectations.

Set the Vision

The most important thing a leader can do for their team is to provide direction: To look ahead at what will be needed and have a point of view on how their team will contribute to future success. Especially in Operations, what your company needs from your team today is very different from what your company will need from you a year from now. Someone (you) has to be able to extract themselves from the weeds of the day-to-day and look ahead toward that future, and design a team structure that will meet and exceed those future needs.

In Chapter 4, we discussed the importance of establishing operating rhythms for the business. You can't just focus on everyone else ("The cobbler's children have no shoes" comes to mind). In this section, we want to discuss the operating rhythms for your team. The exact frequency of these might depend on your team size and geographic locations, but the routines here are applicable across different scenarios:

1 **Quarterly full team meetings:** Reiterate your mission statement. Report against goals from last quarter. Include communication of goals for the current quarter and how they are tied to the company goals. Team building. Celebrations. Recognitions. Team learning.

2 **Monthly group check-ins:** Progress reports of goals. Any updates on goals or priorities. Sharing of knowledge, skills, difficulties, and updates.

3 **Weekly/bi-weekly team meetings:** Informing others of projects, issues, and new priorities. Coordination activities. Preparation for internal customer meetings. Debriefing on meetings held.

4 **1:1s between managers and employees:** This is one of the most critical routines of any team. We believe employees own the 1:1

agenda and should arrive at the 1:1 with topics to discuss. Best practice is to have a written agenda in a shared document, where each week's topics and discussion are kept.

These management philosophies are tools for you to level yourself up, so that everyone around you gets better, too. It may not be hearts and lungs, but we spend a lot of our time and energy at work and we all want that effort to matter.

Chapter Takeaways

1 **Be human first:** Recognize that you, your team, and your customers are human first, with imperfections and external factors affecting reactions and behaviors. Foster psychological safety for authenticity at work.

2 **Be kind and direct:** Directness provides clarity and eliminates guesswork, while kindness ensures a supportive and considerate culture. Avoid extremes—directness without kindness leads to a cut-throat environment, and kindness without directness hinders growth.

3 **Assume good intent and have good intent:** Assume good intentions behind actions, making it easier to process feedback and criticism. Actively cultivate good intentions in your own actions, fostering a positive and productive environment.

4 **Be curious and action-oriented:** Pair curiosity with action, ensuring a balance between understanding and proactive problem-solving.

5 **Have consistently high expectations:** Develop high-performing teams by setting, communicating, and maintaining consistently high expectations.

6 **Set the vision:** Provide direction as a leader by setting a clear vision for your team. Establish regular team operating rhythms for alignment and progress.

22

Speed Isn't Always the Answer: Slow is Smooth, Smooth is Fast

Guess how fast a Formula 1 pit stop takes?

An average of 2.4 seconds.

Yup. Average. As of 2024, the fastest time is 1.80 seconds by the McLaren team.

This is mind-boggling. We really want you to put this book down and go search for some footage of a pit stop. Watch them carefully. Watch the speed at which each individual person moves. It isn't fast. It is deliberate, purposeful, planned, and smooth.

There is a race car motto that is also shared with the Navy SEALs:

Slow is *Smooth*, Smooth is *Fast*.

What can Operations teams learn from this motto? A lot, we believe. The Formula 1 pit stops are only sub-three seconds because the process has been thought out, the activities are orchestrated to be efficient, and every person involved has a well-defined role. There is no rushing, no trying to do someone else's job, no wasted motion. It's not reasonable to believe we can do a Fiscal Year Flip in 2.4 seconds, but we can keep moving towards the direction of planning transitions that are as smooth as a pit stop.

Operations teams are often by nature rapid-responders and there are times that you need them to be. If the quoting system goes down at the end of the quarter, you better hope you have rapid responders getting that system back up and running ASAP If the biggest deal of the quarter comes with an error in the Terms and Conditions, you want the turnaround time for a revision at the top of the priority list. The Board Meeting deck has to go out tonight and the CRO wants a revision to the next quarter projection, yup, you want to have that Johnny/Janie-Ops.-on-the-spot response time.

But we also want to be careful about where we put our Operations team's focus or automation efforts, and assess which things we actually need to optimize. In Chapter 11, we wrote about developing RevOps goals that tie to the overall organization's outcomes. We need to figure out which things need to be smooth and which things are the priority to accomplish the pit stop.

REAL WORLD ROLE MODELS

Taft Love is the Founder of Iceberg RevOps, a Revenue Operations agency, and the leader of Commercial Strategy and Operations at Dropbox. Taft addresses this balance in Episode 110 of the *Operations* podcast, "When 'Good Enough' is Good Enough at Early Stage Companies":

> There's this concept of premature optimization, this idea that you can do too much too early. And it can have pretty negative effects on your ability to build your business. Trying to make everything scale can get in the way of scaling.
>
> It's counterintuitive, but I worked at startups where the first questions in every meeting were, "Does this scale? How do we scale this?" The answer should be, "Do we know that it works? Do we like what we are scaling? Do we even know what it is really? And can we even build a process?"
>
> Once we know this is a thing that should exist, preparing for scale and optimizing things takes time and money and resources. And if you do that before you've proven that something makes sense, you're just driving in the wrong direction very fast.
>
> What are the specific things that early-stage Operators should be working on, if we want to avoid this pitfall of premature optimization?
>
> Here's the framework I use to work backwards that actually has been really valuable. I ask, "What do you need to run your business in terms of information? What's the MVP (minimum viable product)?" Once we have the list, we ask, "If this number goes up, how do you behave? What are you going

to do differently? How do changes in these numbers impact your decisions?" This is the threshold for actually tracking something.

Then I create a spreadsheet of these metrics. Green are the ones where the data is in place. Yellow is where we have the data or we can easily get the data, we just need to move it to the right place to surface it, a couple hours of work to get to this metric. Red is we do not have the infrastructure to surface this today. And now we have a roadmap with a shared understanding of where all these metrics sit and what it will take to get there.[1]

When Rapid-Response Hurts

When one sales manager wants to change the required fields for pricing exception requests, you want a team that knows it may be just a couple of clicks for them to make that change in Salesforce, but they also slow down enough to think… Who else wants this change? Who else will be affected by this change? Who will need to be trained? When is the best time to introduce this? Are there other changes that would be better to do instead of this request or to bundle with this request?

Our Drift Operations team was amazing, truly a marvel to work with. When Laura arrived, though, she saw areas where rapid-response changes in policies, systems, and practices created an environment where it was difficult for our revenue teams to keep up with the changes. Our management team was running a million miles a minute and wanted lots of changes on the run. Systems were being rolled out quickly and we didn't have a lot of revenue team members who knew how to use them. We had to work with the management team to slow things down a bit so that we wouldn't stumble over ourselves. We presented the video of a Formula 1 pit stop to the entire revenue organization to explain how we were planning to introduce changes to them going forward. We built a game plan and started to execute with clearly defined steps.

You can effectively communicate this approach to your teams without it feeling like Operations is slowing down the rest of the organization. When changes happen at such a vicious rate, your end users (internal customers) are the ones who feel this thrashing more than anyone else; inevitably, they'll just give up trying to keep up with everything, which is the worst possible outcome.

When to Slow Down

Rupert Dallas is the Vice President of Revenue Operations at AudioEye. In Episode 101 of the *Operations* podcast, "Why Discipline Makes You a Better Operator," Rupert provides some great advice on how and why to take advantage of some natural opportunities to slow down to learn. He explains:

> Take some time in between events, projects, and campaigns to have a postmortem. Where did we fail? Where did we knock it out of the park? What are the lessons learned? More importantly, what am I taking and applying to the next one? Have a teachable moment.
>
> And if you're on the receiving end, really take those moments to heart. I have had plenty of opportunities to fail and to fall on my face and to be picked up and to make my own mistakes. If someone cares enough about you in your position and puts enough interest in you to keep you from failing, take that to heart. Internalize it. Execute on it. Operate on it. And it will extremely accelerate your career.[2]

One of our quarterly routines right before goal-setting was to have our team do a "Start, Stop, and Continue" exercise to take advantage of the pause between quarters to be deliberate about what we were going to do to be better the next quarter. The exercise was a round table staff meeting where we identified things we want to start the following quarter, what we want to stop doing, and what we felt we should continue doing. This wasn't something where we as leaders just put our to-do lists on the board; each team member was expected to reflect and thoughtfully contribute to the exercise. This helped flesh out the next quarter's goals, but it also offered what Rupert would refer to as teachable moments for us to consider the impact of what we do.

When Slow is Just Slow

You can't go overboard on the slow part, though—Operations does need to have a bias for action (and results) in order to function at its highest levels. Most often we become slow in Operations when we want something perfect. Voltaire was spot on in his statement: "Perfect is the enemy of good."

As Operators, we have to weigh whether something is good enough to ship. It is rare that we can be perfect; we can also lose the window to make the biggest impact if we wait for something to be perfect. But it does have to be good enough to: 1) Make things better, 2) not damage your company/department/personal reputation, and 3) be adequately vetted to ensure we haven't overlooked something in haste.

Perfectionism in Operations is like salt in cooking—you need some to make the dish work, but too much makes you want to toss it out.

Where do you want perfectionistic tendencies in Operations? You want it in compensation. Order processing. Price book uploads.

Where is too much perfectionism a potential hindrance? Training and sales enablement. Process guides. Team communications. Forecast calls. Opportunity strategy meetings.

Where does good enough really shine? Data analytics that tell the main story and don't get bogged down in anomalies. Timely competitive updates with counter responses. New tool pilots with trusted stakeholders.

Speed is sometimes the answer. Slowing down is sometimes the answer. Perfection is sometimes the answer. Good enough is sometimes the answer. The key for us in Revenue Operations is to recognize which of these options will achieve our desired outcomes.

Chapter Takeaways

1 **"Slow is smooth, smooth is fast" motto:** Operations teams can learn from this motto by emphasizing deliberate, purposeful, and planned actions to optimize processes and transitions for smoother (and ultimately faster!) outcomes.

2 **Avoid premature optimization:** Premature optimization—the tendency to focus on scalability before confirming the viability of a process—can hinder business growth. Early-stage Operators should concentrate on establishing key metrics needed to run the business to then prioritize what they build or optimize.

3 **Balance rapid response and thoughtful change:** Rapid-response capabilities are crucial for certain situations, such as system outages or critical errors. However, it's essential to balance speed with thoughtful consideration, especially when implementing changes that impact multiple audiences.

4 **Strategic reflection and continuous improvement:** Take advantage of breaks to conduct post-mortems and implement routines like "start, stop, and continue" for strategic reflection and continuous improvement in Operations. While a bias for action is crucial in Operations, there should be a balance, avoiding excessive perfectionism and recognizing when "good enough" is sufficient to achieve results.

Endnotes

1 *Operations* with Sean Lane (2023) When "Good Enough" is Good Enough at Early Stage Companies, with Taft Love, Episode 110 [podcast]
2 *Operations* with Sean Lane (2023) Why Discipline Makes You a Better Operator, with Rupert Dallas, Episode 101 [podcast]

23

Managing Expectations and Priorities: How to Say No

Does your company use Slack? If so, does your Slack look similar to Figure 23.1?

We're here to give you permission: You do not need to immediately respond to every single person that Slacks you a question. While you may be a wealth of knowledge, this is not your job. And if all you do is respond to constant messages all day, you will certainly be "busy," but you will never get any of the needle-moving work done that will actually drive outcomes for the business.

One of the most attractive parts of being in Revenue Operations is the variety of work that comes across your desk. Every day is different. New problems pop up. Business circumstances change. The problem solvers in these roles relish that range of opportunity.

But that range, that variability, can also lead to a never-ending to-do list. This chapter is about ensuring the work you're doing doesn't just keep you busy; it creates needle-moving outcomes for your business.

As Operators, we want to help. We're enablers by nature. And a strength of Operators is the curiosity to seek out answers to questions that come our way (we just told you so in Chapter 19). But, if all you do is reactively say yes to every person who asks you a question, and don't stop to consider whether that question is even worth answering, you're going to be a very well-liked but very ineffective Operator.

FIGURE 23.1 An Operator's Slack sidebar

With all the swirl that can come with being in Operations, there's a particular arrow that every Operator should have in their quiver, one that when used effectively can be the difference between inevitable burnout and enduring success.

The arrow that you should have in your quiver? Saying no.

Steve Jobs famously said that saying no allows you to focus on the things that are actually important.[1]

In the book, *The One Thing*, authors Gary Keller and Jay Papasan write, "When you give your one thing your most emphatic yes and vigorously say no to the rest, extraordinary results become possible."[2]

It sounds so easy when they say it, doesn't it? We admit that the idea of saying no in a productive way may sound counter-intuitive, but it's critical to your success. There are a few ways to do this well and we look at these now.

Get to the Root of the Request

When a request comes your way, the best Operators take the time to get to the root of the question being asked. Oftentimes that requires some investigation beyond the original request. Keep a list of our own discovery questions handy to help you get to the core of your internal customers' needs:

- What are you trying to solve for?
- What will you do with what you're asking for?
- What have you tried already as alternatives to this?
- Which existing resources might resolve this request in lieu of creating something new?

That last question is critical, and it's also why Part One of this book and advocating for great documentation are so important. The more familiar you are with your existing systems, processes, and resources, the better equipped you are to point your internal customers towards them. You're not even saying no in these instances. You're simply exposing your teammates to knowledge and tools they didn't know were available to them. Great Operators effectively leverage their institutional knowledge and the company's institutional memory to their advantage.

How you do that deeper discovery, or *how* you say no in these moments, is also important. Marketing Operations leader Sara McNamara stresses that empathy and emotional intelligence are the traits she looks to shine through for Operators in these moments. She explains:

> When I look for someone to add to the team that's going to be working directly with the different groups, I can teach them a tool and I can teach them how to ask questions, but what I can't teach them or instill in their personality is a curiosity about how other people are feeling and really listening closely. People need to feel, "You're heard and we're going to do something about this, and I really care about you and the situation that you're in."

Because we're such a new department in a lot of companies, we're looked at with a skeptical eye already and we're trying to prove our value, so it's really important that we don't burn the bridge between any of the different departments. People are people and people can be frustrating, but we can't be a wall of no and be very self-focused. Our customers are the company and the different stakeholders and employees within the company. So we have to find a way to make that connection with them, even if we have to tell them no on something.[3]

Clearly Document Your Goals and Tie Them to Business Outcomes

We wrote in Chapter 11 about the importance of goal-setting in RevOps. Those goals don't just give you a road map for what you are going to do; they are equally useful in declaring what you are not.

Perhaps this has happened to you before. You meticulously craft your goals, you share them, and get feedback and buy-in from all of your key stakeholders, only to have someone come to you two weeks later with a brand new shiny project they want you to work on. If you say no to the new shiny project that comes your way, you need to have a reason why. Goals are the perfect set of priorities to point to and remind your internal customers what you all jointly agreed were the most important things. This way, you can have a more productive conversation that results in one of the following outcomes: 1) You all collectively agree that the goals you originally crafted are still the most important priorities and this new project will have to wait, or 2) the new shiny project is in fact more important than one of the goals already on your list and the new project replaces the project with the lowest impact.

Notice we didn't say the new project just gets tacked on to the list of goals. You, of course, need to consider trade-offs in bandwidth, capacity, and impact when you make these decisions; but once your goals are agreed upon and well documented, it makes these conversations so much easier. While this may feel daunting at first, once you do this once, your internal customers will get used to these types of trade-off conversations.

Remember the "Purpose, Benefit, Check"™ from Chapter 4? That's exactly how to approach conversations about your goals. Your purposes and your benefits are transparent to all of your internal stakeholders. And as long as you did that "check" during your goal-setting process and confirmed buy-in, that gives you license to bring everyone back to those goals and say no to things outside of them.

Saying no to something also implies you're confident that the work you're already doing is important. It can be difficult sometimes to articulate why that workflow you're building is important, or why the data cleanliness project you've spent the last week on had to be prioritized.

We agree that it can be difficult to measure the impact and efficacy of Operations teams, but it's not impossible. Everything you do must be tied back to measurable business outcomes. When you can do this, saying no is easy.

Let's take an example of lead delivery at a company. If you've ever had to design the systems around lead delivery, you know it's not straightforward or simple. You likely have to build lead distribution triggers, distribution rules, list views, and dashboards among other things in order to make it work smoothly. How can we assign measurable numbers to deliverables like those?

First, you need everything you're building to work at any moment of any day; so, one measurable goal could be to reduce the number of daily distribution errors to below X percent. Next, when those leads do get delivered properly, the whole point is that the team can get to them as quickly as possible. So, another goal could be to reduce the average lead response time from X to Y. Third, thanks to everything you've built and the enablement you put in place, you expect to get a higher yield from those leads. So, you document a goal to increase your lead to meeting conversion rate from X to Y.

That's where you start to get closer to revenue. Follow your work down the funnel and eventually you'll be able to clearly articulate a dollar value for the work you're doing. If the answer is still unclear or you're not sure how you're going to measure it, chances are you need to go back to the drawing board and better articulate your goal. That way, if someone else comes along with a new ask that isn't as clearly measured or doesn't impact your company's revenue in a more meaningful way, you pull that valuable arrow out of your quiver and turn them away.

REAL WORLD ROLE MODELS

In Episode 15 of the *Operations* podcast, Sales and Operations leader Jason Reichl explained how he uses "design thinking" when setting goals and the important role Operations can play in cultivating a continuous cycle of prioritization:

> When you look at most legacy Operations teams, there are really two we see. There are velocity-based Operations teams, which have this idea of, "We're going to build it quickly and then we're just going to watch it explode. And once it explodes, we're just going to build it quickly again."
>
> Then there's another group that is all about scalability. They are looking for the most perfect way to ensure their work scales. The problem is they spend forever on something and then they watch no one use it.
>
> Alternatively, there are two design thinking questions you can ask. "Where is this company trying to go? And what are they willing to sacrifice to get there?" Those two questions allow you to build an operational ecosystem around core ideas.
>
> The first question is about determining the direction of the company and its goals. Are you going to go global? Are you trying to scale your marketing efforts? Are you going to go up-market, down-market? Where are you going?
>
> The second question is usually harder for Operations. There are five areas that you can sacrifice in: 1) You can sacrifice in the way you think it should be done, 2) you can sacrifice the duration or time until you hit your next goal, 3) you can sacrifice internal alignment for speed, 4) you can sacrifice innovation, or 5) you can sacrifice customer experience.
>
> The exercise of picking something to sacrifice is a lesson in recognizing that everything has a reaction. It forces you to pick the top priorities of your organization. So, when we look at a solution, how does this impact customer experience? How does it impact our speed to get to where we want to go as an organization or with our business objectives? Is this scalable enough that we can iterate on top of it? Once you do that, you can build a system that feeds itself.

Most businesses don't have teams that come together to have that conversation. Operations can change that. It's about getting people to think in a way that allows Operations to be a value-add to the business. People need to see that Operators are impacting revenue, but more importantly, you need to change the mindset of Operators that they are capable of doing this. If you can start to change that mindset, you can start to change the importance of Operations itself.[4]

Use Your Operating Rhythms to Stay Fluid and Adaptable

Wait, didn't we say that this chapter was all about saying no? We believe in the merits of goal-setting and prioritization, and at the same time, we are realistic enough to recognize that company circumstances change.

If you read this chapter, lock in your priorities, and you're impervious to a changing landscape around you; you're doing yourself and your company a disservice. Instead, what you can do is leverage the operating rhythms from Chapter 4 to stay attuned to the needs of the business.

In the "Operations <> Internal Customer Alignment Routine," for example, use that time together to check in on your priorities, provide updates, and if necessary, reprioritize on the fly (this meeting, by the way, is a great place to practice connecting the work you're doing back to business results!).

Having difficult prioritization conversations in these routines helps ensure that the right stakeholders are involved in the decision, and there are no surprises later when deliverables and outcomes change. It's possible to be both disciplined in your approach and adaptable to the needs of the business.

Your internal customers will appreciate this approach as well. Kate Adams, a Marketing Executive who has led teams at Quickbase, Validity, Drift, and SmartBear, explained:

The problem with Operations people is they want to fix everything and they want to make everybody happy. You can't do that. The best Operations people that I've worked with have been masters at never saying no, but saying, "Which one?" They have an opinion on which thing is most important to the business and how they would prioritize it to ensure that there's alignment.[5]

Conversations like this, especially if you're talking to a more senior executive, can be daunting. No one wants to say no to a VP or C-level colleague who is asking for something. But Taft Love, Founder of Iceberg RevOps, reassuringly explains that when handled properly, these conversations can be effective and important:

> There is a lot of forcing prioritization and setting boundaries. That VP will have an understanding of how businesses work, but you have to be willing to challenge them and set boundaries of what is and isn't doable, so that then they can make smart decisions. They will come to you saying, 'I want this and I want that, and I want it all this quarter.'

> But you have to say, "I can do one of those things this quarter, because it's me and one other person on this team."

> Ask them, "Is that the most important thing? What are you going to do with it? Why do you need it? What's the alternative?" And as you start having these conversations, these very smart people will get in line with you. It's very rare in my experience that people handle that poorly.

> But if you don't set those boundaries, and you don't communicate that well, and you just say yes to everything, it's honestly your fault as the Ops. person for not laying out the structure in which they can work.[6]

Simplify the asks coming to you, focus on your goals and outcomes, and repeat. That recipe will empower you to properly prioritize the right work, say no to everything else, and avoid the never-ending to-do list and inevitable burnout. Sure, saying no is hard, but with these tools at your disposal, it will be just a little bit easier the next time around.

Chapter Takeaways

1 **Importance of goal-setting and prioritization:** Clearly document goals as a roadmap for what to do and, equally important, what not to do. Use these goals as a reference point for deciding whether to take on new projects or tasks. This approach facilitates productive

conversations about priorities and helps in making decisions based on the impact and alignment with previously agreed-upon goals.

2 **Connect priorities to business outcomes:** Tie every task or project back to measurable business outcomes. This practice allows for an easier process of saying no to tasks that don't align with, or create more value than, these outcomes. Quantify the impact of your work and prioritize tasks that contribute most effectively to the company's revenue and strategic goals.

3 **Adaptability and effective communication:** While a disciplined approach to goal-setting and prioritization is critical, it's also important to stay adaptable in changing company circumstances. Use operating rhythms for regular alignment and re-evaluation of priorities with internal stakeholders.

Endnotes

1 P. Burrows. Steve Jobs: He Thinks Different, *Businessweek*, 25 October 2004, www.bloomberg.com/news/articles/2004-10-31/steve-jobs-he-thinks-different (archived at https://perma.cc/RVW7-3XE5)

2 G. Keller and J. Papasan (2013) *The ONE Thing: The Surprisingly Simple Truth About Extraordinary Results*, Bard Press, Portland, OR

3 *Operations* with Sean Lane (2019) Emotional Management vs. Tech Stack Management, with Cloudera's Sara McNamara, Episode 21 [podcast]

4 *Operations* with Sean Lane (2019) What's the Dollar Impact of Ops? (with GoNimbly CEO Jason Reichl) Episode 15 [podcast]

5 *Operations* with Sean Lane (2021) Live from Modern Sales Pros: Why Operations is the Key to Sales and Marketing Alignment, Episode 70 [podcast]

6 *Operations* with Sean Lane (2023) When "Good Enough" is Good Enough at Early Stage Companies, with Taft Love, Episode 110 [podcast]

24

Get Outside of Your Four Walls: The Importance of Seeking Out Role Models

In 2017, when Sean was working at a restaurant technology company, a private equity firm became the majority owner of the company. Sean started sitting in on meetings with the firm's representatives, helping to explain how the company operated and everything that had been built so far. He confidently and proudly presented everything they had accomplished up until that point, but having never been at a company during this type of transaction before, Sean grew defensive when previous decisions were questioned or new process replacements were floated. *I've been here for over five years. I know this business way better than they do. Who are they to tell me what's broken?*

What a mistake.

Fast forward four years. Sean was at a different company, and the same private equity firm announced they were acquiring the company. But this time, Sean's reaction and approach to the acquisition was completely different from the last time around.

So what changed?

It's not that he was no longer proud or confident in the work he had done; it was instead the liberating realization that every problem he encountered had likely been solved already by someone else. Unless you are doing cutting-edge research to cure cancer (if you are, please put down this book and get back to work!), there's someone out there who has been in your shoes and solved the problem you're facing before you. So instead of rebuffing the expertise that came with a portfolio of similar companies all trying to grow and succeed, he embraced the resources and the peers that came with being a part of that portfolio. Instead of getting defensive when previous solutions were questioned, Sean sought out learnings and examples from others, ultimately becoming a "RevOps champion" for the entire portfolio.

The *Operations* podcast is the ultimate manifestation of this mentality. While you don't have to start your own podcast to seek out role models, it created a forum through which Sean could ask smart people about the work they'd done, the lessons they'd learned, and skip over some of the painful mistakes they'd made along the way. Yes, the show is meant for a broader audience of Operators, but it's also a selfish learning exercise for him personally (for example, when he needed to learn about building a professional services team, he would invite guests on the show who had done just that).

Throughout this book, we've purposefully included excerpts from "Real World Role Models" to illustrate the importance of learning from successful Operators who have already solved the problems you might be facing in your business today.

This isn't just something that should only exist in this book or in a podcast you listen to. This approach of seeking out role models and being lifelong learners should be embedded in the DNA of your team and your company. A few ways you can do this yourself or encourage it within your team:

· **Pick role model companies slightly more mature than you:** If you're working at a growing company, assess your company's revenue, stage of maturity, target customer, industry, and size, and go find a company that is a couple years ahead of you in their maturation. Then, identify an Operations peer within that company and connect with them. You'll be amazed at how generous Operators are with their time and their lessons. Set up a recurring time to meet with them, ask each other questions, and share your experiences. Repeat this at each stage of your company's growth. Don't forget to pay it forward and become a role model for others as well!

- **Present findings/recommendations internally with role model examples included:** When you are building something new or presenting a recommendation internally, that recommendation should include the role models you spoke with to arrive at your recommendation. This social proof will dramatically improve the way your colleagues will receive your recommendation because it's backed up by evidence-based results. Also, this doesn't mean you should blindly copy everything your role models have done; your goal should be to take the best aspects of what all of your role models have built and improve upon their previous solutions for your company's specific situation.

- **Seeking out role models doesn't have to mean 1:1 networking:** While we think that developing meaningful connections with peer Operators is crucial to growing your career, we recognize sending cold outreach to strangers isn't for everyone. If you aren't comfortable yet in a 1:1 setting, lean into the myriad of RevOps communities, Slack groups, and message boards that are available to you. The archives of conversations in these communities can be a treasure trove for finding the answers to questions others have asked before you. Many of these groups also have live events you can attend and connect with like-minded Operators in-person.

- **Include networking/role model conversations in your team goals:** The best way to engrain this behavior in your team is to set goals around it. Operators are busy—there will always be something else to do that feels more urgent than taking the time to build out their network of role models. But this is just as (if not more) important to producing meaningful outcomes for your business. Consider what you can measure yourself (and your team members) on in this area: Meet with two role models per month, listen to three podcast episodes this quarter, and attend one Ops. community event before the end of the year.

CONFESSION CORNER

My company sold a product that only had a month-to-month commitment, and we were transitioning from a monthly business to an annual one. That meant that I was tasked with building the first ever renewal motion in the company's history.

I locked myself in a room with my counterpart in customer success, and we mapped out what we believed to be the most elegant, sophisticated renewal process ever created. We scoped out the project, made significant changes to our CRM's architecture to support our new vision, and prepared to launch our new renewal motion to the team.

The launch blew up in our faces.

We didn't ask for guidance or feedback from a single person internally or externally. We thought the two people in that conference room, armed with a whiteboard and a marker, had all the answers. The crux of our mistake was in the complexity of the system we had designed—multiple opportunities to track every possible renewal outcome, with the onus on our colleagues to properly capture and forecast each possible outcome. People were confused, frustrated, and ultimately rejected this new poorly conceived process.

After the debacle that was our launch, a colleague introduced us to someone from their previous company who had designed the renewal system there. When we got on the phone with him to ask about his experiences, the first thing he said was, "You did the multiple opportunity thing, didn't you?"

One call. That's all it would have taken to avoid a project that wasted time, resources, and eroded the team's confidence in whatever solution would come next. For the re-launch, we took the best solutions from a number of role model companies, and improved upon them to create a motion that still exists at the company to this day.

A danger, of course, to seeking out role models is taking advice from the wrong one or applying the wrong solution to your company's situation. It's so easy today to share "thought leadership" that isn't backed up by any real data, experience, or previous success. You can be thoughtful about the individuals you're learning from, and you can also seek out organizations that specialize in benchmarks and data-driven insights due to the nature of their work.

Jeremey Donovan, for example, is the Executive Vice President of Revenue Operations and Strategy at Insight Partners, a global software investor that focuses on high-growth technology start-up and scale-up companies. Insight Partners is uniquely positioned to be a reliable resource for important business metrics and KPIs thanks to the exposure they have through their portfolio companies. Jeremey, a former Operations leader himself, created a maturity assessment to survey companies in hopes of distinguishing between the practices and best practices amongst high-performing organizations. After surveying 122 companies, Insight Partners published the five best practices that top performing go-to-market teams "over-index" on:

1 **Partner**: We actively manage partner channel conflict using rules of engagement and systems (e.g. deal registration).

2 **Process**: Sellers are mapping stakeholders and influencers in the sale.

3 **Pipeline**: We have a large enough pipeline to achieve bookings goals in each period given sales cycles and win rates.

4 **People**: Our seller attrition rate is well below industry standards (<25 percent per year).

5 **Process**: Sales and marketing are aligned on top-of-funnel strategy for each segment.[1]

Jeremey's approach, and the deliberate method through which he gathered and analyzed data, should be what you are looking for when considering benchmarks for your company and whether or not a source is worthy of being a role model (by the way, we covered his survey and its results more deeply on Episode 96 of the *Operations* podcast).[2]

Don't limit yourself to your own experiences or even to the knowledge and experiences of the people who work at your company. If you do, you're destined to make the same painful mistakes so many before you have already made. Get outside of the four walls of your company, seek out role models, skip the pain, and quickly move on to the outcomes you are there to generate.

Chapter Takeaways

1 **Learn from others' mistakes:** Seeking role models and learning from their experiences. Defensiveness should be replaced by the realization that others likely faced similar challenges before you, and you can seek out businesses that have already discovered the solutions you need.

2 **Embed seeking out role models in your DNA:** The practice of seeking out role models is not confined to personal or podcast learning but should be integral to the company's culture. Suggestions include connecting with slightly more mature companies, incorporating role model examples in internal presentations, utilizing available communities and forums, and setting learning goals for teams.

3 **Avoid pitfalls and select reliable sources:** While seeking role models is crucial, don't blindly follow advice from unverified sources. Consider people and organizations that specialize in data-driven insights and benchmarks.

Endnotes

1 J. Donovan (2024) Needles and Haystacks: Which GTM Practices are Actually Best Practice? Downloadable report from: https://www.insightpartners.com/ ideas/secrets-of-top-performers-gtm-strategies/ (archived at https://perma. cc/5P6F-KF32)
2 *Operations* with Sean Lane (2023) Separating Practices from Best Practices, with Insight Partners' Jeremey Donovan, Episode 96 [podcast]

25

Perfection is an Illusion: Instilling the "Better, Better, Never Done" Mentality

Laura once walked into a mess of a systems landscape. There had been a systems overhaul that had gone so very wrong. Data had been corrupted. Processes were manual and broken. The Operations team was scrambling every day to keep things afloat. The users were disgruntled and disbelieving of any promise of change. The topic was raised at every company meeting. What was an Operator to do?

Laura started by interviewing stakeholders across the company. No one had a systems architecture diagram of how all of the systems worked together; so, she started one on a piece of arts and crafts paper using a pencil. After each interview, she would add to the diagram or erase what she had gotten incorrect or highlight where a pain point was. The creases started to deepen on the paper from such regular use, and soon everyone in the organization knew that she carried the diagram with her wherever she went.

The team pulled together a plan to address the biggest pain points and stop the sources of bad data. It was going to likely take them at least six months of incremental improvements. They began the communication plan and sold the improvements to the rest of the organization. But the message was **not**, "We are going to fix every-thing." The message was, "We will never be done working on our systems. But we will be making them better with each of our releases."

Internally, the team used that arts and crafts version of a systems architecture diagram as a measuring stick to see how far it had come even after a real one was created. There was a party at the end of the formal projects where every team member took highlighters to check off their favorite fixes. The team noted that not everything was checked off. This was a toast to **progress**, not perfection. Better, better, never done.

Problems should be embraced, not avoided. The world of an Operator will never stop changing. We believe it's what makes this function so interesting, challenging, fulfilling, and satisfying. Operators will never be finished in their work because we will always look for new ways to make improvements, new technology will appear on the landscape, business needs will change, industry regulations will shift, new people will enter the organization, and customer expectations will evolve. Perfection is impossible to achieve. Improvement is the name of the Operator's game.

The Revenue Operations Mindset means:

- Operators are **strategic** partners, not a support function.

- Operators focus on **outcomes**, not inputs.

- Operators are the perfect blend of **strategic** and **tactical**.

- Operators are **lifelong learners** and not afraid to be proven wrong.

- Operators champion their work and are proud of the **impact** they create.

- Operators believe in constant, incremental **improvements** and a "better, better, never done" approach.

This book is a blueprint for building a world-class Revenue Operations organization. We probably missed some things. Some of our tips won't apply to all companies or situations. And while these pages are a compelling distillation of many years of hard-earned lessons and words of wisdom from Operators we admire, we know that this book doesn't mark the end of our own Revenue Operations education. So, we hope it doesn't mark the end of yours. That's part of our commitment to being lifelong learners.

We were inspired by Karen Borchert, founder and CEO of Alpaca and the former COO at Flywheel, who shared a personal career story:

> The person who impacted me the most in getting the job I have today is Lin-Manuel Miranda.
>
> I was in a job that wasn't challenging me very much. I wasn't doing things that I was really proud of, energized by or excited about. Then I heard for the first time the full original Broadway cast recording of *Hamilton*. I stopped dead in my tracks on a 10-mile run to marvel at that work and that creative accomplishment of his.
>
> I decided that I wasn't doing something that I would marvel at someday, that I was truly proud of.
>
> And so I quit my job. I flew to Chicago. I saw *Hamilton*. I decided that it was the right choice to make. Then I set about finding a job where I could do something that I would marvel at someday and be really proud of.[1]

This book has unapologetically championed the Operator. Operators are at the center of what makes companies run. We believe that the "better, better, never done" approach doesn't just apply to the work we do for a business. It starts with us as individuals. It is an approach to life. Only after you commit to improving yourself can you play a meaningful role in improving your team and your company.

It is not possible to master and implement all of these ideas at once. Seek out the few opportunities to drive the most needle-moving change, and ruthlessly prioritize getting better.

Go make a difference, and do work you'll marvel at someday, knowing the best challenge is in never being done.

Endnote

1 *Operations* with Sean Lane (2019) Imperfection is Commitment's Secret Weapon, with Karen Borchert, Episode 19 [podcast]

Continuing Education: Embrace the "Better, Better, Never Done" Mentality

Want to continue your RevOps learning? You can find select tables, figures and resources from this book on our website at revenueoperationsmanual.com.

INDEX

Note: Page numbers in *italics* refer to tables or figures.

Looking for another book?

Explore our award-winning
books from global business
experts in Marketing and Sales

Scan the code to browse

More from Kogan Page

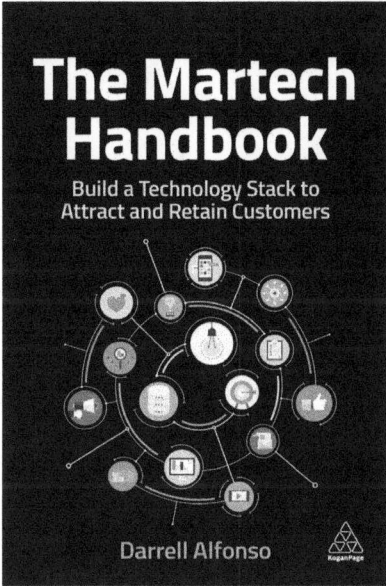

The Martech Handbook
Build a Technology Stack to Attract and Retain Customers
Darrell Alfonso

ISBN: 9781398606449

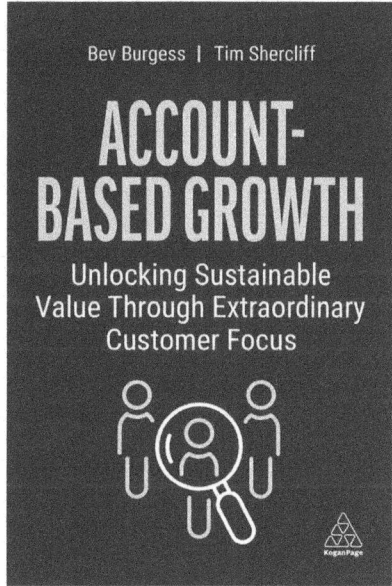

Bev Burgess | Tim Shercliff
ACCOUNT-BASED GROWTH
Unlocking Sustainable Value Through Extraordinary Customer Focus

ISBN: 9781398607446

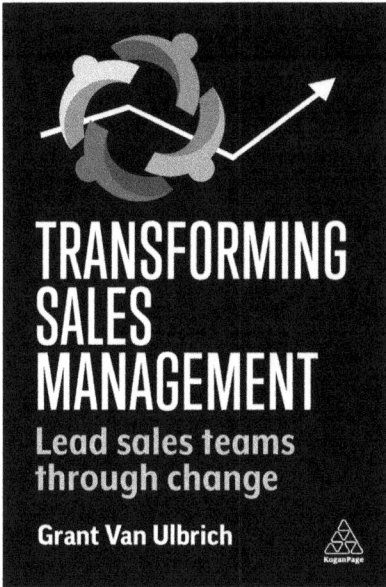

TRANSFORMING SALES MANAGEMENT
Lead sales teams through change
Grant Van Ulbrich

ISBN: 9781398609082

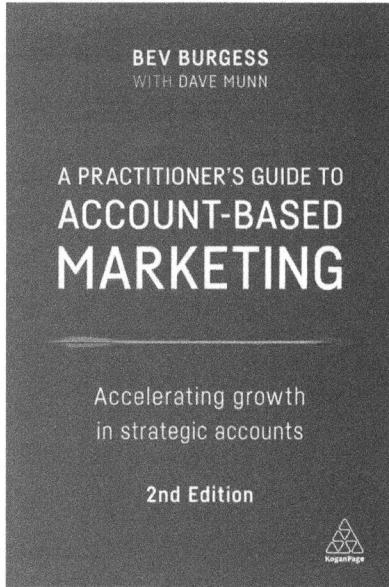

BEV BURGESS
WITH DAVE MUNN
A PRACTITIONER'S GUIDE TO
ACCOUNT-BASED MARKETING
Accelerating growth in strategic accounts
2nd Edition

ISBN: 9781398600874

www.koganpage.com

From 4 December 2025 the EU Responsible Person (GPSR) is:
eucomply oÜ, Pärnu mnt. 139b – 14, 11317 Tallinn, Estonia
www.eucompliancepartner.com

www.ingramcontent.com/pod-product-compliance
Lightning Source LLC
Chambersburg PA
CBHW071541210326
41597CB00019B/3071

9 781398 616769